A 365-Day Journey Walking *with the* Word & the Spirit

A Daily Devotional for Growing from Glory to Glory

DR. JOELLE SUEL

TABLE OF CONTENTS

A Blessing as You Begin — x
Preface — xi
How to Use This Devotional — xiii

Day 1: First Things First — 1
Day 2: Seeking God Early — 2
Day 3: In the Potter's Hand — 3
Day 4: Strength in Stillness — 4
Day 5: Letting Go of the Old — 5
Day 6: Fresh Mercy Each Day — 6
Day 7: Putting On the New Man — 7
Day 8: In the Beauty of Holiness — 8
Day 9: Steps of Faith — 9
Day 10: Streams in the Desert — 10
Day 11: The Faith to Move Mountains — 11
Day 12: Sustained by the Spirit — 12
Day 13: Walking in Truth — 13
Day 14: Counting Him Faithful — 14
Day 15: The Joy of the Lord — 15
Day 16: Keeping the Light On — 16
Day 17: Worship in Spirit and Truth — 17
Day 18: Treasuring Others — 18
Day 19: Catch the Foxes — 19
Day 20: Guarding Your Heart — 20
Day 21: Standing in the Fire — 21
Day 22: Our Leading Shepherd — 22
Day 23: Our Shield of Protection — 23
Day 24: Power of His Indwelling — 24
Day 25: What Are We Saying? — 25
Day 26: Faithful in the Little Things — 26
Day 27: Increase Our Faith — 27
Day 28: Christ Is the Head — 28
Day 29: The God Who Sees — 29
Day 30: Trusting God's Timing — 30
Day 31: Made New by the Spirit — 31
Day 32: Hearing His Lovingkindness — 32
Day 33: Trusting God's Leading — 33
Day 34: Pressing On in Faith — 34
Day 35: Open Doors and Opposition — 35
Day 36: He Knows Each One of Us — 36
Day 37: Shaking Off Resentment — 37
Day 38: The Power of Forgiveness — 38
Day 39: Vintage Wine in the Making — 39
Day 40: Consider Your Ways — 40
Day 41: Burning Compassion — 41
Day 42: The Fire of His Presence — 42
Day 43: Jehovah Jireh, Our Provider — 43
Day 44: Surrendering Our Cups to the Father — 44
Day 45: The Spirit of Revelation — 45
Day 46: The Knowledge of God's Love — 46
Day 47: God's Word Will Stand — 47
Day 48: Broken Cisterns — 48
Day 49: God's Divine Timing — 49
Day 50: Fresh Infillings — 50
Day 51: The Bread of Life — 52
Day 52: Come to Me — 53
Day 53: The Lord Is My Refuge — 54
Day 54: He Will Establish and Guard You — 55
Day 55: Anchored in Love — 56
Day 56: Stand Fast in the Faith — 57
Day 57: The Spirit of Truth — 58
Day 58: Healing Light — 59
Day 59: Do Not Fret — 60
Day 60: Unshakable Faith — 61
Day 61: Removing Barriers — 62
Day 62: Abiding in the True Vine — 63
Day 63: Search My Heart, O God — 64
Day 64: The Strength in Saying No — 65
Day 65: Finding Peace in Stillness — 66
Day 66: Nurturing Your Heart — 67
Day 67: Unity in Prayer — 68
Day 68: Led by the Spirit — 69
Day 69: Embracing Opportunities — 70
Day 70: Reopening Our Spiritual Wells — 71

Day 71: Rooms of Blessing	72	Day 109: The Redeemed of the Lord	111
Day 72: Adoption as Sons	73	Day 110: The Bypass Anointing	112
Day 73: Faith Comes by Hearing	74	Day 111: Commit Your Way	113
Day 74: Praise the Lord	75	Day 112: It Is the Lord	114
Day 75: Crucified with Christ	76	Day 113: Praise Produces Power	115
Day 76: The Power of the Gospel	77	Day 114: Unbound and Set Free	116
Day 77: Walking in the Spirit	78	Day 115: Stretch Out Your Hand to Heal	117
Day 78: Receiving Jesus with Joy	79	Day 116: Victory over Defeat	118
Day 79: Resist Him	80	Day 117: Eternal Weight of Glory	119
Day 80: Belonging to the Lord	81	Day 118: Accepted in the Beloved	120
Day 81: More than Conquerors	82	Day 119: Be Strong and of Good Courage	121
Day 82: The Glorious Race	83	Day 120: The Treasure Within It	122
Day 83: Stepping Into the Promise	84	Day 121: We Are His Workmanship	123
Day 84: Freedom from Condemnation	85	Day 122: Leaving the Comfort Zone	124
Day 85: The Gift of Praise	86	Day 123: Only One Word	125
Day 86: The Incorruptible Seed	87	Day 124: Breaking Free from Offense	126
Day 87: Victory Secured	88	Day 125: Embrace Cheer, Not Fear	127
Day 88: Radiance in Trials	89	Day 126: Worship to Hear	128
Day 89: The Sword of the Spirit	90	Day 127: The Kingdom Is Not in Word	129
Day 90: Strength in Our Weaknesses	91	Day 128: Breaking Free from Vows	130
Day 91: Praising Through Fear	92	Day 129: The Comfort of the Scriptures	131
Day 92: The Power of the Cross	93	Day 130: God's Amazing Love	132
Day 93: Removing the Veil	94	Day 131: Love the Lord Your God	133
Day 94: His Victory, Our Freedom	95	Day 132: Strength to Strength	134
Day 95: Do You Believe This?	96	Day 133: Every Word	135
Day 96: Delivered from Darkness	97	Day 134: Forgiven?	136
Day 97: Divine Exchange	98	Day 135: Shut the Door	137
Day 98: Wise Surrender	99	Day 136: Faithful Progress	138
Day 99: A Future and a Hope	100	Day 137: Fellowship with God	139
Day 100: Daily Renewal	102	Day 138: Go with God	140
Day 101: Immovable	103	Day 139: What Are We Thinking?	141
Day 102: Peace Be Still	104	Day 140: Delight Yourself in the Lord	142
Day 103: Hosanna in the Highest	105	Day 141: Dealing with Unbelief	143
Day 104: What Does God Look At?	106	Day 142: God Confirms His Will	144
Day 105: Power to Heal	107	Day 143: A Still, Small Voice	145
Day 106: The Abiding Anointing	108	Day 144: We Dare Not!	146
Day 107: Nevertheless	109	Day 145: You Are My Hiding Place	147
Day 108: Room for More	110	Day 146: Founded on the Rock	148

Day 147: Unlimited Potential	149	Day 185: Power of Praise	188
Day 148: The Fire of God	150	Day 186: Embrace the Now	189
Day 149: Process of Healing	152	Day 187: Recognizing the Battle	190
Day 150: Spiritual Discernment	153	Day 188: The "Yet" Praise Life	191
Day 151: As Christ Forgave You	154	Day 189: Free to Flee	192
Day 152: The Lord Will Perfect It	155	Day 190: Belonging to Our Redeemer	193
Day 153: Seeking God's Will	156	Day 191: Joy and Peace in Believing	194
Day 154: Rooted and Built Up in Christ	157	Day 192: Speak Life	195
Day 155: Do We Need Wisdom?	158	Day 193: Walking in Wisdom	196
Day 156: Free from Guilt and Shame	159	Day 194: A Song in the Night	197
Day 157: The Spirit of Truth	160	Day 195: Living Water	198
Day 158: One Spirit-Led Moment	161	Day 196: Our Provider	199
Day 159: It Changes Everything	162	Day 197: Looking Unto Jesus	200
Day 160: Blessed Peacemakers	163	Day 198: God of the Impossible	202
Day 161: Enduring Faith	164	Day 199: Knowing Your Weapons	203
Day 162: A Heart After God	165	Day 200: Don't Give Up!	204
Day 163: The Joy of Obedience	166	Day 201: Rivers in the Desert	205
Day 164: Stir Up the Gift	167	Day 202: The Power of Surrender	206
Day 165: Heed to Yourselves	168	Day 203: But You, O Lord	207
Day 166: Breaking Chains	169	Day 204: Unconquered Light	208
Day 167: New Every Morning	170	Day 205: Beholding His Work	209
Day 168: A Teachable Spirit	171	Day 206: Bound in the Spirit	210
Day 169: Witnesses to the World	172	Day 207: Building on Christ	211
Day 170: The Power of Prayer	173	Day 208: He Restores My Soul	212
Day 171: A Vision of Hope	174	Day 209: Genuine Anointing	213
Day 172: Don't Hold On to It	175	Day 210: Free to Be	214
Day 173: God Holds Tomorrow	176	Day 211: Sleeping in the Storm	215
Day 174: Give Thanks to the Lord	177	Day 212: Our Faithful God	216
Day 175: The Pure in Heart	178	Day 213: The Power of His Name	217
Day 176: Seeking Him Diligently	179	Day 214: He Goes with You	218
Day 177: Hallelujah	180	Day 215: Consider the Lilies	219
Day 178: Hard-Pressed on Every Side	181	Day 216: Come Boldly to the Throne	220
Day 179: Putting On Love	182	Day 217: More than Enough	221
Day 180: My Heart Is Overwhelmed	183	Day 218: Our New Identity	222
Day 181: Refined by Fire	184	Day 219: Breaking Through the Cocoon	223
Day 182: He Will Deliver Us	185	Day 220: Walking the Bright Path	224
Day 183: Grace Over Rejection	186	Day 221: The God of Peace	225
Day 184: The Truth Shall Make You Free	187	Day 222: When God Said "Wait"	226

Day 223: Overflowing Grace	227	Day 261: Do We Know He Hears Us?	266
Day 224: The Gift of Peace	228	Day 262: Do We Glorify Jesus?	267
Day 225: Seasons of Growth	229	Day 263: From Glory to Glory	268
Day 226: Standing in Authority	230	Day 264: God Will Provide	269
Day 227: Directed Into God's Love	231	Day 265: Give Me This Mountain	270
Day 228: Anchored in Hope	232	Day 266: The Lord Is My Light	271
Day 229: The Lifter of Your Head	233	Day 267: The Seed and the Harvest	272
Day 230: Don't Quit Before the Harvest	234	Day 268: The Constant in Our Lives	273
Day 231: Strength for Today	235	Day 269: Following God Fully	274
Day 232: Faith Beyond Familiarity	236	Day 270: Strength to Keep Going	275
Day 233: Greater than Our Heart	237	Day 271: God's Open Doors	276
Day 234: Broken for Breakthrough	238	Day 272: Faith in Transition	277
Day 235: Trust and Obey	239	Day 273: Living and Powerful	278
Day 236: Always On Call	240	Day 274: Guided by His Light	279
Day 237: Fear Not, for I Am with You	241	Day 275: Word of Our Testimony	280
Day 238: Watch Out for the Traps	242	Day 276: From Adam to God's Family	281
Day 239: God Gives the Increase	243	Day 277: Daily Bread	282
Day 240: Recognizing the Lies	244	Day 278: Treasure Hunt	283
Day 241: Guarding Your Ears	245	Day 279: Lift Your Eyes	284
Day 242: Greater Is He in You	246	Day 280: Unstoppable Growth	285
Day 243: God Will Make a Way	247	Day 281: Divine Opportunities	286
Day 244: Great and Awesome	248	Day 282: A Secured Path	287
Day 245: Unlocking the Impossible	249	Day 283: Draw Near to God	288
Day 246: The Door of Fellowship	250	Day 284: Powerful Restoration	289
Day 247: The Light of Life	252	Day 285: Above and Beyond	290
Day 248: As We Go	253	Day 286: Love Poured Out	291
Day 249: What Shall We Do?	254	Day 287: God Heals the Brokenhearted	292
Day 250: Turning Aside to See God	255	Day 288: Walls Come Down	293
Day 251: Steps Ordered by the Lord	256	Day 289: Confident in His Work	294
Day 252: Walking in Divine Favor	257	Day 290: Worship That Wars	295
Day 253: Established by Grace	258	Day 291: Light in the Dark	296
Day 254: Prepared for the Test	259	Day 292: Pressing Toward the Prize	297
Day 255: Test the Spirits	260	Day 293: Faithful in the Hidden Season	298
Day 256: Enter the Ark	261	Day 294: Becoming a Chain Breaker	299
Day 257: Launch Into the Deep	262	Day 295: Deep Calls Unto Deep	300
Day 258: Living from His Strength	263	Day 296: A Thankful Heart	302
Day 259: What Are We Building?	264	Day 297: Watered and Refreshed	303
Day 260: God's Thoughts for You	265	Day 298: Overcome Evil with Good	304

Day 299: People of God	305
Day 300: Grace to the Humble	306
Day 301: Seeds of Thought	307
Day 302: Torches in Clay Pots	308
Day 303: Like the Bars of a Castle	309
Day 304: The Touch of Faith	310
Day 305: Abide in the Vine	311
Day 306: Faith, Hope, and Love	312
Day 307: The Ministry of Reconciliation	313
Day 308: Quench All the Fiery Darts	314
Day 309: Haste Makes Waste	315
Day 310: Do You Not Know?	316
Day 311: Receiving Faith Over Fear	317
Day 312: Strength in Submission	318
Day 313: The Power of Redemption	319
Day 314: Seeking the Holy Spirit	320
Day 315: What Do You See?	321
Day 316: Our Dot-to-Dot Journey	322
Day 317: Reach for His Saving Hand	323
Day 318: Set Apart from the Start	324
Day 319: When the Night Shines	325
Day 320: Another Touch	326
Day 321: Hidden in His Quiver	327
Day 322: Be Anxious for Nothing	328
Day 323: What Do You Remember?	329
Day 324: Shake Off the Enemy's Attacks	330
Day 325: Waves of Glory	331
Day 326: Strengthened in the Inner Man	332
Day 327: The Power of Gratitude	333
Day 328: Rejoice, Pray, and Give Thanks	334
Day 329: Reflecting Christ's Love	335
Day 330: Lift Your Eyes	336
Day 331: Held by His Hand	337
Day 332: Standing Out in Faith	338
Day 333: Called Into Fellowship	339
Day 334: Strength in Stillness	340
Day 335: The Sound of Abundance	341
Day 336: Using Our God-Given Gifts	342
Day 337: Your Glory Revealed	343
Day 338: Led by the Spirit	344
Day 339: Filled to the Brim	345
Day 340: The Breaker Goes Before You	346
Day 341: United as One Body	347
Day 342: Called by His Word	348
Day 343: Sowing in Tears	349
Day 344: Mindful of the Things of God	350
Day 345: Cheerful Giving	352
Day 346: Beholding His Glory	353
Day 347: Arrows of Victory	354
Day 348: Seeking the Lord	355
Day 349: The Light of the World	356
Day 350: God's Plan in Disruptions	357
Day 351: The Power of Perfect Love	358
Day 352: Glorious Lights	359
Day 353: The Living Word	360
Day 354: God Knows Our Frame	361
Day 355: Making Room for Jesus	362
Day 356: Loving One Another	363
Day 357: God's Good Gifts	364
Day 358: Worship in Spirit and Truth	365
Day 359: The Greatest Gift	366
Day 360: God With Us	367
Day 361: Inseparable Love	368
Day 362: Wonderfully Made	369
Day 363: Praise at All Times	370
Day 364: Amen to His Promises	371
Day 365: Jesus Upholds All Things	372
A Blessing at the Journey's End	373
About the Author	374
Let's Stay Connected	375
Free Bonus for Readers	376
Scripture Index	377

A Blessing as You Begin

As you begin this journey, may every page draw you closer to the heart of God.

His Word will meet you in the quiet places, strengthen you in the waiting, and refresh you with daily grace.

Whatever the season ahead holds, rest in this truth: He goes before you, walks beside you, and dwells within you.

May each reflection remind you that you are deeply loved, fully known, and securely held in His care.

As the Holy Spirit teaches you the Word and reveals deeper truths to empower your walk, I pray you will run your spiritual race with faith, peace, and the unshakable joy that comes from His presence.

Bless you above and beyond all you ask or think,

Dr. Joelle Suel

Preface

Every journey with God begins with a step—sometimes of faith, sometimes of surrender, always of grace.

This daily devotional was born out of that journey: a desire to help others walk closer with the Lord, not only in moments of worship or study, but in the ordinary rhythm of life.

For years, I have seen how the Word of God, when partnered with the power of the Holy Spirit, transforms hearts from the inside out. In 2012, I began the daily blog *Today with Dr. J.* What started as encouragement soon became Spirit-led teachings—daily drops of living water that many came to anticipate in their inbox and online.

Over time, readers began asking for these timeless messages in book form. This devotional grew from that heartbeat—to create a space where you can walk with the Word and the Spirit each day and see His glory revealed in your own story.

Each devotional entry includes a verse of Scripture, a reflection to draw you deeper, practical steps for application, and a prayer to connect your heart with God's. You'll also find quotes to ponder and journaling prompts to capture those quiet moments when the Lord whispers truth or direction to your spirit.

This is not a study to rush through but a daily walk of faith. Take your time. Some days, you may move forward one step at a time; on others, you may linger on a single verse or phrase. Let the Holy Spirit guide your pace.

Whether you use this book in your quiet time, with family, or in a small group, my prayer is that it becomes a companion for your personal walk—a reminder that every day can be an encounter with God.

As you read, may the Scriptures come alive, and may the Spirit illuminate each page. May the Lord strengthen your heart, renew your vision, and deepen your faith as you continue to grow from glory to glory.

With love and grace,

Dr. Joelle Suel

How to Use This Devotional

This devotional leads to a daily walk, not a race. Each day offers a Scripture, a reflection, an application, and a connection prayer, followed by a quote and journaling prompt to help you listen for what the Holy Spirit is saying personally to you.

Begin with prayer. Ask the Lord to open your heart to His Word and to reveal truth through His Spirit.

Read the **Scripture** slowly, allowing the words to sink in. Then, linger in the **reflection**. Let it lead you into dialogue with God rather than just thought.

Use the **application** points to take practical steps of obedience and growth. Pray through the **connection** prayer, letting it become your own.

Finally, pause with the **quote** and **journaling prompt**.

Write what the Lord impresses upon your spirit: what He's showing you, changing in you, or calling you to trust Him for. Yield to the Holy Spirit's healing and transforming touch.

Don't feel pressured to hurry. On some days, you may revisit a single entry repeatedly; on others, you may flow easily from one to the next.

Let the Holy Spirit set your pace.

Every moment in His presence is part of your walk—from glory to glory.

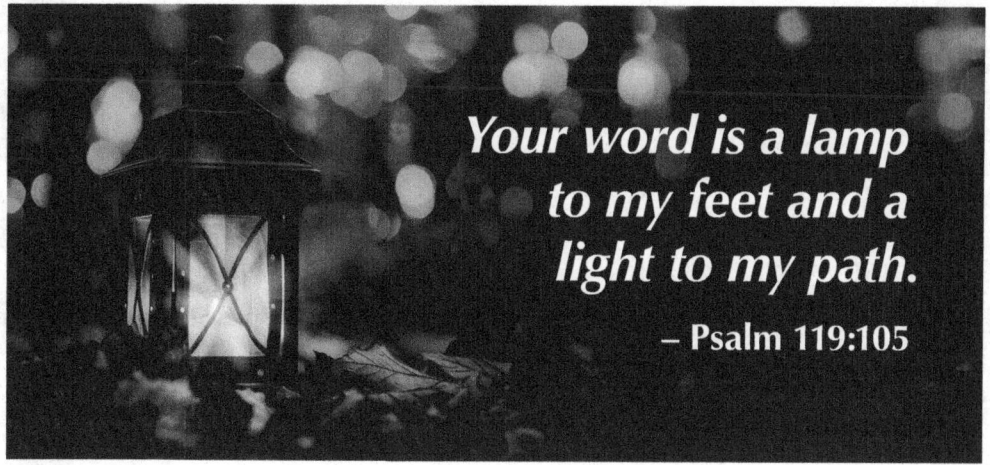

1	2	3	4	5	6	7	8	9	10
11	12	13	14	15	16	17	18	19	20
21	22	23	24	25	26	27	28	29	30
31	32	33	34	35	36	37	38	39	40
41	42	43	44	45	46	47	48	49	50
51	52	53	54	55	56	57	58	59	60
61	62	63	64	65	66	67	68	69	70
71	72	73	74	75	76	77	78	79	80
81	82	83	84	85	86	87	88	89	90
91	92	93	94	95	96	97	98	99	100
101	102	103	104	105	106	107	108	109	110
111	112	113	114	115	116	117	118	119	120
121	122	123	124	125	126	127	128	129	130
131	132	133	134	135	136	137	138	139	140
141	142	143	144	145	146	147	148	149	150
151	152	153	154	155	156	157	158	159	160
161	162	163	164	165	166	167	168	169	170
171	172	173	174	175	176	177	178	179	180
181	182	183	184	185	186	187	188	189	190

191	192	193	194	195	196	197	198	199	200
201	202	203	204	205	206	207	208	209	210
211	212	213	214	215	216	217	218	219	220
221	222	223	224	225	226	227	228	229	230
231	232	233	234	235	236	237	238	239	240
241	242	243	244	245	246	247	248	249	250
251	252	253	254	255	256	257	258	259	260
261	262	263	264	265	266	267	268	269	270
271	272	273	274	275	276	277	278	279	280
281	282	283	284	285	286	287	288	289	290
291	292	293	294	295	296	297	298	299	300
301	302	303	304	305	306	307	308	309	310
311	312	313	314	315	316	317	318	319	320
321	322	323	324	325	326	327	328	329	330
331	332	333	334	335	336	337	338	339	340
341	342	343	344	345	346	3 47	348	349	350
351	352	353	354	355	356	357	358	359	360
361	362	363	364	365					

Use this spread to record your progress.
Color or mark each square as you complete each day.

A 365-Day Journey Walking with the Word & the Spirit

DAY 1
First Things First

But seek first the kingdom of God and His righteousness, and all these things shall be added to you.
— Matthew 6:33

REFLECTION

The Kingdom of God is His reign and rule within our hearts. When we prioritize it, we pursue His will above our own. It transforms how we live and what we value. His Word and His Spirit lead us and deepen our trust in Him. Submitting to the Lordship of Jesus brings clarity, contentment, and the assurance that He will take care of all that concerns us. In the abundance of His peace and purpose, we find our rest.

APPLICATION

† Prioritize time in God's Word and prayer
† Seek His will first in every decision
† Trust in His faithfulness for what you cannot control

CONNECTION

Thank You, Lord, for being my Lord and Savior. Help me seek Your Kingdom above all else. Align my plans and desires with Your will. Teach me to value what You value and to trust You to meet every need. In Jesus' name, Amen.

HIGHLIGHT QUOTE

When we seek God's Kingdom first, our lives find peace and purpose.

JOURNAL PROMPT

What area of your life needs to be realigned with God's Kingdom today?

DAY 2
Seeking God Early

> *My voice You shall hear in the morning, O LORD; In the morning I will direct it to You, And I will look up.*
> *– Psalm 5:3*

REFLECTION

Morning prayer shapes the rhythm of our day. Distractions may compete for our attention, but consistency builds strength. When we seek God early, His presence brings focus, His will brings peace, and His guidance steadies our steps. Each new dawn becomes an invitation to look up, surrender our plans, and welcome His direction with joy.

APPLICATION

- † Acknowledge God upon waking
- † Pray sincerely, sharing your heart with Him
- † Ask for wisdom and guidance for the day ahead

CONNECTION

Thank You, Lord, for meeting me each morning. Forgive me for allowing distractions to come before time with You. Teach me to rise and seek You first. Let Your strength sustain me and Your direction guide my day. In Jesus' name, Amen.

HIGHLIGHT QUOTE

Morning prayer sets the tone for the day ahead.

JOURNAL PROMPT

How can you make your mornings a consistent time to meet with God?

DAY 3
In the Potter's Hand

But now, O LORD, You are our Father; We are the clay, and You our potter; And all we are the work of Your hand.
— Isaiah 64:8

REFLECTION

God's hands shape us through every season of change. Sometimes His process feels uncomfortable, like being stretched, pressed, or reshaped for a new purpose. Yet the Potter knows the design He intends and how every detail will fulfill His plan. When we yield to His shaping and release what no longer fits, He forms us into vessels that reflect His grace and reveal His purpose.

APPLICATION

† Trust God's hands as He shapes your life through change

† Let go of what no longer fits His purpose for you

† Embrace each season as an opportunity for His refining work

CONNECTION

Thank You, Lord, for being the Potter who lovingly shapes my life. Help me yield to Your hand and trust Your purpose in every season of change. Mold me into a vessel that reflects Your design and brings You glory. In Jesus' name, Amen.

HIGHLIGHT QUOTE

Every season of shaping prepares us for God's purpose.

JOURNAL PROMPT

What area of your life might God be reshaping to better reflect His design?

DAY 4
Strength in Stillness

But those who wait on the LORD Shall renew their strength; They shall mount up with wings like eagles, They shall run and not be weary, They shall walk and not faint.
– Isaiah 40:31

REFLECTION

We do not gain strength in the Lord through striving but through waiting on Him. God renews us, not only in our doing but in our being still. When we take the time to rest in His presence, He lifts our weary hearts, and faith soars again. Waiting on the Lord is not time wasted; it is a holy exchange of our weakness for His strength, our restlessness for His peace.

APPLICATION

† Set aside time each day to wait on the Lord and listen for His voice
† Trust His perfect timing, especially when progress feels slow
† Expect renewed strength as you wait in faith

CONNECTION

Thank You, Lord, for renewing my strength as I wait on You. Teach me to be still in Your presence and to rest in Your perfect timing. Lift me above weariness and fill me with the power and peace of Your Spirit. In Jesus' name, Amen.

HIGHLIGHT QUOTE

Waiting on God is not losing time; it's gaining strength.

JOURNAL PROMPT

Where do you need to stop striving and start waiting for God to renew your strength?

DAY 5
Letting Go of the Old

Do not remember the former things, Nor consider the things of old.
— Isaiah 43:18

REFLECTION

It's easy to revisit the past—its failures, regrets, and even its successes. Yet the word *remember* means to make active, and God calls us to move forward, not backward. Past victories can inspire but must not define today's steps. Old mindsets and fears lose their hold when we yield them to Christ. As we release the old, He heals, renews, and leads us into the new thing He is doing.

APPLICATION

- † Release the past, both failures and successes
- † Welcome God's new ways with open faith
- † Trust His grace to guide each step forward

CONNECTION

Thank You, Lord, for healing me from the past. Help me let go of what was and embrace what You are doing today. Renew my heart to walk in faith and hope. In Jesus' name, Amen.

HIGHLIGHT QUOTE

Letting go of the old makes room for God to do something new.

JOURNAL PROMPT

What part of your past might God be asking you to release so He can bring the new?

DAY 6
Fresh Mercy Each Day

> *Through the LORD's mercies we are not consumed, Because His compassions fail not. They are new every morning; Great is Your faithfulness.*
> – Lamentations 3:22–23

REFLECTION

Resolutions fade, but God's mercies never do. Our calendars may mark a new beginning, yet true renewal flows from His compassion. Each morning offers a fresh start—not because we have changed, but because He never fails. His faithfulness meets us in our weakness and restores hope where striving once ruled. Every sunrise becomes a reminder that His mercy is still enough.

APPLICATION

† Trust His mercies when you stumble
† Begin each day afresh in His presence
† Rely on His faithfulness more than your willpower

CONNECTION

Thank You, Lord, that Your mercies are new every morning. Strengthen me to walk in Your grace today and rest in Your unfailing faithfulness. Remind me that Your compassion is always enough. In Jesus' name, Amen.

HIGHLIGHT QUOTE

Every new morning carries the mercy of a faithful God.

JOURNAL PROMPT

Where have you recently experienced God's mercy in a fresh, personal way?

DAY 7
Putting On the New Man

> *That you put off, concerning your former conduct, the old man which grows corrupt according to the deceitful lusts, and be renewed in the spirit of your mind, and that you put on the new man which was created according to God, in true righteousness and holiness.* – Ephesians 4:22–24

REFLECTION

Putting on the new man is like clothing ourselves with Christ. Our old ways belong to who we once were. By faith, we wear His righteousness, forgiveness, and freedom. Satan's lies lose their grip as we wrap ourselves in truth and grace. We no longer hide in shame; we stand covered in Christ's glory. Putting on Christ daily affirms our identity and renews our walk with Him.

APPLICATION

- † Reject the shame and guilt of the old ways
- † Clothe yourself in Christ by faith
- † Walk in your identity of love and freedom

CONNECTION

Thank You, Lord, for clothing me in Your righteousness. Help me put off my old self and put on the new man in Christ every day. Teach me to live from the identity You've given me. In Jesus' name, Amen.

HIGHLIGHT QUOTE

We no longer hide in shame; we stand covered in Christ's glory.

JOURNAL PROMPT

What "old" attitude or habit might you need to put off as you put on Christ by faith?

DAY 8
In the Beauty of Holiness

Worship the LORD in the beauty of holiness.
– Psalm 29:2

REFLECTION

Holiness is not about perfection; it's about devotion. The beauty of holiness shines through hearts fully surrendered to God. As we worship in purity and truth, His presence adorns our lives with peace and grace. True holiness is the work of the Holy Spirit, transforming us from the inside out as we reflect the glory of the Lord.

APPLICATION

- † Commit your thoughts and actions to honor God today
- † Seek a purity of heart through prayer and humility
- † Reflect His beauty by walking in love and grace

CONNECTION

Thank You, Lord, for the beauty of Your holiness. Help me lay aside distractions that draw my heart away from worship. Shape my life through the Holy Spirit so that I may reflect Your glory. In Jesus' name, Amen.

HIGHLIGHT QUOTE

The beauty of holiness shines through a heart fully surrendered to God.

JOURNAL PROMPT

How can your worship today reflect a heart of devotion rather than perfection?

A 365-Day Journey Walking with the Word & the Spirit

DAY 9
Steps of Faith

The steps of a good man are ordered by the LORD, And He delights in his way.
— Psalm 37:23

REFLECTION

God delights in guiding His children. Even detours and delays serve as part of His divine direction. When we surrender our plans to Him, our steps become steady and full of purpose. Though the path may twist and turn, His hand never leaves ours. Each act of obedience leads to a blessing, even when the destination remains unseen.

APPLICATION

† Begin each day by inviting God to direct your plans
† Trust His leading, even when the path ahead feels uncertain
† Rejoice knowing He delights in every step of your journey with Him

CONNECTION

Thank You, Lord, for ordering my steps. Help me walk faithfully in Your direction and trust You when I cannot see the whole path ahead. Strengthen my confidence in Your steady hand and remind me of Your presence. In Jesus' name, Amen.

HIGHLIGHT QUOTE

Our confidence isn't in knowing every step; it's in knowing the One who leads.

JOURNAL PROMPT

Where might God be redirecting your steps toward His greater purpose?

DAY 10
Streams in the Desert

> *I will even make a road in the wilderness And rivers in the desert.*
> – Isaiah 43:19

REFLECTION

God specializes in impossible places. When the wilderness feels endless and the desert is dry, His Spirit brings living water. He creates paths where there were none and refreshes weary souls. Every dry place becomes an opportunity for His glory to flow. In Him, barrenness turns to fruitfulness, and desolation becomes a testimony to His faithfulness.

APPLICATION

† Ask God to refresh your spirit where you feel dry
† Look for His purpose in your wilderness season
† Trust that He's making a way, even when you can't see it

CONNECTION

Thank You, Lord, for making rivers in my desert. Refresh my heart and renew my hope in Your faithfulness. I trust You to bring life where there seems to be none. In Jesus' name, Amen.

HIGHLIGHT QUOTE

In the Lord, barrenness turns to fruitfulness.

JOURNAL PROMPT

Where might God be bringing new life into your dry or waiting season?

DAY 11
The Faith to Move Mountains

> *If you have faith as a mustard seed, you will say to this mountain, 'Move from here to there,' and it will move.*
> – Matthew 17:20

REFLECTION

Faith doesn't deny the mountain; it speaks to it. Even a small amount of faith becomes mighty when placed in a mighty God. Power lies not in the size of our faith but in the focus of it. Jesus is the focus, not us or others. When we speak God's Word with trust and perseverance, obstacles shift, and He reveals His power. Faith moves forward when sight cannot.

APPLICATION

† Speak life and truth over your challenges
† Refuse to magnify the mountain; magnify your God
† Keep believing, even when progress seems small

CONNECTION

Thank You, Lord, for a faith that moves mountains. Increase my faith in You only. Strengthen my trust in Your power and remind me that nothing is impossible for You. In Jesus' name, Amen.

HIGHLIGHT QUOTE

A small faith in a big God can move what fear says will never move.

JOURNAL PROMPT

What mountain do you need to speak to with faith today?

DAY 12
Sustained by the Spirit

> *The spirit of a man will sustain him in sickness, But who can bear a broken spirit?*
> – Proverbs 18:14

REFLECTION

A strong spirit sustains us through sickness, loss, and trials. The Spirit of Christ within strengthens us with love, power, and a sound mind. Though our body and soul may weaken, God upholds us with His mighty hand. Prayer, praise, and His Word fortify our inner lives, giving us endurance and peace. Faith rests not in circumstances but in His sustaining power, which never fails.

APPLICATION

† Strengthen your spirit through prayer and praise
† Stand firm in faith during trials
† Trust God's sustaining power in weakness

CONNECTION

Thank You, Lord, for Your sustaining power. I surrender to Your Spirit to strengthen my inner man to stand firm through every trial. In Jesus' name, Amen.

HIGHLIGHT QUOTE

Though the body weakens, His Spirit sustains the heart that trusts Him.

JOURNAL PROMPT

How can you strengthen your spirit today to stand firm in faith?

DAY 13
Walking in Truth

I have no greater joy than to hear that my children walk in truth.
– 3 John 4

REFLECTION

Unspoken hurts and unresolved matters can fester into bitterness. Sometimes minor arguments mask deeper issues left unhealed. What seems small might be a secret call for aid. Only the Holy Spirit can reveal what is unvoiced, heal root causes, and restore peace. As He leads us, truth brings freedom, forgiveness, and reconciliation.

APPLICATION

† Yield to the Spirit for clarity and healing
† Pray for reconciliation with others
† Walk daily in truth, love, and peace

CONNECTION

Thank You, Lord, for leading me to walk in truth. Heal what's hidden and help me love with grace. Teach me to seek reconciliation and live in peace. In Jesus' name, Amen.

HIGHLIGHT QUOTE

Truth brings healing where love and grace lead.

JOURNAL PROMPT

Where might the Holy Spirit be calling you to seek truth or reconciliation today?

DAY 14
Counting Him Faithful

> *By faith Sarah herself also received strength to conceive seed, and she bore a child when she was past the age, because she judged Him faithful who had promised.*
> – Hebrews 11:11

REFLECTION

Sarah conceived because she trusted God's faithfulness. We also see His promises fulfilled when we remember His past works and believe His Word today. Fear grows when we focus on the lack instead of on the Provider. Like the disciples, we may forget yesterday's miracle in today's trial, but God never changes. His salvation, healing, and provision remain constant for every generation.

APPLICATION

- † Recall God's past faithfulness
- † Shift your focus from lack to the Provider
- † Rest in His unchanging promises

CONNECTION

Thank You, Lord, for Your unfailing faithfulness. Help me remember Your works and trust You fully today. Strengthen my faith to believe that every promise You've made will come to pass. In Jesus' name, Amen.

HIGHLIGHT QUOTE

Faith grows when we remember the faithfulness of God.

JOURNAL PROMPT

What promise are you believing God to fulfill, and how can you count Him faithful?

DAY 15
The Joy of the Lord

For the joy of the LORD is your strength.
– Nehemiah 8:10

REFLECTION

We do not find genuine joy in circumstances but in Christ. His joy strengthens us when emotions fail and renews us when life feels heavy. The joy of the Lord is not shallow happiness; it's a deep assurance that He is good, faithful, and near. When joy becomes our strength, despair loses its grip, illuminating our path even in the darkest moments.

APPLICATION

- † Choose gratitude, even when you don't feel joyful
- † Ask the Holy Spirit to restore your joy in His presence
- † Share encouragement with someone who feels weary

CONNECTION

Thank You, Lord, for being my source of joy and strength. Fill my heart with gladness that rises above circumstances and refreshes those around me. In Jesus' name, Amen.

HIGHLIGHT QUOTE

Joy isn't the absence of struggle; it's God within it.

JOURNAL PROMPT

What simple act of gratitude can you practice today to renew your joy?

A 365-Day Journey Walking with the Word & the Spirit

DAY 16
Keeping the Light On

> *Your word is a lamp to my feet And a light to my path.*
> *– Psalm 119:105*

REFLECTION

God's Word is the light that guides us through darkness. Without it, we stumble; with it, clarity and direction come. The Word feeds our spirit, renews our mind, and strengthens our walk. Daily reading keeps the lamp burning and guards our steps from confusion. Even brief moments in Scripture shine more light than we realize, revealing His presence and direction.

APPLICATION

† Read the Word daily as spiritual nourishment
† Seek Scriptures that speak to your current season
† Walk in the light, not in confusion or fear

CONNECTION

Thank You, Lord, for Your Word that lights my path. Keep me nourished and guided by Your truth daily. May Your light lead me in every decision. In Jesus' name, Amen.

HIGHLIGHT QUOTE

Every step grows clearer when we walk in the light of God's Word.

JOURNAL PROMPT

How can you make time today to read and reflect on God's Word?

DAY 17
Worship in Spirit and Truth

> *But the hour is coming, and now is, when the true worshipers will worship the Father in spirit and truth; ... God is Spirit, and those who worship Him must worship in spirit and truth.*
> – John 4:23–24

REFLECTION

Worship is both intimacy and warfare. It draws us into God's presence, magnifies Him above all else, and causes the enemy to flee. In trials, worship shifts our focus from darkness to light. It isn't dependent on feelings; it's founded on truth. Worship is our eternal calling, so we practice loving, honoring, and surrendering to the Father. In His presence, battles turn into victories.

APPLICATION

† Worship even when you don't feel like it
† Magnify God above your circumstances
† Resist the enemy through praise

CONNECTION

Thank You, Lord, for the gift of worship. Teach me to honor You in spirit and truth and to praise You even in life's battles. In Jesus' name, Amen.

HIGHLIGHT QUOTE

Worship shifts our focus from the battle to the One who brings victory.

JOURNAL PROMPT

How can you make worship your first response rather than your last resort?

A 365-Day Journey Walking with the Word & the Spirit

DAY 18
Treasuring Others

> *Beloved, if God so loved us, we also ought to love one another.*
> – 1 John 4:11

REFLECTION

God's love gives us identity and worth. When we receive His love, we can love others with grace and appreciation. Rejection loses power, and offenses fade away. Too often, we misplace value, overlooking small treasures or overvaluing what is temporary. God's love resets our priorities and helps us treasure what truly matters: Him, His people, and His gifts. Love values, honors, and uplifts.

APPLICATION

† Receive God's love for your worth
† Honor others as priceless to Him
† Treasure His gifts, both big and small

CONNECTION

Thank You, Lord, for loving me perfectly. Forgive me for my misplaced priorities. Help me treasure You and value others through the lens of Your love. In Jesus' name, Amen.

HIGHLIGHT QUOTE

God's love resets our priorities and teaches us to treasure what matters most.

JOURNAL PROMPT

Who in your life might need to be reminded of their worth and value in God's eyes?

A 365-Day Journey Walking with the Word & the Spirit

DAY 19
Catch the Foxes

> *Catch us the foxes, The little foxes that spoil the vines, For our vines have tender grapes.*
> *– Song of Solomon 2:15*

REFLECTION

Small things can spoil fruitfulness if left unchecked. A careless word, a minor offense, or a hidden flaw can hinder growth. Like foxes, they dig unseen holes that threaten what's tender and new. God teaches us to build boundaries that protect His work in our lives. By His grace, we guard what He's planted, nurture growth, and preserve the fruit of His Spirit.

APPLICATION

† Identify minor issues before they grow
† Set healthy boundaries by God's grace
† Guard your heart and protect what God has planted

CONNECTION

Thank You, Lord, for helping me guard my vineyard. Show me what needs attention and strengthen me to protect the fruit of Your work in my life. In Jesus' name, Amen.

HIGHLIGHT QUOTE

Small compromises can spoil great fruit, so guard what God has planted.

JOURNAL PROMPT

What small foxes might the Holy Spirit be prompting you to address before they grow?

DAY 20
Guarding Your Heart

Keep your heart with all diligence, For out of it spring the issues of life.
– Proverbs 4:23

REFLECTION

Our hearts are the wellspring of life, shaping our words, actions, and relationships. What we allow in determines what flows out. Guarding the heart means protecting peace, filtering influences, and keeping love alive. It requires wisdom and intentionally setting healthy boundaries in love and truth. A heart anchored in God remains pure, fruitful, and steadfast.

APPLICATION

† Be mindful of what you allow to influence your heart
† Forgive quickly to keep your heart free
† Let God's Word shape your thoughts and motives

CONNECTION

Thank You, Lord, for giving me a new heart. Help me guard it carefully and fill it with Your truth and peace. Keep my love pure and my motives right before You. In Jesus' name, Amen.

HIGHLIGHT QUOTE

What we guard in our hearts determines what flows from our lives.

JOURNAL PROMPT

What habit or thought do you need to remove to better guard your heart?

DAY 21
Standing in the Fire

> *Our God whom we serve is able to deliver us from the burning fiery furnace, and He will deliver us from your hand, O king.*
> – Daniel 3:17

REFLECTION

In trials, our focus determines our faith. Looking at the fire or its cause brings fear, but looking at the Lord brings peace and victory. The enemy amplifies the noise of adversity to distract us, yet God's presence is our assurance. As we magnify Him above the flames, the fire loses its power to consume. He is with us, and His peace guards our hearts in the heat of every test.

APPLICATION

- † Focus on the Lord, not the fire
- † Magnify His presence above adversity
- † Stand firm against pressure to bow

CONNECTION

Thank You, Lord, for being with me in every fire. Help me magnify You above the flames and trust in Your deliverance. In Jesus' name, Amen.

HIGHLIGHT QUOTE

As we magnify Him above the flames, the fire loses its power to consume.

JOURNAL PROMPT

Where is God asking you to shift your focus from the fire to His faithful presence?

DAY 22
Our Leading Shepherd

> *The LORD is my shepherd; I shall not want.*
> – Psalm 23:1

REFLECTION

As our Shepherd, God lovingly leads us to still waters and restores our souls. In His care, we truly lack nothing. When we follow His voice, we find safety, rest, and renewal. His presence turns valleys into green pastures and replaces fear with peace. He guides with love, guards with grace, and meets every need along the way.

APPLICATION

- † Trust His guidance, even when the way seems uncertain
- † Express gratitude for His daily provision and peace
- † Prioritize His voice above all others in your life

CONNECTION

Thank You, Lord, for being my Shepherd. Lead me beside still waters and restore my soul. Help me trust You completely and rest in Your peace. In Jesus' name, Amen.

HIGHLIGHT QUOTE

The Shepherd's presence turns every valley into a place of peace.

JOURNAL PROMPT

Where do you sense the Shepherd is leading you to rest and trust His care?

A 365-Day Journey Walking with the Word & the Spirit

DAY 23
Our Shield of Protection

> *But You, O LORD, are a shield for me, My glory and the One who lifts up my head.*
> *– Psalm 3:3*

REFLECTION

David called God his shield, not a partial covering but a complete, surrounding protection. The Lord shields us above and beneath, before and behind, and on every side. This doesn't mean we never face trials but that every challenge must pass through His care. God even uses difficulties to refine our trust and display His glory. When we remember He is our defender, fear loses its grip, and faith steadies our hearts again.

APPLICATION

- † Rest in the truth that God's protection covers every side
- † Trust His sovereignty when you feel vulnerable
- † Thank Him for turning every trial into spiritual growth

CONNECTION

Thank You, Lord, for surrounding me with Your perfect protection. Teach me to rest in Your care and stand secure beneath Your covering. My safety and confidence are in You alone. In Jesus' name, Amen.

HIGHLIGHT QUOTE

God even uses difficulties to refine our trust and display His glory.

JOURNAL PROMPT

Where do you need to lift your shield of faith today?

A 365-Day Journey Walking with the Word & the Spirit

DAY 24
Power of His Indwelling

But you are not in the flesh but in the Spirit, if indeed the Spirit of God dwells in you.
– Romans 8:9

REFLECTION

The same Spirit who raised Jesus from the dead dwells within us, even when our flesh feels weak. Guilt and doubt may whisper otherwise, but His presence never departs. Confidence in His indwelling power enables us to rise above fear and frailty. In our weakness, He strengthens us and equips us to live boldly and love deeply. God's Word, not our circumstances, defines our identity.

APPLICATION

- † Believe that the Holy Spirit dwells in you
- † Trust His power in your weakness
- † Walk in the identity He has given you

CONNECTION

Thank You, Lord, for the power of Your Spirit within me. Help me walk in Your strength and reflect Your life each day. In Jesus' name, Amen.

HIGHLIGHT QUOTE

The Holy Spirit within us is greater than our weakness.

JOURNAL PROMPT

What area of your life needs to be strengthened by remembering that the Spirit dwells in you?

DAY 25
What Are We Saying?

Whoever guards his mouth and tongue Keeps his soul from troubles.
– Proverbs 21:23

REFLECTION

Words carry the power to wound or to heal. Unchecked speech can harm, but surrendered words become vessels of grace. The enemy tempts us toward gossip or complaint, yet silence often brings greater peace. Guarding our words requires the help of the Holy Spirit, enabling us to speak truth in love. When our tongues align with His heart, our words bring light and life to those around us.

APPLICATION

† Pray for grace to guard your tongue
† Avoid gossip and careless words
† Speak the truth in love through the Spirit's guidance

CONNECTION

Thank You, Lord, for the power of words. Help me guard my tongue and use my speech to build up, not tear down. In Jesus' name, Amen.

HIGHLIGHT QUOTE

Words surrendered to God become vessels of His grace.

JOURNAL PROMPT

What conversation might God be asking you to surrender to Him?

DAY 26
Faithful in the Little Things

> *He who is faithful in what is least is faithful also in much.*
> *– Luke 16:10*

REFLECTION

God measures greatness by faithfulness, not size. Every minor act of obedience lays the foundation for greater things. When we serve Him with humility in what seems insignificant, He prepares us for influence we cannot yet see. Faithfulness in little things proves our readiness for the greater. He lets nothing done for Him go to waste.

APPLICATION

† Be faithful in today's tasks, no matter how small

† Trust God to see what others overlook

† Commit to consistency over recognition

CONNECTION

Thank You, Lord, for taking what looks small and making it big in Your hands. Help me serve You wholeheartedly in every assignment, knowing You see and reward every act done in love. In Jesus' name, Amen.

HIGHLIGHT QUOTE

Faithfulness in small things prepares us for the miracles of greater ones.

JOURNAL PROMPT

Where can you practice quiet faithfulness today, even if no one notices but God?

A 365-Day Journey Walking with the Word & the Spirit

DAY 27
Increase Our Faith

> *And the apostles said to the Lord, "Increase our faith."*
> *– Luke 17:5*

REFLECTION

The disciples understood that forgiveness requires faith beyond human strength. Their request mirrors our own struggles to forgive when wounded. Faith grows as we recall God's faithfulness and yield our hurts to His transforming power. Love fuels faith, and faith results in forgiveness—this love comes from the Holy Spirit, which He puts in our hearts.

APPLICATION

† Pray for increased faith where you need to forgive
† Remember God's faithfulness in shaping your heart
† Release offenses and trust His power to transform

CONNECTION

Thank You, Lord, for being the Author and Finisher of my faith. Increase my faith where forgiveness feels impossible. Teach me to trust You fully to heal and renew my heart. In Jesus' name, Amen.

HIGHLIGHT QUOTE

Faith grows as we recall God's faithfulness and yield our hurts to Him.

JOURNAL PROMPT

Where might God be asking you to extend forgiveness as an act of faith?

A 365-Day Journey Walking with the Word & the Spirit

DAY 28
Christ Is the Head

And He is the head of the body, the church ... that in all things He may have the preeminence.
— Colossians 1:18

REFLECTION

Jesus is the head of His church, and under His authority, we walk in unity. Division reveals the enemy's schemes, but unity magnifies His presence. Like a body out of alignment, we lose balance when disconnected from Him. As we realign through prayer and worship, His peace restores us, and His presence flows freely.

APPLICATION

- † Resist division and pursue unity through love
- † Reconnect to Christ daily through prayer and worship
- † Abide in Him as your constant source of life

CONNECTION

Thank You, Lord, for being the Head of Your Church. Align my heart with Yours and help me walk in unity with others. In Jesus' name, Amen.

HIGHLIGHT QUOTE

When Christ is our focus, unity becomes our fruit.

JOURNAL PROMPT

What area of your life needs to realign with Christ's leadership and peace?

DAY 29
The God Who Sees

> *Then she called the name of the LORD who spoke to her, You-Are-the-God-Who-Sees.*
> – Genesis 16:13

REFLECTION

Hagar's story reminds us that God sees what others overlook. In lonely or forgotten places, His eyes never leave us. The God who sees also redeems and restores. His gaze isn't one of judgment but compassion. When we feel unseen, we can rest in His care, confident that His plans are for our good. The more we recognize His eyes upon us, the clearer we see Him.

APPLICATION

† Remember God fully knows you and loves you deeply
† Thank Him for noticing what others may miss
† Encourage someone you sense feels overlooked

CONNECTION

Thank You, Lord, for being the God who sees me. Help me rest in Your compassionate gaze and extend that same care to others. In Jesus' name, Amen.

HIGHLIGHT QUOTE

Even when we feel invisible, God sees, and He never looks away.

JOURNAL PROMPT

Where have you felt unseen lately, and how is God revealing His care in that place?

DAY 30
Trusting God's Timing

> *To everything there is a season, A time for every purpose under heaven.*
> – Ecclesiastes 3:1

REFLECTION

God's timing is never late, though it often stretches our patience. He works behind the scenes, aligning every detail for good. Delays are not denials; they prepare us for what's ahead. Trusting His timing means resting in His wisdom and believing that every season carries a purpose. When we wait in faith, we position ourselves for fulfillment in His perfect plan.

APPLICATION

† Surrender your timeline to God's perfect plan
† Praise Him in the waiting, not just the arrival
† Remember that His preparation is part of His promise

CONNECTION

Thank You, Lord, for being right on time in every season. Teach me to wait with peace and trust in Your plan. Strengthen my patience and deepen my faith. In Jesus' name, Amen.

HIGHLIGHT QUOTE

God's timing may test our patience, but it never fails in His purpose.

JOURNAL PROMPT

What promise are you waiting on that requires renewed trust in God's timing?

A 365-Day Journey Walking with the Word & the Spirit

DAY 31
Made New by the Spirit

> *I say then: Walk in the Spirit, and you shall not fulfill the lust of the flesh.*
> – Galatians 5:16

REFLECTION

Walking in the Spirit changes how we live, think, and respond. The battle between the flesh and the spirit is real, but God's power within us is stronger than our weakness. As we feed on His Word, pray, and draw near in worship, our spirit grows, and the old nature loses its pull. Each day of surrender renews us in His grace, teaching us to walk in freedom and joy.

APPLICATION

† Feed your spirit daily through Scripture and prayer
† Surrender old habits and rely on the Spirit's strength
† Walk in the freedom that comes from your new life in Christ

CONNECTION

Thank You, Lord, for renewing me by Your Spirit. Help me surrender daily, walk in Your strength, and reflect Your grace. In Jesus' name, Amen.

HIGHLIGHT QUOTE

As we walk in the Spirit, our weakness meets His strength.

JOURNAL PROMPT

How can you depend on the Spirit's strength instead of your own today?

DAY 32
Hearing His Lovingkindness

Cause me to hear Your lovingkindness in the morning, For in You do I trust; Cause me to know the way in which I should walk.
– Psalm 143:8

REFLECTION

Each new morning offers us the chance to tune our hearts to God's voice. His lovingkindness is constant, but it takes intention to pause and listen amid life's noise. He longs to lead us in ways we cannot see, gently guiding us with His care. Trust grows as we listen daily, allowing Him to redirect us with His wisdom and love.

APPLICATION

† Listen to His voice, not only your own
† Pause for His guidance before rushing into plans
† Stay open to His redirection throughout the day

CONNECTION

Thank You, Lord, for Your love, care, and guidance. I trust You and desire to trust You more. Cause me to know which way I should walk and how I should glorify You. In Jesus' name, Amen.

HIGHLIGHT QUOTE

His lovingkindness leads us with gentle care each morning.

JOURNAL PROMPT

How can you set aside a few moments each morning to hear His voice more clearly?

DAY 33
Trusting God's Leading

> *Trust in the LORD with all your heart, And lean not on your own understanding; In all your ways acknowledge Him, And He shall direct your paths.*
> – Proverbs 3:5–6

REFLECTION

Trusting God often means surrendering our own reasoning. His ways may lead us where logic would not, teaching us to rely on the Holy Spirit more than on our instincts. Every act of obedience becomes an expression of trust, showing faith in His direction. When we acknowledge Him, He faithfully aligns our steps with His perfect will.

APPLICATION

† Pause and pray before each important decision
† Ask God for confirmation before moving forward
† Choose trust, even when His way feels uncertain

CONNECTION

Thank You, Lord, for sharpening my hearing and increasing my confidence in You. Forgive me for leaning on my own understanding. Help me to acknowledge You quickly and follow Your leading. In Jesus' name, Amen.

HIGHLIGHT QUOTE

Trusting God often means surrendering our own reasoning.

JOURNAL PROMPT

What step of faith is God asking you to take today that stretches your understanding?

DAY 34
Pressing On in Faith

> *Not that I have already attained, or am already perfected; but I press on, that I may lay hold of that for which Christ Jesus has also laid hold of me.*
> – Philippians 3:12

REFLECTION

The Christian life is not about instant perfection but continual progress. God shapes our hearts through both triumphs and trials, teaching us to rely on His strength more than our own. Pressing on means trusting Him in the unseen process and believing He's working, even when results are pending. Each step forward, no matter how small, is evidence of His grace at work within us.

APPLICATION

- † Celebrate small victories as signs of His ongoing work
- † Surrender impatience and rest in His perfect timing
- † Remain faithful when progress feels slow or hidden

CONNECTION

Thank You, Lord, for Your patient grace shaping my journey. Help me persevere when progress seems slow, and help me to keep pressing toward the purpose You've prepared for me. In Jesus' name, Amen.

HIGHLIGHT QUOTE

The Christian life is not about instant perfection but continual progress.

JOURNAL PROMPT

Where in your life do you need to press on in faith despite slow progress?

A 365-Day Journey Walking with the Word & the Spirit

DAY 35
Open Doors and Opposition

> *For a great and effective door has opened to me, and there are many adversaries.*
> – 1 Corinthians 16:9

REFLECTION

With every God-given opportunity, there often comes resistance. The enemy seeks to oppose what God has set before us, but his efforts cannot prevail against God's plan. Opposition should not discourage us but remind us that the door is significant. By standing firm in His Word, led by the Holy Spirit, we walk boldly through the doors He opens.

APPLICATION

- † Pray for discernment when opportunities arise
- † Prepare spiritually for the resistance that may come
- † Stand firm in God's promises when facing challenges

CONNECTION

Thank You, Lord, for the opportunities You place before me. Strengthen me to withstand opposition and remain steadfast in Your Word. I choose to walk in the purpose You have prepared. In Jesus' name, Amen.

HIGHLIGHT QUOTE

Adversity confirms God's opportunities.

JOURNAL PROMPT

What opportunities has God opened to you that require perseverance against resistance?

DAY 36
He Knows Each One of Us

I am the good shepherd; and I know My sheep, and am known by My own.
– John 10:14

REFLECTION

Jesus, our Good Shepherd, knows us intimately by name and cherishes every detail of our lives. His unwavering love envelops us as He protects us from harm and guides us to safety. As His sheep, we learn to trust more deeply as we recognize His voice and follow Him. In His presence, we discover rest, security, and the fullness of the life He offers.

APPLICATION

- † Take time today to thank Jesus for His personal care
- † Practice listening for His voice through prayer and Scripture
- † Choose to rest in His presence instead of worrying

CONNECTION

Thank You, Lord, for being my Good Shepherd. Your care fills me with awe and peace. Forgive me for worrying as though You are not with me. Help me follow Your voice with trust. In Jesus' name, Amen.

HIGHLIGHT QUOTE

He who knows you best loves you most.

JOURNAL PROMPT

How can you grow in recognizing and following the Shepherd's voice this week?

DAY 37
Shaking Off Resentment

*"Be angry, and do not sin":
do not let the sun go down
on your wrath.*
– Ephesians 4:26

REFLECTION

Resentment often starts small but can grow into bitterness if not addressed. God calls us to release anger quickly, preventing it from taking root in our hearts. Embracing forgiveness brings restoration and protects us from the enemy's schemes. Daily surrender to the Holy Spirit enables us to shake off offenses and walk in freedom.

APPLICATION

† Examine your heart for any hidden resentment
† Choose to forgive quickly rather than harbor anger
† Invite the Holy Spirit to heal and soften your heart

CONNECTION

Thank You, Lord, for Your wisdom in protecting my heart. Help me release anger quickly and walk in forgiveness. Heal any wounds that may nurture resentment and fill me with Your peace. In Jesus' name, Amen.

HIGHLIGHT QUOTE

Unresolved anger is the seedbed of bitterness, but forgiveness uproots it.

JOURNAL PROMPT

Is there someone you need to forgive to release any resentment?

DAY 38
The Power of Forgiveness

> Now whom you forgive anything, I also forgive. For if indeed I have forgiven anything, I have forgiven that one for your sakes in the presence of Christ.
> – 2 Corinthians 2:10

REFLECTION

Forgiveness is both a command and a gift of freedom. It is not merely a gesture toward others but a necessary release for our own souls. Holding onto offenses quenches the Holy Spirit's flow in our lives. We must strive to forgive as Christ forgave us, opening the door to healing and peace. It's a powerful key that, left unused, keeps us stuck.

APPLICATION

† Pray for strength to forgive those who have wronged you
† Release offenses into God's hands daily
† Embrace the freedom that comes with forgiveness

CONNECTION

Thank You, Lord, for the incredible gift of forgiveness through the cross. I forgive others and myself by Your grace. May I walk daily in the freedom of Your Spirit. In Jesus' name, Amen.

HIGHLIGHT QUOTE

Holding onto offenses quenches the Holy Spirit's flow in our lives.

JOURNAL PROMPT

Who is God prompting you to forgive today so you can walk in greater freedom?

DAY 39
Vintage Wine in the Making

Wait on the LORD; Be of good courage, And He shall strengthen your heart; Wait, I say, on the LORD!
— Psalm 27:14

REFLECTION

Waiting is one of God's refining tools, shaping us into vessels of faith and endurance. Like vintage wine, He cannot rush His work in us, for He is producing something lasting and beautiful. Impatience tempts us to act on our own, but waiting on Him strengthens our hearts. His perfect timing ensures the fruit will be rich, pure, and complete.

APPLICATION

† Surrender impatience and choose to wait on His timing
† Trust that God is preparing something far greater than you see
† Use waiting seasons to deepen prayer and reliance on Him

CONNECTION

Thank You, Lord, for what You are perfecting in me. Forgive my hastiness and empower me to wait on Your manifestation. Strengthen my heart to trust in Your timing and praise You always. In Jesus' name, Amen.

HIGHLIGHT QUOTE

Impatience tempts us to act on our own, but waiting on Him strengthens our hearts.

JOURNAL PROMPT

Where is God asking you to wait and trust His timing instead of rushing ahead?

DAY 40
Consider Your Ways

> *Now therefore, thus says the LORD of hosts: "Consider your ways! ...*
> *– Haggai 1:5*

REFLECTION

Our human tendency often leans toward examining the actions and flaws of others rather than reflecting on our own. When the Holy Spirit reveals the lack of His presence around us, it serves as a divine invitation to pray and evaluate our own hearts. He calls us to self-examination, humility, and repentance, aligning our lives again with His truth.

APPLICATION

† Humbly surrender to the Holy Spirit
† Reflect on your own behavior and attitudes
† Yield to His power for healing and transformation

CONNECTION

Thank You, Lord, for Your constant presence. Help me focus on my way rather than on the ways of others. Reveal what only You can heal, and restore my joy and peace. In Jesus' name, Amen.

HIGHLIGHT QUOTE

God reveals what only He can heal.

JOURNAL PROMPT

In what area of your life is the Holy Spirit prompting you to consider your own way?

DAY 41
Burning Compassion

> *The LORD is gracious and full of compassion, Slow to anger and great in mercy.*
> – Psalm 145:8

REFLECTION

God calls us to walk in compassion and abundance, just like Him. Compassion stirs healing, miracles, and manifestations of His glory. As we grasp His forgiveness, our love for Him deepens, fueling compassion for others. Genuine compassion is not based on others' responses but flows from the Holy Spirit through us. Like Christ, we are called to represent Him with mercy, passion, and love.

APPLICATION

† Receive God's compassion and forgiveness
† Extend mercy regardless of response
† Represent Christ with passion and love

CONNECTION

Thank You, Lord, for Your endless compassion. Empower me to represent You with mercy, passion, and love, by Your grace. In Jesus' name, Amen.

HIGHLIGHT QUOTE

As we grasp His forgiveness, love fuels compassion.

JOURNAL PROMPT

How can you extend God's compassion today, even when it's not returned by others?

DAY 42
The Fire of His Presence

> *And they said to one another, "Did not our heart burn within us while He talked with us on the road, and while He opened the Scriptures to us?"*
> – Luke 24:32

REFLECTION

When Jesus spoke to His disciples, their hearts burned with the fire of His presence. That same fire kindles within us today through His Word and Spirit. This holy heartburn awakens our faith and renews our passion for God's truth. The Holy Spirit stirs within us a divine flame that brings revelation, courage, and joy; a fire nothing can extinguish.

APPLICATION

† Spend time in the Word, inviting the fire of His presence
† Follow the Spirit's stirring as confirmation of His leading
† Guard your passion by staying close to Jesus in daily fellowship

CONNECTION

Thank You, Lord, for igniting within me the fire of Your presence. Stir my heart to burn for Your Word and Your will. Empower me to release every hindrance that dulls my passion for You. In Jesus' name, Amen.

HIGHLIGHT QUOTE

His presence sets hearts aflame with passion, clarity, and joy.

JOURNAL PROMPT

When was the last time you felt the fire of His presence? How can you rekindle it today?

A 365-Day Journey Walking with the Word & the Spirit

DAY 43
Jehovah Jireh, Our Provider

And Abraham called the name of the place, The-LORD-Will-Provide.
– Genesis 22:14

REFLECTION

God's provision flows from His infinite riches, not from our limited resources. Often, He releases provision on the other side of surrender. When we trust Him fully, He provides abundantly, sometimes in ways we never expect. We can lean into His unfailing faithfulness and rest in His care, knowing that He carries us and supplies every genuine need in His perfect timing.

APPLICATION

- † Thank God for His provision in past seasons
- † Trust Him with current needs through prayer and surrender
- † Encourage someone else by sharing a testimony of His faithfulness

CONNECTION

Thank You, Lord, for being my faithful Provider. You carry me through life's challenges and supply all my needs. Help me trust Your riches in glory and rest in Your care. In Jesus' name, Amen.

HIGHLIGHT QUOTE

God's supply is limitless, and His provision never fails.

JOURNAL PROMPT

What need can you surrender to God today and trust Him to provide?

DAY 44
Surrendering Our Cups to the Father

Abba, Father, all things are possible for You. Take this cup away from Me; nevertheless, not what I will, but what You will."
– Mark 14:36

REFLECTION

Even Jesus brought His deepest anguish before the Father, demonstrating the power of surrender in moments of suffering. True peace flows when we consciously release our "cups" into His hands and trust His divine will. As we yield our struggles to His control, we find His ability to carry our burdens with grace.

APPLICATION

† Bring your deepest struggles before God in prayer with honesty
† Release control and place your trust in His will above your own
† Lean into His strength and embrace His power in your life

CONNECTION

Thank You, Lord, for being my loving Father. I surrender my struggles into Your hands, trusting in Your perfect plan and timing. Empower me to carry my burdens, knowing they are safe in Your care. In Jesus' name, Amen.

HIGHLIGHT QUOTE

As we yield our struggles to God's control, we find His grace to carry on.

JOURNAL PROMPT

What struggles are you led to release into His hands today?

A 365-Day Journey Walking with the Word & the Spirit

DAY 45
The Spirit of Revelation

> Simon Peter answered and said, "You are the Christ, the Son of the living God." Jesus answered and said to him, "Blessed are you, Simon Bar-Jonah, for flesh and blood has not revealed this to you, but My Father who is in heaven ... – Matthew 16:16–17

REFLECTION

Peter's confession came by revelation, not human reasoning. Revelation is the rock upon which faith grows and deception crumbles. When we try to understand God's will, the Holy Spirit shines truth into our hearts. Revelation is beyond human instruction. Doubt may challenge revelation, but persistence in seeking God strengthens faith.

APPLICATION

† Pray for revelation in every decision
† Trust God to confirm His truth
† Encourage others on their journeys of revelation

CONNECTION

Thank You, Lord, for revealing truth to me by Your Spirit. Open my heart and guide me with revelation knowledge. Keep me steadfast in Your truth and sensitive to Your voice. In Jesus' name, Amen.

HIGHLIGHT QUOTE

Revelation is the rock upon which faith grows.

JOURNAL PROMPT

What has God recently revealed to your heart, and how will you respond in faith?

DAY 46
The Knowledge of God's Love

> *To know the love of Christ which passes knowledge; that you may be filled with all the fullness of God.*
> – Ephesians 3:19

REFLECTION

God's love is steadfast, unconditional, and not tied to our performance. We cannot earn it, nor can we lose it; it is a gift given through Christ. Resting in this truth frees us from striving and self-condemnation. When we receive His love, we unwrap the fullness of Jesus Christ and rest in the assurance that His love is unwavering and complete.

APPLICATION

† Release the belief that God's love depends on your performance
† Receive His forgiveness and let go of self-condemnation
† Rest in His steadfast love through your gratitude and worship

CONNECTION

Thank You, Lord, for Your unconditional, steadfast love. Help me receive and rest in it by faith. I desire to walk in the fullness of it, trusting that nothing can separate me from You. In Jesus' name, Amen.

HIGHLIGHT QUOTE

To know His love is to live in His fullness.

JOURNAL PROMPT

Where do you still struggle to believe His love is truly unconditional?

DAY 47
God's Word Will Stand

> *The grass withers, the flower fades, But the word of our God stands forever.*
> – Isaiah 40:8

REFLECTION

Trends and seasons come and go, but God's Word endures unchanging. His promises remain true no matter what surrounds us. When we build our lives on His Word, storms may come, but our foundation stands firm. The eternal Word who created the world also sustains our hearts; His forever helps us endure our temporary trials.

APPLICATION

† Anchor your thoughts and decisions in God's Word
† Memorize a verse that strengthens your faith this week
† Declare His promises when doubt tries to speak louder

CONNECTION

Thank You, Lord, that Your Word endures forever. Help me to stand on it with unshakable faith and live each day according to Your truth. In Jesus' name, Amen.

HIGHLIGHT QUOTE

His Word endures when everything else fades.

JOURNAL PROMPT

What truth from God's Word anchors you when life feels uncertain?

DAY 48
Broken Cisterns

> *For My people have committed two evils: They have forsaken Me, the fountain of living waters, And hewn themselves cisterns—broken cisterns that can hold no water.*
> – Jeremiah 2:13

REFLECTION

The Holy Spirit fills us not only to refresh us but to overflow through us, bringing life to others. When we surrender fully to Him, His living water revives our dry places and breathes hope into weary souls. God calls us to be rivers, not reservoirs, and channels of His abundance. As His Spirit flows freely through us, our emptiness turns to overflow and our dryness to renewal.

APPLICATION

- † Be still before God and receive His refreshing
- † Ask the Holy Spirit to flow through you to others
- † Share encouragement that brings life and hope

CONNECTION

Thank You, Lord, for the Holy Spirit. Remove any hindrance to His flow in and through me. Help me not to store what You intend to share. Let my life bring glory to You. In Jesus' name, Amen.

HIGHLIGHT QUOTE

When we let the Spirit flow freely, dryness becomes overflow.

JOURNAL PROMPT

Where is God asking you to be a source of His living water to someone else?

DAY 49
God's Divine Timing

> *For the vision is yet for an appointed time; But at the end it will speak, and it will not lie. Though it tarries, wait for it; Because it will surely come, It will not tarry.*
> – Habakkuk 2:3

REFLECTION

God's timing never fails. What He sets as extensions, He plans to use as expansions to bring about His perfect plan. Sometimes, His Spirit moves suddenly, accelerating blessings, healing, and breakthrough beyond what we could imagine. At other times, He teaches us patience while preparing us for the promise. When it is God's appointed time, everything aligns smoothly, quickly, and perfectly according to His will.

APPLICATION

† Fix your focus on God instead of your timeline
† Trust that He is working behind the scenes
† Expect surprises and swift answers to prayer

CONNECTION

Thank You, Lord, for Your perfect timing. Help me release discouragement and trust Your process. Teach me to wait with faith and recognize divine acceleration when it comes. In Jesus' name, Amen.

HIGHLIGHT QUOTE

God's timing is precise, never delayed, and never rushed.

JOURNAL PROMPT

Where might God be aligning things in His perfect time, even if you cannot yet see it?

DAY 50
Fresh Infillings

> *And they were all filled with the Holy Spirit, and they spoke the word of God with boldness.*
> – Acts 4:31

REFLECTION

The Holy Spirit empowers us beyond our natural strength. As He fills us afresh, boldness rises to live and speak for Christ. Just as the early disciples experienced shaking and renewal, we too can welcome His presence in greater measure. Every fresh infilling renews our courage, passion, and power to glorify God in our daily lives.

APPLICATION

† Pray for a fresh filling of the Holy Spirit
† Surrender control and let Him move as He desires
† Step out in boldness as the Spirit leads you

CONNECTION

Thank You, Lord, for the gift of the Holy Spirit. I surrender my will to You. Fill me afresh with Your power and boldness to live for You. In Jesus' name, Amen.

HIGHLIGHT QUOTE

A fresh filling of the Holy Spirit births bold faith.

JOURNAL PROMPT

When was the last time you asked God for a fresh filling of His Spirit, and how did it change you?

*I will even make a road
in the wilderness
And rivers in the desert.*

– Isaiah 43:19

DAY 51
The Bread of Life

> *I am the bread of life. He who comes to Me shall never hunger, and he who believes in Me shall never thirst.*
> – John 6:35

REFLECTION

Jesus alone satisfies the hunger and thirst of our souls. While the world leaves us empty, He fills us with purpose, peace, and joy. As we feed on His Word and dwell in His presence, we find lasting fulfillment. He is our ultimate nourishment and the source of abundant life. Only in Him do we find deep, abiding satisfaction.

APPLICATION

- † Spend time in Scripture as daily nourishment for your soul
- † Turn away from empty substitutes that cannot satisfy
- † Rely on Christ to meet both spiritual and practical needs

CONNECTION

Thank You, Lord, for being my Bread of Life. Help me seek You daily for my spiritual nourishment. Satisfy my soul with Your presence, keeping me from reaching for what cannot fulfill. In Jesus' name, Amen.

HIGHLIGHT QUOTE

Only Jesus satisfies the deepest hunger of the heart.

JOURNAL PROMPT

Are there any areas of your life where you have been seeking fulfillment apart from Him?

DAY 52
Come to Me

> Come to Me, all you who labor and are heavy laden, and I will give you rest.
> – Matthew 11:28

REFLECTION

Jesus' invitation, "Come to Me," is deeply personal. He doesn't just offer rest *from* something; He offers rest *in* Himself. True peace begins when we draw near Him, not only when our circumstances change. His rest flows out of relationship, not relief. When we come first into His presence, we find strength for the day and comfort that quiets the soul.

APPLICATION

- † Spend time simply being with Jesus, not asking for anything
- † Let His presence quiet your heart before you begin your day
- † Receive His rest as a gift of relationship, not a reward for effort

CONNECTION

Thank You, Lord, for inviting me to draw closer. Teach me to rest in Your presence and find peace through my relationship with You. May my heart always respond to Your gentle call. In Jesus' name, Amen.

HIGHLIGHT QUOTE

Jesus doesn't just give rest; He *is* our rest.

JOURNAL PROMPT

How can you make space each day to rest in Jesus Himself?

DAY 53
The Lord Is My Refuge

God is our refuge and strength, A very present help in trouble.
– Psalm 46:1

REFLECTION

In times of trouble, God does not watch from afar; He draws near. He is our refuge when life feels uncertain and our strength when we have none left. During spiritual warfare, we can run to Him and find safety in His presence. When everything else shakes, His stability remains, and His peace anchors our souls.

APPLICATION

† Turn to prayer as your first response, not your last resort
† Remember that God's presence is your safest refuge
† Encourage someone else to find strength in Him today

CONNECTION

Thank You, Lord, for being my refuge and strength. Help me run to You above all else. Shelter me in Your love and remind me that Your presence is my peace. In Jesus' name, Amen.

HIGHLIGHT QUOTE

God doesn't just give peace; He is peace, our refuge in every storm.

JOURNAL PROMPT

What trouble or fear do you need to bring under God's refuge today?

DAY 54
He Will Establish and Guard You

> *But the Lord is faithful, who will establish you and guard you from the evil one.*
> – 2 Thessalonians 3:3

REFLECTION

God's faithfulness secures and strengthens us, even in seasons of trial or battle. He not only establishes us on solid ground but also guards us from the enemy's attacks. This assurance gives us confidence to walk boldly, knowing His power holds us steady. Nothing can undo the sealed victory we have in Christ.

APPLICATION

- † Remember the times when God protected and strengthened you
- † Trust His faithfulness when facing spiritual challenges
- † Walk boldly today, confident in His victory over the enemy

CONNECTION

Thank You, Lord, for Your unwavering faithfulness. You establish me and guard me from evil. Help me remain steadfast in faith and depend on Your protection every day. In Jesus' name, Amen.

HIGHLIGHT QUOTE

Nothing can undo the sealed victory we have in Christ.

JOURNAL PROMPT

Where do you need to stand firm in the assurance of His protection?

DAY 55
Anchored in Love

> *That Christ may dwell in your hearts through faith; that you, being rooted and grounded in love.*
> – Ephesians 3:17

REFLECTION

God's love not only nurtures us; it anchors us. When we rest in His unchanging affection, insecurity and fear lose their grip. His love defines our worth and steadies our faith through life's storms. Rooted in this truth, we stand unshaken, confident that nothing can separate us from His care. The deeper our trust in His love, the stronger our peace becomes.

APPLICATION

- † Fix your heart on God's love when uncertainty arises
- † Let His truth define your identity, not comparison or opinion
- † Rest daily in the assurance that His love will not fail

CONNECTION

Thank You, Lord, for anchoring me in Your unfailing love. When doubts or storms arise, remind me that Your affection is my security. Teach me to rest fully in who You are. In Jesus' name, Amen.

HIGHLIGHT QUOTE

God's love is the anchor that steadies every heart.

JOURNAL PROMPT

Where do you need to rest more deeply in the security of God's love?

DAY 56
Stand Fast in the Faith

Watch, stand fast in the faith, be brave, be strong.
– 1 Corinthians 16:13

REFLECTION

In a world filled with distractions and pressure, God calls us to remain steadfast in faith. Standing firm means staying spiritually alert, courageous, and anchored in Christ. Challenges may come, but when our foundation is in Him, nothing can shake us. Faith makes us strong to endure and overcome every test.

APPLICATION

† Begin your day by asking God to keep you spiritually alert
† Respond to challenges with courage instead of fear
† Stand firm on His promises when pressures surround you

CONNECTION

Thank You, Lord, for empowering me to stay watchful and unwavering in my faith. Give me the strength to stand firm under pressure. Keep me courageous and steadfast through every trial. In Jesus' name, Amen.

HIGHLIGHT QUOTE

Faith stands strong when it's rooted in Christ.

JOURNAL PROMPT

What situation today requires you to stand strong in faith?

DAY 57
The Spirit of Truth

> By this we know the spirit of truth and the spirit of error.
> – 1 John 4:6

REFLECTION

In a world clouded by deception, the Spirit of Truth brings clarity and discernment. The Holy Spirit helps us distinguish God's voice from the surrounding noise. Testing every spirit ensures we remain anchored in truth and protected from error. Intimacy with Him sharpens our discernment and strengthens our walk with Christ.

APPLICATION

- † Spend time in Scripture to grow in recognizing God's truth
- † Pray for discernment before making important decisions
- † Guard your heart by testing what you hear against God's Word

CONNECTION

Thank You, Lord, for giving me the Spirit of Truth. Help me discern clearly what is of You, remain unmoved by deception, and stay steadfast in Your Word. In Jesus' name, Amen.

HIGHLIGHT QUOTE

The Spirit of Truth keeps us steady in a world of deception.

JOURNAL PROMPT

Where do you need discernment today to recognize God's truth clearly?

DAY 58
Healing Light

Unto the upright there arises light in the darkness; He is gracious, and full of compassion, and righteous.
– Psalm 112:4

REFLECTION

God's light does more than expose; it heals. When His truth enters the hidden corners of the heart, shame loses its grip and freedom begins. His light reveals not to condemn but to restore, bringing wholeness where brokenness once lived. As we walk honestly before Him, grace replaces guilt, and His compassion renews our story.

APPLICATION

† Invite God's light to touch any hidden or hurting place
† Let His truth bring freedom instead of fear
† Walk in transparency and grace with others

CONNECTION

Thank You, Lord, for Your healing touch. Shine into every shadow of my life and make me whole. Let Your compassion flow through me to bring hope to others. In Jesus' name, Amen.

HIGHLIGHT QUOTE

God's light exposes to heal, not to harm.

JOURNAL PROMPT

Where do you need His light to bring truth and healing today?

DAY 59
Do Not Fret

> *Do not fret because of evildoers, Nor be envious of the workers of iniquity. For they shall soon be cut down like the grass, And wither as the green herb.*
> – Psalm 37:1–2

REFLECTION

It's easy to grow discouraged when the wicked seem to prosper, but God's Word reminds us to stay calm and trust His justice. The victory of evil is temporary, but His righteousness endures forever. When we fix our eyes on the Lord, He fills our hearts with peace that overcomes worry and envy. God's plan always prevails in the end.

APPLICATION

† Shift your focus to God when you fret
† Remind yourself that His plan and justice always prevail
† Encourage others who may struggle with discouragement

CONNECTION

Thank You, Lord, for being victorious in all things. Help me keep my eyes on You and not the surrounding evil. Replace anxiety with peace and envy with trust. Remind me daily that Your power is greater than any evil I see. In Jesus' name, Amen.

HIGHLIGHT QUOTE

God's justice may wait, but it never fails.

JOURNAL PROMPT

What situation tempts you to fret, and how can you release it to God's peace today?

DAY 60
Unshakable Faith

> *If that is the case, our God whom we serve is able to deliver us from the burning fiery furnace, and He will deliver us from your hand, O king. But if not, let it be known to you, O king, that we do not serve your gods, nor will we worship the gold image which you have set up.* – Daniel 3:17–18

REFLECTION

Shadrach, Meshach, and Abednego exemplified a faith that was not dependent on outcome. Their confidence rested in God's sovereignty, not in the certainty of their rescue. Great faith endures through both triumph and trials, deliverance, and difficulty. When we trust Him regardless, we show an unshakable and pure worship.

APPLICATION

- † Reflect on the challenges that test your faith today
- † Declare your trust in God's sovereignty above outcomes
- † Stand firm in faith, even if circumstances remain unchanged

CONNECTION

Thank You, Lord, for Your grace and sustaining power. Help me remain faithful to You, no matter the outcome. Increase my trust in You. In Jesus' name, Amen.

HIGHLIGHT QUOTE

Faith that endures regardless of outcome reveals a heart fully surrendered to God.

JOURNAL PROMPT

What situations in your life require you to trust God, even if the outcome is uncertain?

DAY 61
Removing Barriers

Finally, brethren, pray for us, that the word of the Lord may run swiftly and be glorified.
– 2 Thessalonians 3:1

REFLECTION

Barriers often seek to hinder the flow of God's Word in our lives. Through prayer, we break down these spiritual obstacles and release His truth into our circumstances. When received in faith, God's Word is powerful and unstoppable. Prayer paves the way for His promises to come to fruition. We share the Word by faith, for His glory!

APPLICATION

† Pray for God's Word to flow freely in your life
† Declare His truth over any obstacles that appear resistant
† Stay steadfast in prayer when you face spiritual hindrances

CONNECTION

Thank You, Lord, for the unstoppable power of Your Word. Break every barrier and let Your truth flow freely in my life. Help me share it boldly. In Jesus' name, Amen.

HIGHLIGHT QUOTE

Prayer removes barriers so the Word of God can move freely and bear fruit.

JOURNAL PROMPT

What spiritual barrier might God be calling you to remove through prayer this week?

DAY 62
Abiding in the True Vine

I am the true vine, and My Father is the vinedresser.
– John 15:1

REFLECTION

Just as a branch flourishes by remaining connected to the vine, we too thrive by abiding in Christ. He is our source of life, strength, and fruitfulness. Abiding in Him nourishes our faith and produces enduring fruit. Without Him, our efforts wither, but in Him, we find sustenance and abundance, from glory to glory.

APPLICATION

- † Dedicate time each day to connect with Christ
- † Draw strength from Him instead of relying on yourself
- † Depend on His Word to nourish and guide your steps

CONNECTION

Thank You, Lord, for being my true vine. Help me stay deeply connected to You and draw strength from Your abiding presence. In Jesus' name, Amen.

HIGHLIGHT QUOTE

Fruitfulness flows naturally from a heart that abides continually in Christ.

JOURNAL PROMPT

How can you strengthen your daily connection with Christ this week?

DAY 63
Search My Heart, O God

Search me, O God, and know my heart; Try me, and know my anxieties.
– Psalm 139:23

REFLECTION

When we invite God to search our hearts, He gently reveals the areas that need transformation. The Holy Spirit brings to light hidden thoughts, motives, and wounds. By allowing Him to reshape us from within, we can experience the freedom and wholeness only He can provide. Surrendering to His healing brings freedom and wholeness.

APPLICATION

† Ask God to search your heart honestly and fully
† Acknowledge hidden thoughts and surrender them to Him
† Allow the Holy Spirit to heal and transform you

CONNECTION

Thank You, Lord, for lovingly searching my heart. Please reveal what needs to change and transform me by Your Spirit. I surrender all to You. In Jesus' name, Amen.

HIGHLIGHT QUOTE

Transformation begins when we let God reveal and heal what's hidden within.

JOURNAL PROMPT

What area of your heart is God inviting you to surrender for deeper healing?

DAY 64
The Strength in Saying No

> *But let your 'Yes' be 'Yes,' and your 'No,' 'No.' For whatever is more than these is from the evil one.*
> – Matthew 5:37

REFLECTION

God calls us to practice integrity and discernment in our commitments. Saying no can be just as holy as saying yes, especially when it aligns with His will. Establishing healthy boundaries protects our hearts and gives us space to walk in obedience to Him. The Holy Spirit empowers us to speak truth with grace, reflecting His divine wisdom in our lives.

APPLICATION

- † Seek the Holy Spirit's guidance before giving your yes or no
- † Set healthy boundaries that honor God and guard your heart
- † Walk in honesty and integrity in every decision you make

CONNECTION

Thank You, Lord, for giving me discernment and courage. Help me set boundaries that honor You with my words and choices. In Jesus' name, Amen.

HIGHLIGHT QUOTE

A Spirit-led no is a boundary that protects God's best for your life.

JOURNAL PROMPT

Where might God be asking you to say no so that you can honor Him fully?

DAY 65
Finding Peace in Stillness

Be still, and know that I am God.
– Psalm 46:10

REFLECTION

Stillness is the pathway to a deeper understanding of God. When we quiet our hearts, we become aware of His presence and find refuge in His power. Our doubts diminish when we focus on who He is instead of what surrounds us. In this stillness, peace replaces striving, faith grows stronger, and He transforms us from glory to glory.

APPLICATION

† Pause throughout your day to rest in His presence
† Release distractions and focus on His greatness
† Practice stillness as worship and gratitude to Him

CONNECTION

Thank You, Lord, for providing supernatural peace. Teach me to be still and know You are God. Forgive me for yielding to distraction, and help me rest in Your Spirit's empowerment. Let Your peace rule in my heart. In Jesus' name, Amen.

HIGHLIGHT QUOTE

Stillness invites the peace of God to quiet the noise within.

JOURNAL PROMPT

Where can you intentionally pause and be still with God today?

DAY 66
Nurturing Your Heart

Keep your heart with all diligence, For out of it spring the issues of life.
— Proverbs 4:23

REFLECTION

Our hearts shape our words, actions, and decisions. It is essential to guard them to live our lives that reflect Christ. Protecting our hearts involves watching out for harmful influences and filling them with truth. A heart diligently nurtured overflows with joy, peace, and love rooted in Him. The Holy Spirit is the One who guides and shapes our inner lives.

APPLICATION

† Assess the influences that shape your heart and thoughts
† Safeguard your peace and spiritual well-being
† Immerse yourself in God's Word so it overflows into your life

CONNECTION

Thank You, Lord, for giving me a new heart. Help me guard it from wrong influences and keep it tender toward You. May my words and actions reflect Your presence within me. In Jesus' name, Amen.

HIGHLIGHT QUOTE

A nurtured heart becomes fertile ground for God's peace and love.

JOURNAL PROMPT

What influences most affect your heart, and how can you guard it better?

DAY 67
Unity in Prayer

Assuredly, I say to you, whatever you bind on earth will be bound in heaven, and whatever you loose on earth will be loosed in heaven.
– Matthew 18:18

REFLECTION

When we pray in agreement, we unlock Heaven's authority here on earth. Unity in prayer fortifies our resolve and aligns us with God's will. Agreement in prayer is both a powerful weapon against the enemy and an avenue for God to fulfill His divine purposes. When believers unite in faith, Heaven responds with a mighty intervention.

APPLICATION

† Seek a prayer partner and engage in agreement today
† Commit to praying over areas where you need clarity and strength
† Stand firm in the authority Christ has given you through prayer

CONNECTION

Thank You, Lord, for the strength we find in unity through prayer. Bring fresh fire upon our intercession and let Your Kingdom come and manifest Your will as we unite in faith. In Jesus' name, Amen.

HIGHLIGHT QUOTE

Agreement in prayer releases Heaven's authority on earth.

JOURNAL PROMPT

Who can you join with in prayer this week to stand in faith together?

DAY 68
Led by the Spirit

For as many as are led by the Spirit of God, these are sons of God.
– Romans 8:14

REFLECTION

The Holy Spirit leads us into a deeper relationship with God, guiding each step of our journey. His direction may not always align with our logic, but it always reflects His truth. The more we yield to His influence, the more attuned we become to His gentle prompting. Walking by the Spirit affirms our identity as beloved children of God.

APPLICATION

† Invite the Holy Spirit to guide your decisions, both big and small
† Journal how you sense His leading in your daily life
† Practice obedience, even when His way feels unfamiliar

CONNECTION

Thank You, Lord, for directing me by Your Spirit. Help me stay sensitive to Your wisdom and peace. Grant me strength to walk in daily obedience to You. In Jesus' name, Amen.

HIGHLIGHT QUOTE

Being led by the Spirit confirms our identity as God's children.

JOURNAL PROMPT

How can you grow in sensitivity to the Spirit's leading this week?

DAY 69
Embracing Opportunities

> *Therefore, as we have opportunity, let us do good to all, especially to those who are of the household of faith.*
> – Galatians 6:10

REFLECTION

God presents us with opportunities each day—some small, others life-changing. He uniquely prepares these divine appointments for us to walk in. By His grace, He has already equipped us to step into them by faith. By recognizing and seizing these moments, we allow His goodness to shine through us and bless others.

APPLICATION

† Ask the Holy Spirit to open your eyes to daily opportunities
† Respond quickly in obedience when He nudges your heart
† Celebrate the impact of even minor acts of kindness

CONNECTION

Thank You, Lord, for the divine opportunities You place before me. Help me recognize them clearly and act in faith, without doubt or fear. In Jesus' name, Amen.

HIGHLIGHT QUOTE

Every opportunity to do good is a doorway for God's goodness to flow through you.

JOURNAL PROMPT

What opportunity might God be placing before you today?

DAY 70
Reopening Our Spiritual Wells

> Now the Philistines had stopped up all the wells which his father's servants had dug in the days of Abraham his father, and they had filled them with earth.
> – Genesis 26:15

REFLECTION

When Isaac discovered that the enemies had filled his father's wells with earth, he faced the loss of vital sources of life. The enemy still seeks to block our spiritual flow, our wells of grace, hope, and strength. When we sense dryness, God calls us to reopen what disappointment, distraction, or fear has buried. As we dig again, His living water flows afresh within us.

APPLICATION

† Reflect on any spiritual "wells" that feel obstructed
† Choose one area to revisit and restore
† Seek the Holy Spirit's guidance as you dig again

CONNECTION

Thank You, Lord, for the abundance of Your spiritual blessings. Reveal the wells in my life that the enemy has plugged and give me courage to reopen them. Let Your living water refresh and renew my soul. In Jesus' name, Amen.

HIGHLIGHT QUOTE

When you reopen old wells, living water flows again where dryness once existed.

JOURNAL PROMPT

Which spiritual well in your life needs to be reopened and restored?

DAY 71
Rooms of Blessing

> *And he moved from there and dug another well, and they did not quarrel over it. So he called its name Rehoboth, because he said, "For now the LORD has made room for us, and we shall be fruitful in the land."*
> – Genesis 26:22

REFLECTION

After seasons of contention and struggle, Isaac finally reached a place of peace and fruitfulness. Rehoboth represents the spacious place where God's favor removes opposition and makes room for His blessing. Through perseverance and faith, He leads us into environments of growth and rest. Even in times of conflict, He is preparing our Rehoboth, our room of blessing.

APPLICATION

- † Remain steadfast when faced with opposition
- † Quiet the critical voices within and around you
- † Stand firm in faith, trusting God to make room for you

CONNECTION

Thank You, Lord, for the places of fruitfulness You have prepared for me. Forgive my complaints during seasons of struggle. Lead me into spacious places of peace and strengthen my faith as I wait for my Rehoboth. In Jesus' name, Amen.

HIGHLIGHT QUOTE

Through perseverance and faith, God leads us into environments of growth and rest.

JOURNAL PROMPT

Where might God be leading you from contention into a new place of peace and fruitfulness?

DAY 72
Adoption as Sons

> *Having predestined us to adoption as sons by Jesus Christ to Himself, according to the good pleasure of His will.*
> – Ephesians 1:5

REFLECTION

Through Christ, God adopted us with grace into His family and secured us in His unchanging love. This new identity liberates us from insecurity and fills our hearts with confidence rooted in His grace. Our adoption in Christ is not symbolic but a permanent position of belonging. This truth dispels fear and fills us with lasting joy.

APPLICATION

† Celebrate your identity as a cherished child of God

† Release feelings of insecurity, and rest in His steadfast grace

† Share His love with others, reflecting the adoption you've received in Christ

CONNECTION

Thank You, Lord, for welcoming me into Your family. Help me live confidently in my new identity and extend Your love to those around me. In Jesus' name, Amen.

HIGHLIGHT QUOTE

Being adopted by God replaces fear with the security of His unchanging love.

JOURNAL PROMPT

How does knowing you are God's child change the way you see yourself and others?

DAY 73
Faith Comes by Hearing

> *So then faith comes by hearing, and hearing by the word of God.*
> — Romans 10:17

REFLECTION

Faith flourishes when we immerse ourselves in God's Word. In a world filled with distractions and many voices, His voice brings clarity and strength. Hearing the Word again and again deepens our relationship with Christ and equips us to face every challenge. The more we embrace His truth, the more we walk by faith and not by sight.

APPLICATION

† Set aside intentional time to read and meditate on Scripture
† Listen for God's voice in the quiet moments of your day
† Write insights from His Word to anchor your faith

CONNECTION

Thank You, Lord, for Your powerful Word. Help me prioritize hearing Your voice above all others. Nurture my faith and let Your truth shape my days. In Jesus' name, Amen.

HIGHLIGHT QUOTE

Faith grows stronger when God's Word becomes the loudest voice in our hearts.

JOURNAL PROMPT

What Scripture is God using right now to strengthen your faith?

DAY 74
Praise the Lord

> *Praise the LORD, call upon His name; Declare His deeds among the peoples, Make mention that His name is exalted.*
> – Isaiah 12:4

REFLECTION

The ordinary can blind us, but Christ makes everything fresh. He revives our appreciation for what's familiar and adds newness to our habits. Relationships, routines, and surroundings gain new significance when illuminated by His Spirit. Gratitude opens our eyes to notice what we once overlooked and keeps our hearts soft before Him.

APPLICATION

† Be attentive to God's work in your everyday surroundings

† Walk in love with a heart full of renewed gratitude

† Embrace the continual newness offered by His Spirit

CONNECTION

Thank You, Lord, for making all things new. Open my eyes to see Your hand in every detail of life and fill me with gratitude in every season. In Jesus' name, Amen.

HIGHLIGHT QUOTE

Gratitude refreshes the heart and restores wonder to the ordinary.

JOURNAL PROMPT

Where have you seen God's renewing presence in your daily life this week?

DAY 75
Crucified with Christ

> *I have been crucified with Christ; it is no longer I who live, but Christ lives in me; and the life which I now live in the flesh I live by faith in the Son of God, who loved me and gave Himself for me.*
> – Galatians 2:20

REFLECTION

Surrender and transformation characterize our new life in Christ. To be crucified with Him means releasing our old nature and allowing the Holy Spirit to shape us from within. This is the essence of walking by faith, trusting His life within us rather than our own strength. His love empowers us to live courageously, reflecting His presence in every circumstance.

APPLICATION

- † Surrender areas where you still rely on your own strength
- † Use Scripture to stand against doubt and discouragement
- † Walk boldly, trusting His Spirit to empower you daily

CONNECTION

Thank You, Lord, for the new life I have in You. Help me yield every part of myself so Christ may live through me. Strengthen my faith to rely fully on Your Spirit. In Jesus' name, Amen.

HIGHLIGHT QUOTE

To live by faith is to let Christ live His life through us.

JOURNAL PROMPT

Where do you need to surrender control and allow Christ to live through you today?

DAY 76
The Power of the Gospel

> *For I am not ashamed of the gospel of Christ, for it is the power of God to salvation for everyone who believes, for the Jew first and also for the Greek.*
> – Romans 1:16

REFLECTION

The gospel is not merely words; it is the power of God that saves and transforms lives. It breaks every barrier and offers righteousness to all who believe. As we live unashamedly, our faith deepens, and we grow from one level of belief to another. The gospel defines our identity and fuels our passion to share God's truth with the world.

APPLICATION

† Reflect on how the gospel has transformed your life
† Ask God for boldness to share His message without fear
† Live unashamedly in the gospel's truth each day

CONNECTION

Thank You, Lord, for the transforming power of the gospel. Strengthen me to live courageously and share Your truth with love and boldness. Let my life reflect the hope found only in You. In Jesus' name, Amen.

HIGHLIGHT QUOTE

The gospel isn't just news; it's God's power to change every heart that believes.

JOURNAL PROMPT

Where is God calling you to live or speak more boldly for His gospel?

DAY 77
Walking in the Spirit

Are you so foolish? Having begun in the Spirit, are you now being made perfect by the flesh?
– Galatians 3:3

REFLECTION

The Christian life begins by the Spirit and can only continue by His power. Yet we often drift toward self-effort, forgetting the grace that sustains us. Walking in the Spirit means surrendering daily and depending on His strength rather than our own. When we let Him lead, He brings freedom, growth, and victory over the flesh, transforming us from glory to glory.

APPLICATION

† Examine areas where you rely on your own strength instead of God's
† Surrender control and invite the Spirit to lead you today
† Walk in the freedom and grace that only He provides

CONNECTION

Thank You, Lord, for the gift of Your Spirit. Forgive me for trying to walk in my strength instead of Yours. Empower me to yield completely and depend on Your grace in each moment. In Jesus' name, Amen.

HIGHLIGHT QUOTE

Walking in the Spirit turns daily surrender into lasting victory.

JOURNAL PROMPT

Where are you being invited to release control and let the Spirit lead today?

DAY 78
Receiving Jesus with Joy

> *And when Jesus came to the place, He looked up and saw him, and said to him, "Zacchaeus, make haste and come down, for today I must stay at your house." So he made haste and came down, and received Him joyfully.* – Luke 19:5–6

REFLECTION

When we seek Jesus earnestly, He meets us with grace and transforms us with joy. Like Zacchaeus, we are called to open our hearts completely and allow His presence to dwell within. Welcoming Him fully renews our purpose, restores our hope, and fills our lives with freedom. Joy is the natural response of a heart truly surrendered to Christ.

APPLICATION

† Examine your heart for distractions that keep you from a closeness with Jesus
† Invite Him to dwell deeply in every area of your life
† Seek Him with eagerness and joy, expecting His transforming presence

CONNECTION

Thank You, Lord, for drawing near when I seek You. Help me to welcome You in every part of my life and rejoice in Your presence. Fill me with lasting joy that flows from knowing You. In Jesus' name, Amen.

HIGHLIGHT QUOTE

Joy overflows when we welcome Jesus into every part of our lives.

JOURNAL PROMPT

How can you make room for Jesus to dwell more deeply in your heart this week?

DAY 79
Resist Him

> *Be sober, be vigilant; because your adversary the devil walks about like a roaring lion, seeking whom he may devour. Resist him, steadfast in the faith, knowing that the same sufferings are experienced by your brotherhood in the world.* – 1 Peter 5:8–9

REFLECTION

The enemy seeks to weaken us through fear and distraction, but steadfast faith disarms his attacks. Christ's victory empowers us to stand firm against every scheme of darkness. As we remain alert and grounded in His promises, we find strength, courage, and endurance. Resistance becomes an act of worship when rooted in unwavering faith.

APPLICATION

† Use God's Word to recognize and resist the enemy's lies
† Stand firm in the victory Christ has already secured for you
† Encourage others to remain steadfast in faith through trials

CONNECTION

Thank You, Lord, for Your victory that silences every roar of the enemy. Help me stay alert and steadfast in faith, relying on Your power and peace. Strengthen my heart to stand firm in every battle. In Jesus' name, Amen.

HIGHLIGHT QUOTE

Faith that stands firm silences the roar of the enemy.

JOURNAL PROMPT

What step can you take today to resist the enemy and stand strong in faith?

DAY 80
Belonging to the Lord

> *Know that the LORD, He is God; It is He who has made us, and not we ourselves; We are His people and the sheep of His pasture.*
> *– Psalm 100:3*

REFLECTION

Belonging to God reshapes how we live and how we steward all that we have. We are His creation, loved, guided, and cared for as His own. This truth anchors our identity and compels us to honor Him in every area of life. When we remember we are His treasured possession, gratitude naturally flows and transforms our actions.

APPLICATION

- † Affirm daily that you belong to the Lord and not to yourself
- † Use your time and resources to glorify Him
- † Live with gratitude as His beloved child and creation

CONNECTION

Thank You, Lord, for making me Your own. Help me live as Your treasured possession and reflect gratitude in all I do. In Jesus' name, Amen.

HIGHLIGHT QUOTE

Belonging to God reshapes how we live and how we steward all that we have.

JOURNAL PROMPT

How does remembering that you belong to God change the way you live today?

DAY 81
More than Conquerors

> *Yet in all these things we are more than conquerors through Him who loved us.*
> – Romans 8:37

REFLECTION

Life's battles may leave scars, but Christ's love secures our ultimate victory. The Holy Spirit strengthens and heals us, reminding us of who we are in Him. We are not merely survivors; we are more than conquerors, equipped to overcome every challenge. His love turns every struggle into a testimony of grace and power.

APPLICATION

- † Lean on the Holy Spirit when facing challenges
- † Focus on Christ's victory instead of setbacks
- † Let struggles deepen your trust and strengthen your faith

CONNECTION

Thank You, Lord, for making me more than a conqueror through Your love. Strengthen my faith and empower me to walk in Your victory each day. In Jesus' name, Amen.

HIGHLIGHT QUOTE

Through Christ's love, every battle becomes a steppingstone to victory.

JOURNAL PROMPT

How has God used past challenges to reveal your strength in Him?

A 365-Day Journey Walking with the Word & the Spirit

DAY 82
The Glorious Race

Do you not know that those who run in a race all run, but one receives the prize? Run in such a way that you may obtain it.
– 1 Corinthians 9:24

REFLECTION

Like runners pressing toward the goal, we pursue Christ's call with perseverance and faith. The Holy Spirit empowers us to push past obstacles and distractions. Each step becomes a testimony of His sustaining grace. Even when the path feels uncertain, we run with purpose, fixing our eyes on Jesus, the ultimate prize and reward.

APPLICATION

† Embrace challenges as opportunities to grow in faith

† Trust that God's grip holds you steady when you falter

† Expect His strength to renew you when you feel weary

CONNECTION

Thank You, Lord, for holding me steady as I run the race set before me. Strengthen me to persevere and finish well, keeping my focus on You. In Jesus' name, Amen.

HIGHLIGHT QUOTE

When we run with Christ as our prize, perseverance becomes an act of worship.

JOURNAL PROMPT

What helps you stay focused and faithful in the race God has called you to run?

DAY 83
Stepping Into the Promise

Arise, walk in the land through its length and its width, for I give it to you.
– Genesis 13:17

REFLECTION

God called Abraham to rise and walk in the promise, and He extends that same invitation to us. Our Promised Land is filled with blessings prepared by His hand, but stepping into it requires faith that moves beyond what we see. As we trust Him with courage, He leads us into provision, purpose, and a manifestation of His promises.

APPLICATION

† Visualize God's promises fulfilled in your life
† Step forward in faith instead of staying in doubt
† Thank Him for victories before they appear

CONNECTION

Thank You, Lord, for the promises You spoke over my life. Give me bold faith to arise and walk in them, trusting Your timing and plan. In Jesus' name, Amen.

HIGHLIGHT QUOTE

People of faith walk boldly into God's promises long before they see them.

JOURNAL PROMPT

What promise from God are you being called to step into with greater faith today?

DAY 84
Freedom from Condemnation

> *There is therefore now no condemnation to those who are in Christ Jesus, who do not walk according to the flesh, but according to the Spirit.*
> – Romans 8:1

REFLECTION

In Christ, guilt and shame no longer define us. He bore our condemnation on the cross so we can walk free in His Spirit. Self-condemnation often weighs heavier than God's judgment, but His truth declares us forgiven and loved. Through Him, we discover the beauty of our new identity, enabling us to live purposefully, guided by His grace.

APPLICATION

- † Reject self-condemnation and embrace God's grace
- † Remind yourself daily of your identity in Christ
- † Walk by the Spirit instead of dwelling on past mistakes

CONNECTION

Thank You, Lord, for freeing me from condemnation. Help me rest in my identity in You and walk daily in Your Spirit. In Jesus' name, Amen.

HIGHLIGHT QUOTE

Grace silences condemnation and restores confidence in who we are in Christ.

JOURNAL PROMPT

Where are you still holding on to guilt that Christ has already forgiven?

DAY 85
The Gift of Praise

> *Therefore by Him let us continually offer the sacrifice of praise to God, that is, the fruit of our lips, giving thanks to His name.*
> – Hebrews 13:15

REFLECTION

Praise shifts our focus from our struggles to the greatness of God. He is worthy of our adoration. Offering praise in hardship becomes a sacrifice that strengthens faith and releases joy. As we lift His name, our perspective changes, and His peace fills our hearts. Gratitude expressed through praise becomes a powerful weapon against discouragement.

APPLICATION

† Offer praise to God, even when it feels difficult
† Declare His goodness aloud in times of doubt
† Make gratitude a daily habit to strengthen faith

CONNECTION

Thank You, Lord, for the transforming power of praise. Fill my lips with thanksgiving in every season and help me recognize Your goodness all around me. In Jesus' name, Amen.

HIGHLIGHT QUOTE

Praise transforms trials into opportunities to magnify God's faithfulness.

JOURNAL PROMPT

What can you praise God for today, even before my circumstances change?

A 365-Day Journey Walking with the Word & the Spirit

DAY 86

DAY 86
The Incorruptible Seed

Being born again, not of corruptible seed but incorruptible, through the word of God which lives and abides forever.
– 1 Peter 1:23

REFLECTION

The Word of God is a living, incorruptible seed that brings new life. Once planted in our hearts, it grows unseen but steadily, producing transformation from within. Even when progress feels hidden, His Word continues its perfect work. What God begins, He faithfully completes, bringing forth fruit that endures for eternity.

APPLICATION

† Treasure the Word as God's eternal seed in your heart
† Trust His work in you, even when growth is unseen
† Nurture the seed daily through prayer and Scripture

CONNECTION

Thank You, Lord, for planting Your incorruptible seed in me. Help me nurture it faithfully, trusting it to bear lasting fruit. Let Your Word shape my thoughts, words, and actions. In Jesus' name, Amen.

HIGHLIGHT QUOTE

Even when progress feels hidden, God's Word continues its perfect work.

JOURNAL PROMPT

How can you better cultivate the seed of God's Word planted in your heart?

DAY 87
Victory Secured

> So the LORD saved Israel that day out of the hand of the Egyptians, and Israel saw the Egyptians dead on the seashore.
> – Exodus 14:30

REFLECTION

The Red Sea parted for Israel but closed upon their enemies, a powerful picture of God's deliverance. Jesus Christ secured our victory; sin and shame no longer have power over us. The cross has silenced every accusation, and His resurrection has sealed our freedom. We now walk forward in the confidence of His finished work.

APPLICATION

- † Declare your freedom in Christ daily
- † Let go of past struggles that no longer define you
- † Walk in the victory His grace has secured for you

CONNECTION

Thank You, Lord, for securing my victory through Christ. Help me walk boldly in the freedom You have given me, rejoicing in Your unshakable love. In Jesus' name, Amen.

HIGHLIGHT QUOTE

Christ's finished work makes every step we take a walk in victory.

JOURNAL PROMPT

What past struggle do you need to leave behind to walk fully in Christ's victory?

DAY 88
Radiance in Trials

> *But the path of the just is like the morning sun, That shines ever brighter unto the perfect day.*
> – Proverbs 4:18

REFLECTION

Trials may try to dim our light, but God's purpose turns adversity into radiance. Each test refines our faith, polishing away fear and revealing His glory within us. As we walk with Christ, even hardship becomes the canvas where His faithfulness glows the brightest. Darkness cannot overpower a surrendered heart; God's light always shines through.

APPLICATION

- † Hold fast to your identity in Christ during trials
- † Remember how God has already revealed His faithfulness
- † Trust the Holy Spirit to strengthen your light in every test

CONNECTION

Thank You, Lord, for making my life a reflection of Your light. Shine through me in seasons of trial so others see Your strength and grace. Let Your radiance overcome every shadow. In Jesus' name, Amen.

HIGHLIGHT QUOTE

God's light shines brightest through hearts refined by trust.

JOURNAL PROMPT

How has a tough season deepened the light of Christ in your life?

DAY 89
The Sword of the Spirit

> *And take the helmet of salvation, and the sword of the Spirit, which is the word of God.*
> – Ephesians 6:17

REFLECTION

God's Word is a living weapon—sharp, active, and full of power. The Holy Spirit breathes life into Scripture, equipping us to confront lies with truth and fear with faith. The enemy twists what God says, but when we speak His Word with conviction, we cut through every deception. A believer's sword should never stay sheathed; it is our daily defense and source of victory.

APPLICATION

† Meditate on Scripture and hide it in your heart
† Speak God's Word aloud when faced with fear or temptation
† Pray Scripture daily as a declaration of faith and victory

CONNECTION

Thank You, Lord, for the Sword of the Spirit, Your Word alive in me. Teach me to wield it with boldness and wisdom, letting truth guide my thoughts and actions. In Jesus' name, Amen.

HIGHLIGHT QUOTE

The Word of God in a believer's mouth is a sword that darkness cannot withstand.

JOURNAL PROMPT

What Scripture can you speak over your life today to stand strong in truth?

DAY 90
Strength in Our Weaknesses

> *My flesh and my heart fail; But God is the strength of my heart and my portion forever.*
> *– Psalm 73:26*

REFLECTION

Weakness reminds us of our deep dependence on God's grace. When our strength fades, His power fills the gap. What feels like failure becomes fertile ground for His glory to grow. In every limitation, God's presence becomes our portion—steady, sufficient, and eternal. We find our greatest strength when we surrender fully to Him.

APPLICATION

- † Ask God what He is teaching you through your struggles
- † Extend grace to yourself and release burdens into His care
- † Trust Him to transform weakness into strength for His glory

CONNECTION

Thank You, Lord, for being my strength when I am weak. Teach me to rest in Your sufficiency and trust that Your power works perfectly in my weakness. In Jesus' name, Amen.

HIGHLIGHT QUOTE

Our weakness is the doorway through which God's strength enters.

JOURNAL PROMPT

Where is God inviting you to depend more fully on His strength today?

DAY 91
Praising Through Fear

> *Then they cried out to the LORD in their trouble, And He saved them out of their distresses.*
> *– Psalm 107:13*

REFLECTION

Fear loses its hold in an atmosphere of praise. When we lift our voices to honor God, our focus shifts from what threatens us to the One who delivers us. Praise magnifies His greatness until fear grows small and powerless. In worship, we remember His faithfulness and rest in His peace. Where praise rises, fear retreats, and His presence fills every anxious space with strength and calm.

APPLICATION

† Speak words of praise when fear tries to whisper
† Recall times when God has rescued you in the past
† Fill your home and heart with songs of thanksgiving

CONNECTION

Thank You, Lord, that fear cannot stay where You dwell. Fill my heart with praise that silences anxiety and strengthens faith. Let Your presence bring peace that no fear can undo. In Jesus' name, Amen.

HIGHLIGHT QUOTE

Fear cannot stay where praise lives.

JOURNAL PROMPT

What can you thank God for today that reminds you He is greater than your fear?

DAY 92
The Power of the Cross

> *For the message of the cross is foolishness to those who are perishing, but to us who are being saved it is the power of God.*
> – 1 Corinthians 1:18

REFLECTION

The cross is more than a symbol; it is the living power of God at work in us. Jesus' sacrifice broke the grip of sin, and a new life began. Each day, we walk in the grace that flows from Calvary, reshaped by mercy and renewed by love. The Holy Spirit reminds us that our identity rests not in what we've done, but in what Christ has finished. His cross continues to transform us from glory to glory.

APPLICATION

† Reflect deeply on the meaning of the cross in your life
† Receive healing and peace through Christ's sacrifice
† Live and share the resurrection life Jesus gave you

CONNECTION

Thank You, Lord, for the power of the cross. Help me live daily in Your victory and grace, remembering that Your sacrifice has made me new. May Your Spirit keep transforming my heart. In Jesus' name, Amen.

HIGHLIGHT QUOTE

The cross is God's power transforming us daily.

JOURNAL PROMPT

How can you more fully embrace the power of the cross today?

DAY 93
Removing the Veil

> *Nevertheless when one turns to the Lord, the veil is taken away.*
> – 2 Corinthians 3:16

REFLECTION

Shame and deception often cloud our hearts, keeping us from seeing God's grace clearly. But when we turn to Christ, He lifts the veil, and truth restores our sight. In His presence, we are free to behold His glory and reflect His nature. Each moment with Him reshapes us, exchanging guilt for peace and confusion for clarity. The more we look to Jesus, the more we walk in the freedom He has already given.

APPLICATION

- † Turn from self-focus to the light of His grace
- † Spend time daily in worship and reflection
- † Walk boldly in the identity He's already spoken over you

CONNECTION

Thank You, Lord, for removing the veil and setting me free. Open my eyes to see who I am in You and help me live with unveiled faith. In Jesus' name, Amen.

HIGHLIGHT QUOTE

Turning to Jesus removes the veil and restores our vision.

JOURNAL PROMPT

What veil has the enemy tried to place over your life that Jesus has already lifted?

DAY 94
His Victory, Our Freedom

> *But thanks be to God, who gives us the victory through our Lord Jesus Christ.*
> – 1 Corinthians 15:57

REFLECTION

Christ's victory defines our freedom. We do not earn it through striving; we receive it through surrender. His finished work on the cross has already secured every promise of grace. Even in struggle, His Spirit shapes us into His likeness, teaching us to rest in divine strength. Our task is not to fight for victory but to live from it, anchored in faith, filled with gratitude, and confident that His triumph is complete.

APPLICATION

- † Surrender every struggle to the Holy Spirit's guidance
- † Rest in Christ's finished work instead of your effort
- † Rejoice daily in the freedom you already have in Him

CONNECTION

Thank You, Lord, for the victory I have in You. Teach me to walk fully in Your freedom and rejoice in Your unfailing grace. Let Your Spirit remind me You have already won every battle. In Jesus' name, Amen.

HIGHLIGHT QUOTE

Victory is ours not by striving but by surrendering to Christ.

JOURNAL PROMPT

What area of your life do you need to surrender to His victory today?

DAY 95
Do You Believe This?

> Jesus said to her, "I am the resurrection and the life. He who believes in Me, though he may die, he shall live. And whoever lives and believes in Me shall never die. Do you believe this?" – John 11:25–26

REFLECTION

Jesus doesn't merely offer resurrection—He *is* Resurrection itself. His triumph over death secures our eternal hope and infuses every present moment with power. Because He lives, despair loses its last word. The same Spirit that raised Christ now breathes courage into us, transforming fear into faith and sorrow into strength. To believe is more than agreement; it is a daily trust in the living Christ, whose life defines our victory.

APPLICATION

- † Believe in the resurrection power already at work in you
- † Trust that His Spirit transforms sorrow into strength
- † Rejoice that eternal life is yours today through Him

CONNECTION

Thank You, Lord, for the power of Your resurrection. Yes, Lord, I believe! Help me yield to Your life within me each day and rest in its reality. In Jesus' name, Amen.

HIGHLIGHT QUOTE

Jesus' resurrection guarantees our hope and victory.

JOURNAL PROMPT

How does His resurrection give you hope in today's struggles?

DAY 96
Delivered from Darkness

> *He has delivered us from the power of darkness and conveyed us into the kingdom of the Son of His love, in whom we have redemption through His blood, the forgiveness of sins.*
> – Colossians 1:13–14

REFLECTION

Darkness loses its claim when we remember whose kingdom we belong to. Christ has already transferred us from fear's domain into His marvelous light. Though evil may appear loud, His blood broke its authority. We walk as redeemed children—secure, forgiven, and empowered to shine. The light of His love dispels confusion and reveals our purpose. In every place we step, His Kingdom advances through us.

APPLICATION

† Declare your identity and position in Christ when fear arises
† Walk daily in the confidence of His Kingdom light
† Let His love shine through you wherever He sends you

CONNECTION

Thank You, Lord, for delivering me from darkness. Keep me attentive to Your presence, not fear's voice. Help me walk boldly in Your light and trust Your authority. In Jesus' name, Amen.

HIGHLIGHT QUOTE

The light of Christ conquers darkness and claims us as His own.

JOURNAL PROMPT

Where can you bring His light today to push back the darkness?

DAY 97
Divine Exchange

> *To console those who mourn in Zion, To give them beauty for ashes, The oil of joy for mourning, The garment of praise for the spirit of heaviness.*
> – Isaiah 61:3

REFLECTION

God invites us to exchange our heaviness for the lightness of His presence. Grief and discouragement may weigh the soul, yet His love restores joy. Praise lifts our eyes from what burdens us to the One who bears our sorrows. Worship is not denial but declaration, an act of faith that releases peace and renewal. When we choose praise, His Spirit replaces weariness with divine strength and quiet joy.

APPLICATION

† Choose praise instead of complaints today
† Thank God for His faithfulness in past seasons
† Speak His promises aloud when heaviness lingers

CONNECTION

Thank You, Lord, for exchanging my heaviness for joy. Teach me to clothe myself in praise and find freedom in Your presence. Help me keep my eyes on You. In Jesus' name, Amen.

HIGHLIGHT QUOTE

Praise replaces the weight of heaviness with the wonder of His presence.

JOURNAL PROMPT

What burden do you need to trade for the garment of praise today?

DAY 98
Wise Surrender

> *O My Father, if this cup cannot pass away from Me unless I drink it, Your will be done.*
> – Matthew 26:42

REFLECTION

Deception often begins when desire outruns surrender. Even pleasant dreams can mislead us if they eclipse our devotion to God's will. Jesus modeled perfect submission in Gethsemane, choosing obedience over comfort. That same humility guards our hearts today. When we yield our ambitions to His wisdom, He redirects our paths with truth and peace. Surrender is protection, aligning us with divine purpose and lasting joy.

APPLICATION

† Surrender your desires that compete with God's will
† Ask the Spirit to reveal subtle deceptions in your heart
† Trust His timing instead of forcing your way forward

CONNECTION

Thank You, Lord, for watching over me with mercy. Help me release every desire that distracts me so I can embrace Your perfect will with faith. In Jesus' name, Amen.

HIGHLIGHT QUOTE

Surrendered desires protect us from deception and idolatry.

JOURNAL PROMPT

What desire might compete with God's will in your life?

DAY 99
A Future and a Hope

> *For I know the thoughts that I think toward you, says the LORD, thoughts of peace and not of evil, to give you a future and a hope.*
> – Jeremiah 29:11

REFLECTION

God's plans for us overflow with peace and promise. Even when circumstances whisper doubt, His Word stands as a steady reminder of His goodness. Those who trust His timing never lose hope. Faith rests not in knowing every detail, but in knowing His heart. When we release fear and lean into His care, we discover that every ending in His plan leads to peace and hope.

APPLICATION

- † Meditate on God's promises until peace replaces fear
- † Speak His truth when anxiety about the future arises
- † Rest in the assurance that He is working for your good

CONNECTION

Thank You, Lord, for planning a future rich in peace and hope. Help me rest in Your promises and trust in Your faithful care each day. In Jesus' name, Amen.

HIGHLIGHT QUOTE

God's plans always lead to peace and hope.

JOURNAL PROMPT

Where do you need to replace fear with trust in His promises today?

For the message of the cross is foolishness to those who are perishing, but to us who are being saved it is the power of God.

– 1 Corinthians 1:18

DAY 100
Daily Renewal

> *Therefore we do not lose heart. Even though our outward man is perishing, yet the inward man is being renewed day by day.*
> – 2 Corinthians 4:16

REFLECTION

Though the body may tire and life's pressures weigh heavily, God's Spirit renews us from within. His unseen work strengthens what we cannot see: our faith, our endurance, and our hope. This quiet renewal reminds us that spiritual progress often happens beneath the surface. Each day, He restores what weariness tries to steal, breathing fresh strength into our hearts as we wait on Him in trust and worship.

APPLICATION

† Ask the Holy Spirit daily to renew your inner strength
† Worship through moments of discouragement
† Trust that unseen renewal is still divine progress

CONNECTION

Thank You, Lord, for renewing me from the inside out. Strengthen my inner being and refresh my heart with Your presence. In Jesus' name, Amen.

HIGHLIGHT QUOTE

God renews us inwardly every single day.

JOURNAL PROMPT

Where do you sense God renewing you beneath the surface?

DAY 101
Immovable

> *But none of these things move me; nor do I count my life dear to myself, so that I may finish my race with joy.*
> – Acts 20:24

REFLECTION

We do not attain steadfastness through willpower but through surrender to the Holy Spirit. Life's storms may shake the world, yet in Christ we stand secure. His peace anchors our hearts when emotions waver. To remain immovable is to abide in His strength and trust His faithfulness. Those who rest in Him endure to the end and finish their race with lasting joy.

APPLICATION

† Abide daily in prayer, worship, and the Word
† Return to God's presence whenever fear or doubt stirs
† Trust Him to anchor your heart in perfect peace

CONNECTION

Thank You, Lord, for anchoring me in Your peace. Keep me steady in faith and help me finish my race with joy. In Jesus' name, Amen.

HIGHLIGHT QUOTE

God makes us steadfast when life tries to shake us.

JOURNAL PROMPT

What practice helps you stay anchored in God's peace?

DAY 102
Peace Be Still

> *Then He arose and rebuked the wind, and said to the sea, "Peace, be still!" And the wind ceased and there was a great calm.*
> – Mark 4:39

REFLECTION

Storms reveal what we truly believe about God's nearness. Jesus never promised calm seas, but He promised His peace within them. His authority brings order where fear brings chaos. When we invite Him into our unrest, His Word stills the noise and restores our confidence. Faith grows in the calm that follows obedience—when His presence speaks louder than the storm.

APPLICATION

- † Invite Jesus into every storm of your heart and mind
- † Speak peace instead of panic over your situation
- † Rest in the truth that His presence brings calm

CONNECTION

Thank You, Lord, for calming every storm within and around me. Speak peace to my heart and help me trust that You are in control. In Jesus' name, Amen.

HIGHLIGHT QUOTE

When Jesus speaks, "Peace," every storm must obey.

JOURNAL PROMPT

What current storm do you need to surrender to Jesus' calming power?

DAY 103
Hosanna in the Highest

> *Hosanna to the Son of David! 'Blessed is He who comes in the name of the Lord!'*
> – Matthew 21:9

REFLECTION

Even though crowds shouted *Hosanna!* many turned away when Jesus defied their expectations. True worship is not driven by results but by surrender. It flows from love, honor, and trust in who He is, whether we understand what He allows. Worship grounded in faith endures through every season, declaring His goodness before we know the results, and rejoicing in Him always.

APPLICATION

† Praise God in faith before seeing results
† Surrender your expectations to His perfect will
† Trust His purpose over your preferences

CONNECTION

Thank You, Lord, for knowing what's best for me. Help me worship through uncertainty and surrender fully to You. In Jesus' name, Amen.

HIGHLIGHT QUOTE

True worship praises God beyond expectations.

JOURNAL PROMPT

When was the last time you praised God before seeing results?

DAY 104
What Does God Look At?

> *For the LORD does not see as man sees; for man looks at the outward appearance, but the LORD looks at the heart.*
> – 1 Samuel 16:7

REFLECTION

While people often focus on the outward appearance, God searches the heart. Abiding in Him gives us eyes of grace, able to see beyond performance or pretense. Hidden faith, unseen tears, and quiet obedience are precious to Him. What matters most is not impressing others but living sincerely before the One who knows us fully and loves us completely. A heart that seeks His pleasure is true beauty in His sight.

APPLICATION

- † Fix your heart on pleasing God above all else
- † Lay unseen burdens before Him in prayer
- † See others with the grace God has shown you

CONNECTION

Thank You, Lord, for seeing and loving my heart. Teach me to walk by faith and view others with grace. In Jesus' name, Amen.

HIGHLIGHT QUOTE

God values the heart more than appearances.

JOURNAL PROMPT

What unseen act of faith do you need to bring before God today?

A 365-Day Journey Walking with the Word & the Spirit

DAY 105
Power to Heal

> He sent His word and healed them, And delivered them from their destructions.
> – Psalm 107:20

REFLECTION

God's Word carries power to heal the heart and restore the weary soul. When heaviness lingers, His truth pierces despair and breathes hope where pain once ruled. Each time we receive His Word in faith, healing begins, slowly loosening the grip of sorrow and filling us with peace. The more we meditate on His promises, the deeper His presence roots within us and brings renewal.

APPLICATION

† Read Scripture aloud to refresh your spirit
† Let His Word replace anxious thoughts
† Trust His healing power to touch and restore you

CONNECTION

Thank You, Lord, for sending Your Word to heal and deliver. Replace every burden I carry with Your peace and steadfast truth. Help me embrace the freedom You offer. In Jesus' name, Amen.

HIGHLIGHT QUOTE

His Word heals what heaviness has broken and restores peace to the soul.

JOURNAL PROMPT

Which promise from Scripture brings healing to your heart right now?

DAY 106
The Abiding Anointing

> But the anointing which you have received from Him abides in you, and you do not need that anyone teach you; but as the same anointing teaches you concerning all things, and is true, and is not a lie, and just as it has taught you, you will abide in Him. – 1 John 2:27

REFLECTION

The Holy Spirit is our divine Teacher, dwelling within to reveal truth and guide our steps. Though God may use voices around us, our ultimate reliance rests on His anointing within. The Holy Spirit gives discernment, warns of deception, and confirms peace when the path is right. His teaching never wavers but leads us steadily, transforming us from glory to glory in Christ.

APPLICATION

† Yield daily to the Holy Spirit's anointing
† Seek wisdom with humility and childlike faith
† Follow the Spirit's peace as your trusted guide

CONNECTION

Thank You, Lord, for the Spirit's abiding anointing. Teach me Your truth and guide me each day by Your peace. In Jesus' name, Amen.

HIGHLIGHT QUOTE

The Spirit's anointing leads us into truth and wisdom.

JOURNAL PROMPT

How can you yield more fully to the Spirit's guidance today?

DAY 107
Nevertheless

> *O My Father … nevertheless, not as I will, but as You will.*
> – Matthew 26:39

REFLECTION

Surrender is the pathway to true victory. In Gethsemane, Jesus yielded His will with one powerful word—"Nevertheless." That word turned agony into purpose and submission into redemption. Each time we echo it, Heaven moves. Our own "nevertheless" becomes an invitation for God's strength to enter our weakness, transforming resistance into trust and uncertainty into peace. Surrender doesn't diminish us; it reveals His power within us.

APPLICATION

† Surrender your will to God in prayer
† Say "nevertheless" when comfort conflicts with obedience
† Trust His plan, even when it costs you personally

CONNECTION

Thank You, Lord, for modeling surrender in the Garden. Help me embrace "nevertheless" moments with faith and trust. In Jesus' name, Amen.

HIGHLIGHT QUOTE

Surrender unlocks God's power in our weakness.

JOURNAL PROMPT

Where do you need to say "nevertheless" to God today?

DAY 108
Room for More

> *Now in the morning, having risen a long while before daylight, He went out and departed to a solitary place; and there He prayed.*
> – Mark 1:35

REFLECTION

Jesus rose early to pray, showing us the value of dedicating space for God. Making room for Him changes everything: priorities shift, strength renews, and peace settles in. Yet we must never become content with yesterday's measure of His presence. God always has more to reveal. Even the smallest offering of time or surrender creates an opening for His fullness to dwell within us. There is always more of Christ to receive.

APPLICATION

- † Set aside dedicated time and space for God each day
- † Hunger continually for more of His presence
- † Trust that every minor change invites greater intimacy

CONNECTION

Thank You, Lord, for filling every space I make for You. Increase my hunger and help me create more room for Your presence. In Jesus' name, Amen.

HIGHLIGHT QUOTE

Even small spaces of surrender allow more of Him.

JOURNAL PROMPT

Where can you create more room for God in your daily rhythm?

DAY 109
The Redeemed of the Lord

> *Let the redeemed of the LORD say so, Whom He has redeemed from the hand of the enemy.*
> – Psalm 107:2

REFLECTION

Through His death and resurrection, Jesus redeemed us completely, setting us free from sin's power and restoring us to new life. Redemption isn't just a past event; it's a living reality we're called to declare with joy. Every day is an opportunity to remember what His blood accomplished and to walk boldly in that freedom. Let the redeemed of the Lord say so. Our lives are proof of His victory.

APPLICATION

† Declare boldly your redemption in Christ
† Rejoice daily in the salvation He secured for you
† Live freely, without guilt or condemnation

CONNECTION

Thank You, Lord, for redeeming me with Your blood. I joyfully declare that I am redeemed! Help me walk in that freedom every day. In Jesus' name, Amen.

HIGHLIGHT QUOTE

Redemption is our freedom and song of victory.

JOURNAL PROMPT

What area of your life needs the bold reminder: I am redeemed?

DAY 110
The Bypass Anointing

> *My grace is sufficient for you, for My strength is made perfect in weakness.*
> – 2 Corinthians 12:9

REFLECTION

Our weaknesses can discourage us, yet they are the very spaces where grace shines brightest. When we step forward despite fatigue or limitation, the Holy Spirit flows through surrendered vessels with supernatural power. God's "bypass anointing" moves beyond our ability, displaying His strength for His glory. We don't need to be perfect, only yielded. His sufficiency transforms our lack into evidence of His limitless grace.

APPLICATION

† Say yes to God, even when you feel weak
† Trust His Spirit to accomplish what you cannot
† Celebrate His strength working through your weakness

CONNECTION

Thank You, Lord, for perfecting Your strength in my weakness. Use me as Your vessel of grace and reveal Your glory through my life. In Jesus' name, Amen.

HIGHLIGHT QUOTE

God's grace bypasses our weakness to reveal His strength.

JOURNAL PROMPT

Where can you say yes to God today, despite your weakness?

DAY 111
Commit Your Way

Commit your way to the LORD, Trust also in Him, And He shall bring it to pass.
– Psalm 37:5

REFLECTION

Life offers many paths, but we find peace when we commit ours to the Lord. Trusting Him with our direction keeps us from drifting into distraction. When we surrender our plans, His wisdom orders our steps and establishes what matters most. God's timing may stretch our patience, yet His ways always lead to fulfillment and rest. Each surrendered plan becomes a pathway of divine purpose and quiet peace.

APPLICATION

† Invite the Lord into your daily planning
† Seek His wisdom to discern distractions
† Trust Him to establish your steps in every season

CONNECTION

Thank You, Lord, for guiding my way. Help me commit every plan to You and walk in Your wisdom. In Jesus' name, Amen.

HIGHLIGHT QUOTE

When we commit our way to God, He turns our direction into destiny.

JOURNAL PROMPT

What plan or goal do you need to commit fully into God's hands today?

A 365-Day Journey Walking with the Word & the Spirit

DAY 112
It Is the Lord

It is the Lord!
– John 21:7

REFLECTION

Jesus often reveals Himself in ordinary moments that become extraordinary through His presence. He moves with quiet authority, filling our hearts with awe and recognition. When we sense His peace or see His hand at work, our response echoes that of the disciples, "It is the Lord!" He still draws near to remind us He is active, present, and faithful. Every encounter invites us to expect His miraculous touch in daily life.

APPLICATION

† Stay alert for God's presence in unexpected places
† Respond to His touch with awe and gratitude
† Expect Him to move beyond your expectations

CONNECTION

Thank You, Lord, for showing up in ways I don't expect. Help me recognize Your presence and respond with joy. In Jesus' name, Amen.

HIGHLIGHT QUOTE

Awareness of His presence turns ordinary moments into holy ones.

JOURNAL PROMPT

Where might God be revealing Himself in your ordinary day today?

DAY 113
Praise Produces Power

Then they cry out to the LORD in their trouble, And He brings them out of their distresses.
– Psalm 107:28

REFLECTION

Praise under pressure releases divine power. Like gold refined by fire, our worship deepens when tested by trials. Instead of letting hardship produce despair, praise can turn pain into strength and confusion into clarity. Every song of trust becomes a weapon against fear. As we glorify God in the middle of the storm, His power reshapes our hearts and brings peace where turmoil once reigned.

APPLICATION

† Praise God under pressure
† Declare His greatness louder than your problem
† Trust that every trial can produce strength

CONNECTION

Thank You, Lord, for Your power that rises through praise. Help me worship You when life feels heavy, and let my praise invite Your strength to move. In Jesus' name, Amen.

HIGHLIGHT QUOTE

Praise under pressure becomes the power that turns trials into triumphs.

JOURNAL PROMPT

How can you choose praise in the middle of what feels hard or uncertain today?

DAY 114
Unbound and Set Free

> *Now when He had said these things, He cried with a loud voice, "Lazarus, come forth!" And he who had died came out bound hand and foot with graveclothes ... Jesus said to them, "Loose him, and let him go." – John 11:43–44*

REFLECTION

Jesus not only raised Lazarus from death, but He also commanded his release from what still bound him. In the same way, salvation frees us, but His Spirit continues to remove the graveclothes of fear, guilt, or limitation. Each layer that falls away reveals a greater life in Christ. Freedom is not just deliverance from death, but the daily unfolding of grace that lets us walk unhindered in His victory.

APPLICATION

† Press through resistance with prayer and worship
† Declare freedom over areas still bound
† Step forward in faith, trusting Christ's command

CONNECTION

Thank You, Lord, for breaking every hindrance in my life. Help me walk boldly in Your power, fully released from anything that holds me back. In Jesus' name, Amen.

HIGHLIGHT QUOTE

Jesus not only raises us to life; He also removes what still binds us.

JOURNAL PROMPT

What area of your life needs to be loosed so you can walk freely in His victory?

DAY 115
Stretch Out Your Hand to Heal

> Now, Lord, look on their threats, and grant to Your servants that with all boldness they may speak Your word, by stretching out Your hand to heal, and that signs and wonders may be done through the name of Your holy Servant Jesus. – Acts 4:29–30

REFLECTION

The hands of Jesus, once stretched wide on the cross, now reach toward us in mercy and power. His touch still heals, restores, and delivers. Our confidence rests not in our fragile grasp of Him but in His unwavering hold on us. In every trial, His extended hand invites us to trust His grace, to believe in His healing, and to rest secure in His steadfast love.

APPLICATION

† Ask the Lord to stretch out His hand over your need
† Trust His hold when fear rises
† Rest in His power to heal and restore

CONNECTION

Thank You, Lord, for the power of Your saving hand. Keep me secure in Your embrace and confident in Your healing. In Jesus' name, Amen.

HIGHLIGHT QUOTE

The same hands that were pierced for us still reach to heal and restore.

JOURNAL PROMPT

What area of your life needs the healing touch of His hand today?

DAY 116
Victory over Defeat

> *For a righteous man may fall seven times And rise again.*
> – Proverbs 24:16

REFLECTION

True victory is not the absence of failure but the courage to rise again through faith. Every fall becomes an invitation for grace to lift us higher. The Holy Spirit strengthens us to persevere, turning discouragement into determination and weakness into renewed strength. No defeat is final when we belong to the One who redeems and restores. In Christ, every setback can lead to a stronger comeback.

APPLICATION

- † Respond to defeat with renewed faith
- † Step forward again where fear once held you back
- † Embrace the Spirit's strength for a fresh start

CONNECTION

Thank You, Lord, for the victory we have in Christ. When defeat weighs me down, lift me up and renew my courage to move forward in Your name. In Jesus' name, Amen.

HIGHLIGHT QUOTE

Every fall becomes an opportunity for grace to lift us higher.

JOURNAL PROMPT

What recent setback can become your next step of victory through Christ?

DAY 117
Eternal Weight of Glory

> *For our light affliction, which is but for a moment, is working for us a far more exceeding and eternal weight of glory, while we do not look at the things which are seen, but at the things which are not seen. For the things which are seen are temporary, but the things which are not seen are eternal.* – 2 Corinthians 4:17–18

REFLECTION

When we fix our eyes on eternity, today's troubles lose their grip. God's glory outweighs every burden, transforming affliction into growth. Faith gives us perspective beyond the moment, reminding us that what's unseen is everlasting. As we look to Christ, the eternal outweighs the temporary, and our hearts find peace in the promise that He is shaping all things for glory.

APPLICATION

† Shift your focus from problems to promises
† Meditate on eternity rather than temporary struggles
† Magnify the Lord in worship and faith

CONNECTION

Thank You, Lord, for helping me see with eternal vision. Lift my focus above the temporary and anchor my hope in Your lasting glory. In Jesus' name, Amen.

HIGHLIGHT QUOTE

An eternal perspective turns momentary pain into lasting purpose.

JOURNAL PROMPT

How can a focus on eternity change the way you face today's challenges?

DAY 118
Accepted in the Beloved

> *To the praise of the glory of His grace, by which He made us accepted in the Beloved.*
> – Ephesians 1:6

REFLECTION

Being accepted in Christ silences the need for human approval. We are fully loved, chosen, and secured in His grace. The wounds of rejection lose their sting when we rest in His affirmation. In the Beloved, we are not striving for worth; we are living from it. This identity frees us to love others and to walk in confidence, knowing we are already enough in Him.

APPLICATION

- † Reject the lie that your worth depends on others' approval
- † Rest in the security of your identity in Christ
- † Extend love without the fear of rejection

CONNECTION

Thank You, Lord, for accepting me in Christ. Anchor my heart in Your love and help me live free from the need for approval. In Jesus' name, Amen.

HIGHLIGHT QUOTE

Acceptance in Christ replaces striving with settled belonging.

JOURNAL PROMPT

Where have you been seeking approval that God has already given you in Christ?

DAY 119
Be Strong and of Good Courage

> Have I not commanded you? Be strong and of good courage; do not be afraid, nor be dismayed, for the LORD your God is with you wherever you go.
> – Joshua 1:9

REFLECTION

We show our faith not in the way we start, but in the way we stay. Persistence is the quiet strength that keeps moving forward when emotion fades. God calls us to endure—not through willpower but through His Spirit within us. When opposition rises, courage grows stronger in His presence. Renewal comes as we pray, persevere, and remember that His faithfulness outlasts every battle we face.

APPLICATION

† Identify an area where your persistence has faded
† Surrender it to God and ask for renewed strength
† Continue forward in prayer and steadfast faith

CONNECTION

Thank You, Lord, for Your constant presence and strength. Empower me with courage to persist and to press on in faith. In Jesus' name, Amen.

HIGHLIGHT QUOTE

We show our faith not in the way we start, but in the way we stay.

JOURNAL PROMPT

Where is God inviting you to keep going with renewed courage?

DAY 120
The Treasure Within It

> *But we have this treasure in earthen vessels, that the excellence of the power may be of God and not of us.*
> – 2 Corinthians 4:7

REFLECTION

God places His divine treasure within fragile vessels like us to reveal His glory, not our own. Our weaknesses become the backdrop for His strength. We are carriers of light in a world that longs for hope. When we yield to His Spirit, His power shines through every crack and imperfection. In humility, we reflect on His excellence and show that all the glory belongs to Him alone.

APPLICATION

† Release self-dependence and trust in God's power
† Declare that the glory belongs to Him alone
† Shine His light boldly as His chosen vessel

CONNECTION

Thank You, Lord, for placing Your treasure within me. Help me yield to Your Spirit so Your glory shines through my life. In Jesus' name, Amen.

HIGHLIGHT QUOTE

Our weakness becomes the stage where God's glory shines brightest.

JOURNAL PROMPT

How can you reflect God's glory more fully through your ordinary life?

DAY 121
We Are His Workmanship

> *For we are His workmanship, created in Christ Jesus for good works, which God prepared beforehand that we should walk in them.*
> – Ephesians 2:10

REFLECTION

Insecurity creeps in when we base our worth on shifting circumstances instead of God's unchanging love. Anchored in Christ, our confidence grows, and fear loses its grip. His gentle restoration rebuilds what insecurity tears down, renewing our courage and peace. He leads us into the good works He has prepared for us, empowering us to walk in them, secure in who we are in Him.

APPLICATION

† Trust God with your insecurities today

† Focus on His faithfulness when fears rise

† Follow His leading with peace

CONNECTION

Thank You, Lord, for who You created me to be in Christ Jesus. Help me yield my insecurities to You and walk with confidence in Your purpose. May all I am bring You glory. In Jesus' name, Amen.

HIGHLIGHT QUOTE

Anchored in Christ, our confidence grows, and fear loses its grip.

JOURNAL PROMPT

How can you step into the good works God has prepared for you?

DAY 122
Leaving the Comfort Zone

> *As an eagle stirs up its nest, Hovers over its young, Spreading out its wings, taking them up, Carrying them on its wings, So the LORD alone led him, And there was no foreign god with him.*
> **– Deuteronomy 32:11–12**

REFLECTION

God often stirs our comfort to strengthen our faith. Like the eagle nudging its young to fly, He teaches us to rise above what feels safe and familiar. The stretch of faith feels uncertain, yet it's where wings grow strong. When we trust His leading, the discomfort becomes a divine push toward greater purpose. What feels risky to us is often the very place He intends to reveal His faithfulness.

APPLICATION

- † Step out when God prompts you
- † Trust that He will catch and carry you
- † Keep your eyes fixed on the eternal, not the temporary

CONNECTION

Thank You, Lord, for leading me into higher places in You. Help me release the comfort of the familiar and trust Your Spirit to carry me through every unknown. In Jesus' name, Amen.

HIGHLIGHT QUOTE

God often stirs our comfort to strengthen our faith.

JOURNAL PROMPT

What comfortable place might God be asking you to leave so your faith can grow?

DAY 123
Only One Word

> *But only speak a word, and my servant will be healed.*
> – Matthew 8:8

REFLECTION

The centurion's faith moved Jesus because he trusted fully in His authority. He knew one word from Christ carried the power to heal, restore, and make whole. That same authority still speaks over us today. We don't need visible proof, only steadfast belief in the One who is faithful. Great faith rests in the certainty that when God speaks, His Word accomplishes what it declares.

APPLICATION

- † Believe before you see results
- † Stand on His Word regardless of feelings
- † Declare His promises over your life

CONNECTION

Thank You, Lord, for the power of Your Word. Strengthen my faith to trust what You have spoken, even when I cannot see the outcome. Let Your Word bring life and healing in me. In Jesus' name, Amen.

HIGHLIGHT QUOTE

We don't need visible proof, only steadfast belief in the One who is faithful.

JOURNAL PROMPT

What promise from God do you need to believe today, with no need to see it first?

DAY 124
Breaking Free from Offense

> *The yoke will be destroyed because of the anointing oil.*
> – Isaiah 10:27

REFLECTION

Offense is a heavy burden that binds the heart and clouds our spirit. Yet the anointing of God has the power to break every yoke, freeing us from bitterness and resentment. Forgiveness is the doorway to healing and restoration, inviting the Holy Spirit to fill us with peace. When we choose to release over resentment, the weight lifts and the flow of grace returns unhindered.

APPLICATION

- † Identify and release lingering offenses
- † Ask the Holy Spirit to empower forgiveness
- † Move forward unhindered by bitterness

CONNECTION

Thank You, Lord, for breaking the yoke of offense through Your anointing. Teach me to forgive quickly and walk in the freedom Your Spirit provides. Keep my heart soft and pure before You. In Jesus' name, Amen.

HIGHLIGHT QUOTE

Forgiveness breaks the chains that offense forges.

JOURNAL PROMPT

Who or what do you need to release today so you can walk freely in God's peace?

DAY 125
Embrace Cheer, Not Fear

> *In the world you will have tribulation; but be of good cheer, I have overcome the world.*
> – John 16:33

REFLECTION

Trouble is certain, but so is Christ's victory. The peace He gives does not ignore pain; it transcends it. When fear threatens to cloud our faith, we remember Jesus has already overcome. Cheer is not shallow happiness but steady confidence in His triumph. In every challenge, we can walk with courage, trusting that the One who conquered the world now lives within us.

APPLICATION

- † Speak His Word in moments of fear
- † Sing His praises during storms
- † Encourage others with His victory

CONNECTION

Thank You, Lord, for Your peace that steadies my heart in every trial. Help me walk in cheer, not fear, and reflect the courage that comes from knowing You've already overcome. In Jesus' name, Amen.

HIGHLIGHT QUOTE

Cheer grows from confidence in Christ's victory, not the absence of trouble.

JOURNAL PROMPT

How can you choose cheer over fear in a challenge you're facing today?

DAY 126
Worship to Hear

> When the musician played, that the hand of the LORD came upon him.
> – 2 Kings 3:15

REFLECTION

Worship prepares the heart to hear from God. When Elisha needed clarity, music ushered him into God's presence, stilling distractions and opening his spirit to receive the Word. The same happens when we worship; the noise fades, His presence fills the room, and our hearts become attuned to His voice. In worship, revelation flows and obedience becomes our response.

APPLICATION

- † Begin decisions with worship
- † Invite His presence through quiet praise
- † Let worship prepare your heart to obey

CONNECTION

Thank You, Lord, for the way You speak through worship. Help me make space to listen for Your voice and follow what You reveal with a willing heart. In Jesus' name, Amen.

HIGHLIGHT QUOTE

Worship clears the noise so we can hear God's voice.

JOURNAL PROMPT

What changes when you worship before seeking God's direction?

DAY 127
The Kingdom Is Not in Word

For the kingdom of God is not in word but in power.
– 1 Corinthians 4:20

REFLECTION

The Kingdom of God is more than talk; it's the living power of Christ at work in surrendered hearts. Words may inspire, but His Spirit transforms. As we yield to His will, His power flows through us with grace and authority. Each act of obedience becomes evidence of His reign within. The world recognizes His Kingdom when His power is displayed through humble lives.

APPLICATION

- † Live in surrender, not self-effort
- † Demonstrate His Kingdom through love in action
- † Allow His Spirit to shine brightly through your life

CONNECTION

Thank You, Lord, for Your Kingdom power alive within me. Reign in my heart and let Your Spirit move through my words and deeds for Your glory. In Jesus' name, Amen.

HIGHLIGHT QUOTE

Words may inspire, but His Spirit transforms.

JOURNAL PROMPT

Where can you allow God's power, not your effort, to lead today?

DAY 128
Breaking Free from Vows

He heals the brokenhearted And binds up their wounds.
– Psalm 147:3

REFLECTION

Pain sometimes drives us to make inner vows, silent promises meant to protect us, but that instead imprison the heart. These words can limit faith, joy, and trust. Yet God's truth breaks every chain when we surrender those hidden agreements to Him. The Holy Spirit exposes lies, heals wounds, and restores our confidence in His perfect love and freedom.

APPLICATION

† Ask the Lord to reveal any inner vows, spoken or unspoken
† Surrender them to Him and declare His truth over your heart
† Trust the Holy Spirit to heal and restore your freedom

CONNECTION

Thank You, Lord, for healing my heart and breaking every vow made in pain. I release those words and embrace Your truth that sets me free. Restore my faith and confidence in Your love. In Jesus' name, Amen.

HIGHLIGHT QUOTE

God's truth shatters the vows that pain once forged.

JOURNAL PROMPT

What inner promise or defense might God be asking you to release into His healing?

DAY 129
The Comfort of the Scriptures

> *For whatever things were written before were written for our learning, that we through the patience and comfort of the Scriptures might have hope.*
> – Romans 15:4

REFLECTION

The Word of God has a way of quietly lifting what burdens us. When discouragement settles in, Scripture breathes strength and steadiness back into our spirits. The Holy Spirit uses the Word to renew and realign our hearts with truth. Even when we don't have a Bible in hand, the Word hidden within us rises to remind us of hope, patience, and promise.

APPLICATION

† Take time for a spiritual check-in and let the Word bring healing
† Meditate on even one verse that speaks life to you today
† Write what the Holy Spirit highlights as you read and reflect

CONNECTION

Thank You, Lord, for the comfort and strength Your Word brings. Help me reach for it in every moment and carry it within my heart each day. Let it shape my thoughts and renew my hope. In Jesus' name, Amen.

HIGHLIGHT QUOTE

Hidden Scripture becomes living comfort when the heart grows weary.

JOURNAL PROMPT

What verse has recently renewed your peace or lifted a weight from your heart?

DAY 130
God's Amazing Love

Love suffers long and is kind ... Love never fails.
– 1 Corinthians 13:4, 8

REFLECTION

God's love sees fully, endures patiently, and never ceases to believe. We don't earn God's agape love but receive it by faith, poured into our hearts through the Holy Spirit. When we rest in that perfect love, we become vessels of its flow. Even when others do not return our love, His love within us remains constant, shaping our character and drawing others to His heart.

APPLICATION

† Receive God's love anew by faith today
† Meditate on His limitless love that never fails
† Extend His love freely to others, even when it costs you

CONNECTION

Thank You, Lord, for surrounding me with Your amazing, unending love. Teach me to dwell in it daily and to love others with the same grace You've shown me. In Jesus' name, Amen.

HIGHLIGHT QUOTE

God's love doesn't overlook faults; it overcomes them.

JOURNAL PROMPT

How can you intentionally express God's kind, enduring love to someone today?

DAY 131
Love the Lord Your God

> *You shall love the LORD your God with all your heart, with all your soul, and with all your mind.*
> – Matthew 22:37

REFLECTION

To love God wholly is to center every desire, thought, and action on Him. The enemy tries to dull that love through fear or distraction, but the Holy Spirit reignites it with truth. Love for God grows as we know Him more deeply and respond in worship. When our hearts are fully His, love becomes not just emotion but obedience and devotion in motion.

APPLICATION

- † Pray to receive more of God's love today
- † Spend time in worship, surrendering your heart fully
- † Allow His love to quiet every lie and to overflow to others

CONNECTION

Thank You, Lord, for Your steadfast love that never fails. Draw me closer so I may love You with all my heart, soul, and mind, and so I may share that love generously. In Jesus' name, Amen.

HIGHLIGHT QUOTE

Loving God fully begins with letting His love fill every part of you.

JOURNAL PROMPT

What helps your heart stay centered on loving God with all that you are?

DAY 132
Strength to Strength

> *Blessed is the man whose strength is in You, Whose heart is set on pilgrimage. As they pass through the Valley of Baca, They make it a spring; The rain also covers it with pools. They go from strength to strength; Each one appears before God in Zion.* – Psalm 84:5–7

REFLECTION

When we set our hearts on the journey with God, valleys become places of renewal. What once felt dry becomes a spring of strength. The Holy Spirit meets us in weakness, turning tears into testimonies of His faithfulness. Every trial becomes another step forward, moving us from our own limited ability into the sustaining power of His presence.

APPLICATION

- † Call upon His strength when yours fades
- † Rest in Him and trust His Spirit to carry you forward
- † Let your tears water the ground for God's blessing in your life

CONNECTION

Thank You, Lord, for carrying me from strength to strength. Keep my heart fixed on You and teach me to rely on Your power in every valley and victory. In Jesus' name, Amen.

HIGHLIGHT QUOTE

Each step of faith moves us from our strength into God's unlimited power.

JOURNAL PROMPT

Where do you sense God inviting you to draw from His strength instead of your own?

DAY 133
Every Word

> *No weapon formed against you shall prosper, And every tongue which rises against you in judgment You shall condemn.*
> – Isaiah 54:17

REFLECTION

Words can wound deeply, especially when they come from those we trust. Some are unspoken, and others are felt but never said, yet all can weigh the heart. God offers freedom through the healing power of His Spirit and the truth of His Word. When we forgive and declare what He says about us, every lie loses its strength, and peace returns to our souls.

APPLICATION

† Daily, condemn every word spoken against you in judgment
† Forgive those who've spoken hurtfully and release them to God
† Affirm your identity in Christ by declaring His truth over your life

CONNECTION

Thank You, Lord, for silencing every false word and for healing my heart. I forgive those who have spoken against me, and I receive the freedom of Your truth. Help me walk confidently in who I am in You. In Jesus' name, Amen.

HIGHLIGHT QUOTE

Freedom begins when God's truth speaks louder than wounded words.

JOURNAL PROMPT

What negative word or judgment do you need to replace with God's truth today?

DAY 134
Forgiven?

> *Therefore I say to you, her sins, which are many, are forgiven, for she loved much. But to whom little is forgiven, the same loves little.*
> – Luke 7:46–47

REFLECTION

God's forgiveness reaches beyond our failures and silences shame. We often wonder if He could still love us after what we've done, yet the cross answers every doubt. We are not forgiven because we've improved but because Jesus paid our debt in full. When we receive that grace deeply, love overflows, transforming guilt into gratitude and worship.

APPLICATION

- † Rest in His forgiveness today and release all regret
- † Walk in the freedom of His grace and mercy
- † Let His forgiveness deepen your love for Him and others

CONNECTION

Thank You, Lord, for the mercy that covers every sin. Help me live free from guilt and filled with gratitude for Your grace. Let Your forgiveness flow through me to others. In Jesus' name, Amen.

HIGHLIGHT QUOTE

Forgiveness received becomes love released.

JOURNAL PROMPT

How can receiving God's full forgiveness change the way you love others?

DAY 135
Shut the Door

When you pray, go into your room, and when you have shut your door... your Father who sees in secret will reward you.
– Matthew 6:6

REFLECTION

When life overwhelms, true retreat isn't escape; it's communion. The world urges us to withdraw in despair, but God invites us to the secret place of prayer. Behind the closed door, distractions fade and His presence fills the room. He restores our perspective, renews our strength, and reminds us that intimacy precedes breakthrough.

APPLICATION

† Don't run away; run to Him
† Find a quiet place, close the door, and open your heart
† Let Him renew your strength and guide your next steps

CONNECTION

Thank You, Lord, for meeting me in the secret place. Teach me to shut out the noise and draw near to You. Refresh my heart and fill me with Your peace and direction. In Jesus' name, Amen.

HIGHLIGHT QUOTE

Behind every shut door of prayer, God opens new strength.

JOURNAL PROMPT

How can you make space this week to meet God in the secret place?

DAY 136
Faithful Progress

> But I want you to know, brethren, that the things which happened to me have actually turned out for the furtherance of the gospel.
> – Philippians 1:12

REFLECTION

Progress in God's eyes often looks different from our expectations. Waiting, enduring, or staying steady in faith are all forms of forward motion. He weaves purpose into seasons that feel unproductive, shaping our hearts through patience and perseverance. Every unseen moment of faithfulness moves His story forward, producing growth that He will one day reveal.

APPLICATION

† Don't judge your progress by what you see today
† Keep doing good and trust God for fruit in due season
† Reflect on how far He has already brought you

CONNECTION

Thank You, Lord, for turning every circumstance toward Your purpose. Strengthen my faith when progress feels slow and remind me that steady obedience still advances Your plan. In Jesus' name, Amen.

HIGHLIGHT QUOTE

Faithful waiting is progress in disguise.

JOURNAL PROMPT

Where might God be growing you quietly while you wait for visible progress?

DAY 137
Fellowship with God

> *The grace of the Lord Jesus Christ, and the love of God, and the communion of the Holy Spirit be with you all.*
> *– 2 Corinthians 13:14*

REFLECTION

When we stumble, we may feel distant from God, but He never leaves us. Our relationship with Him is secure, though our fellowship can waver. The enemy uses guilt to isolate, but the Holy Spirit gently draws us near again. Like a child returning to a loving parent, we find Him waiting to restore us. In fellowship, the Lord renews our hearts with joy, peace, and purpose.

APPLICATION

† If you feel disconnected, run to God instead of away from Him
† Confess, receive His grace, and restore your fellowship
† Stay close through prayer, worship, and daily trust

CONNECTION

Thank You, Lord, for never leaving me, even when I drift. Draw me back into close fellowship with You each day. Help me walk in constant awareness of Your love and presence. In Jesus' name, Amen.

HIGHLIGHT QUOTE

In fellowship, the Lord renews our hearts with joy, peace, and purpose.

JOURNAL PROMPT

What helps you stay aware of God's presence throughout the day?

DAY 138
Go with God

> Then he said to Him, "If Your Presence does not go with us, do not bring us up from here …
> – Exodus 33:15

REFLECTION

When the direction feels uncertain, assurance comes from knowing Who goes with us. Moses refused to move without God's presence because the journey without Him held no purpose. The same is true for us today. When His presence is our focus, anxiety fades and peace takes root. Every path becomes sacred ground when walked with the Lord beside us.

APPLICATION

† Focus on Who you are going with, not where you are going
† Acknowledge His presence in every step you take
† Let trust in Him replace anxiety about the unknown

CONNECTION

Thank You, Lord, for walking every path with me. Help me treasure Your presence more than any destination. I surrender my plans and rest in the peace of Your companionship. In Jesus' name, Amen.

HIGHLIGHT QUOTE

When His presence is our focus, anxiety fades and peace takes root.

JOURNAL PROMPT

Where do you need to focus more on God's presence than on the outcome?

DAY 139
What Are We Thinking?

Bringing every thought into captivity to the obedience of Christ.
– 2 Corinthians 10:5

REFLECTION

Our thoughts shape our perspective, yet not all thoughts come from truth. Past wounds or fears can distort what we perceive. The enemy thrives on confusion, but the Holy Spirit restores clarity when we pause and invite His insight. Submitting our thinking to Christ realigns our minds with peace, replacing assumptions and anxieties with His wisdom and calm.

APPLICATION

- † Pause before you respond or react
- † Ask God for clarity instead of assuming
- † Bring every thought before the Lord for truth and peace

CONNECTION

Thank You, Lord, for renewing my mind with truth. Help me recognize every thought that doesn't reflect Your heart and replace it with what is pure and peace-filled. In Jesus' name, Amen.

HIGHLIGHT QUOTE

Peace begins when every thought bows to truth.

JOURNAL PROMPT

What recurring thought do you need to surrender to Christ today?

DAY 140
Delight Yourself in the Lord

Delight yourself also in the LORD, And He shall give you the desires of your heart.
– Psalm 37:4

REFLECTION

Delighting in the Lord means finding joy in who He is, not just in what He gives. As our hearts rest in His goodness, He reshapes our desires to reflect His will. The more we delight in His presence, the more our ambitions align with His purposes. What once seemed important fades, and His joy becomes our true pursuit and reward.

APPLICATION

† Commit your ways to Him today
† Delight in who He is, not just what He does
† Trust Him to shape your desires according to His will

CONNECTION

Thank You, Lord, for being my delight and my desire. Shape my heart to love what You love and to find lasting joy in Your presence. Align my will with Yours. In Jesus' name, Amen.

HIGHLIGHT QUOTE

Delight in God transforms desires into divine direction.

JOURNAL PROMPT

How can you intentionally delight in God's presence today?

DAY 141
Dealing with Unbelief

> *Now He did not do many mighty works there because of their unbelief.*
> – Matthew 13:58

REFLECTION

Unbelief limits what God desires to do through us. When we begin to walk in our new identity, those closest to us may not understand or accept the change. Yet our call is to forgive and keep obeying the Spirit. Only the Holy Spirit can reveal who we truly are in Christ and strengthen our faith to continue forward, even when others cannot yet see.

APPLICATION

- † Recognize that unbelief quenches the manifestation of Christ
- † Forgive those who reject or misunderstand you
- † Stay filled with the Spirit and obey God's leading, regardless of others' reactions

CONNECTION

Thank You, Lord, for helping me walk in truth, even when I'm misunderstood. Remove every trace of unbelief and deepen my faith to trust Your Word completely. In Jesus' name, Amen.

HIGHLIGHT QUOTE

Faith keeps moving, even when others cannot yet believe.

JOURNAL PROMPT

Where might God be asking you to keep walking by faith, despite others' doubts?

DAY 142
God Confirms His Will

> *Now indeed, Elizabeth your relative has also conceived a son in her old age; and this is now the sixth month for her who was called barren. For with God nothing will be impossible.* – Luke 1:36–37

REFLECTION

God confirms His will through divine timing and gentle assurance. Just as Elizabeth's miracle encouraged Mary, God often sends reminders that strengthen our trust. These confirmations—through people, Scripture, or circumstance—anchor our hearts in faith. What He begins, He sustains. When we rest in His timing, each confirmation becomes evidence of His unfailing promise.

APPLICATION

- † Seek God's will above all
- † Trust His timing and the confirmations He provides
- † Rest in His promises and walk with peace

CONNECTION

Thank You, Lord, for confirming Your Word in perfect timing. Help me recognize Your encouragement and walk forward with confidence in what You've spoken. In Jesus' name, Amen.

HIGHLIGHT QUOTE

God's confirmations are quiet echoes of His spoken Word.

JOURNAL PROMPT

What recent encouragement or "confirmation" did God give you to help you stand?

DAY 143
A Still, Small Voice

After the fire a still small voice.
– 1 Kings 19:12

REFLECTION

God rarely speaks through noise and spectacle; He whispers to hearts that make space to listen. In silence, His presence becomes unmistakable. When we withdraw from the world's volume, His still, small voice brings peace and direction. His whispers carry more power than the loudest storm, calling us not to strive but to draw near in quiet trust.

APPLICATION

- † Withdraw from noise and distraction
- † Make space daily to hear God's whisper
- † Trust His steady presence above every other voice

CONNECTION

Thank You, Lord, for speaking gently yet powerfully. Quiet my mind and steady my heart so I can hear Your voice clearly and follow it with peace. In Jesus' name, Amen.

HIGHLIGHT QUOTE

God often speaks through a whisper, not a storm.

JOURNAL PROMPT

Where can you quiet distractions this week to better hear God's whisper?

DAY 144
We Dare Not!

> *For we dare not class ourselves or compare ourselves with those who commend themselves. But they, measuring themselves by themselves, and comparing themselves among themselves, are not wise.* – 2 Corinthians 10:12

REFLECTION

Comparison clouds contentment. God calls us to unity, not rivalry, and to complete one another, not compete. When we compare, we lose sight of grace and the unique call He has placed on our lives. The Spirit frees us to celebrate others while remaining secure in our assignment. We dare not compare because our Christ alone defines our worth.

APPLICATION

- † Celebrate your uniqueness in Christ
- † Let go of comparison and embrace gratitude
- † Walk in unity, resting in God's purpose and timing

CONNECTION

Thank You, Lord, for creating me with purpose and distinction. Free me from comparison and help me rejoice in others' blessings as I fulfill my calling. In Jesus' name, Amen.

HIGHLIGHT QUOTE

Comparison fades when gratitude takes its place.

JOURNAL PROMPT

How can you replace comparison with gratitude in your current season?

DAY 145
You Are My Hiding Place

> *You are my hiding place; You shall preserve me from trouble; You shall surround me with songs of deliverance.*
> – Psalm 32:7

REFLECTION

When shame whispers and weakness overwhelms, God calls us not to hide from Him but to hide in Him. His presence becomes our refuge, a place of mercy, not judgment. There, He covers our failures with grace and replaces regret with peace. Every time we run to Him, deliverance meets us and the song of His love silences every voice of condemnation.

APPLICATION

- † When guilt rises, run to God, not from Him
- † Let His love cover your shame
- † Receive His peace and deliverance in His presence

CONNECTION

Thank You, Lord, for being my refuge and my hiding place. Draw me quickly into Your presence when I fall short, and let Your mercy surround me with peace and deliverance. In Jesus' name, Amen.

HIGHLIGHT QUOTE

We don't hide from God; we hide in Him.

JOURNAL PROMPT

Where do you need to stop hiding from God and start hiding in Him?

DAY 146
Founded on the Rock

> *He is like a man building a house, who dug deep and laid the foundation on the rock. And when the flood arose, the stream beat vehemently against that house, and could not shake it, for it was founded on the rock.* – Luke 6:48

REFLECTION

Every life faces storms, but those rooted in Christ stand unshaken. Obedience to His Word anchors us when pressure rises. Through prayer, worship, and faithfulness, the Spirit strengthens our foundation and steadies our hearts. Trials test what's built, revealing that stability comes not from circumstance but from surrender. When Christ is our Rock, even fierce winds prove His strength within us.

APPLICATION

- † Build daily habits that deepen your obedience to Christ
- † Allow the Spirit to strengthen weak areas in your foundation
- † Stand confident in the Rock when storms arise

CONNECTION

Thank You, Lord, for being my steadfast foundation. Anchor my heart in Your Word so I remain secure through every test. Strengthen my faith until nothing can shake my trust in You. In Jesus' name, Amen.

HIGHLIGHT QUOTE

Storms reveal the strength of the Rock beneath us.

JOURNAL PROMPT

What recent storm has shown you how secure your faith truly is?

DAY 147
Unlimited Potential

> But as it is written: "Eye has not seen, nor ear heard, Nor have entered into the heart of man The things which God has prepared for those who love Him."
> – 1 Corinthians 2:9

REFLECTION

God's plans for us far exceed what we can imagine. Our potential in Christ isn't measured by human limits but revealed through surrender to His Spirit. Transformation is an unfolding process—each step of obedience unveils more of what He's prepared. The "not yet" seasons are not delays but invitations to trust, grow, and expect the greater things to come.

APPLICATION

† Embrace the process of transformation
† Trust the Spirit's ongoing work within you
† Expect that God's best is still to come

CONNECTION

Thank You, Lord, for the limitless potential found in You. Help me rejoice in what You've done and expect what You are still shaping within me. Keep my heart full of faith and expectation. In Jesus' name, Amen.

HIGHLIGHT QUOTE

God's "not yet" is an invitation to expect greater things.

JOURNAL PROMPT

What dream or promise has God placed in your heart that still requires faith to see fulfilled?

DAY 148
The Fire of God

> *But He turned and rebuked them, and said, "You do not know what manner of spirit you are of ...*
> *– Luke 9:55*

REFLECTION

The fire of God purifies; it doesn't destroy. His refining fire burns away fear, pride, and impurity, making us vessels of holiness. Not all fire is from Him, but His fire always brings life. When we yield to His refining, the glow of His Spirit burns brighter, and His presence consumes everything not aligned with His will.

APPLICATION

† Discern between God's refining fire and the enemy's destruction
† Welcome God's purifying work with humility
† Let His Spirit burn away anything that hinders love

CONNECTION

Thank You, Lord, for the fire of Your Spirit. Help me yield to Your cleansing and healing. Purify my heart and let Your holy fire burn within me to walk in Your purpose. In Jesus' name, Amen.

HIGHLIGHT QUOTE

God's fire doesn't consume us; it refines us until we shine like gold.

JOURNAL PROMPT

What might God be refining in you through His holy fire?

For whatever things were written before were written for our learning, that we through the patience and comfort of the Scriptures might have hope.

– **Romans 15:4**

DAY 149
Process of Healing

> *In my distress I called upon the LORD, And cried out to my God; He heard my voice from His temple, And my cry came before Him, even to His ears.*
> – Psalm 18:6

REFLECTION

Forgiveness releases the offender, but only God's love can heal the wound. Healing unfolds as His presence fills the places where pain once ruled. Where rejection lingered, He brings acceptance; where sorrow settled, He restores joy. The process may take time, but each prayer, each moment in His Word, and every act of worship draws us closer to wholeness in Him.

APPLICATION

- † Press through to His presence in prayer and worship
- † Allow God's love to fill the wounded places
- † Remain close to Him for healing and breakthrough

CONNECTION

Thank You, Lord, for hearing my cry and healing my heart. I choose to forgive and receive Your love in every broken place. Restore my joy and lead me into freedom and peace. In Jesus' name, Amen.

HIGHLIGHT QUOTE

Forgiveness releases the offender, but only God's love heals the wound.

JOURNAL PROMPT

What area of your heart still needs God's healing love today?

A 365-Day Journey Walking with the Word & the Spirit

DAY 150
Spiritual Discernment

> *But God has revealed them to us through His Spirit. For the Spirit searches all things, yes, the deep things of God.*
> – 1 Corinthians 2:10

REFLECTION

True discernment grows from intimacy with God. As we walk closely with the Holy Spirit, He unveils truth and gives wisdom beyond what human understanding can see. His revelation is never for pride or exposure but for restoration and grace. When we handle what He shows with humility, our discernment becomes a channel of healing and light.

APPLICATION

† Bring what you discern to God first
† Yield to the Holy Spirit for how and when to act
† Steward insight with humility and love

CONNECTION

Thank You, Lord, for revealing truth through Your Spirit. Teach me to handle revelation with wisdom and compassion so that my words and actions reflect Your heart. In Jesus' name, Amen.

HIGHLIGHT QUOTE

Discernment without love becomes judgment; discernment with love becomes ministry.

JOURNAL PROMPT

How can you ensure that your discernment today leads to healing rather than criticism?

DAY 151
As Christ Forgave You

> Bearing with one another, and forgiving one another, if anyone has a complaint against another; even as Christ forgave you, so you also must do. But above all these things put on love, which is the bond of perfection. – Colossians 3:13–14

REFLECTION

Forgiveness is the release of what we feel others owe us. It's not minimizing the wrong; it's entrusting justice to God. When we reflect on Christ's immeasurable forgiveness toward us, our hearts soften toward others. In forgiving, love becomes both the cause and the result. It frees us from the weight of offense and restores clarity, peace, and purpose in our walk with Him.

APPLICATION

- † Release the debts of others through forgiveness
- † Reflect on the depth of Christ's forgiveness toward you
- † Walk in the Spirit, unhindered by offense

CONNECTION

Thank You, Lord, for forgiving me completely. Help me forgive others as You have forgiven me. Free my heart from offense and fill it with Your perfect love. In Jesus' name, Amen.

HIGHLIGHT QUOTE

Forgiveness frees the heart to love again.

JOURNAL PROMPT

Who might God be asking you to forgive today so you can walk in freedom?

DAY 152
The Lord Will Perfect It

> *The LORD will perfect that which concerns me; Your mercy, O LORD, endures forever; Do not forsake the works of Your hands.*
> – Psalm 138:8

REFLECTION

God is not distant from what concerns you; He is fully present and powerfully involved. Every worry, need, and unfinished area of your life matters to Him. His promise is to perfect what He started. As we surrender, trust, and obey, He brings us into alignment with His will. His mercy never fails, and His timing is perfect.

APPLICATION

† Surrender every concern, big or small, to God
† Trust that He will bring it to completion and keep your heart anchored in peace
† Speak His promises when doubts arise, remembering that He has not forgotten you

CONNECTION

Thank You, Lord, for perfecting all that concerns me. When I don't see the progress, help me remember You are still working behind the scenes. Strengthen my trust in You as I rest in Your process and praise You through it all. In Jesus' name, Amen.

HIGHLIGHT QUOTE

God promises to perfect what He started; His mercy never fails.

JOURNAL PROMPT

What concern do you need to surrender fully to God and trust Him to perfect in His timing?

DAY 153
Seeking God's Will

> *So I say to you, ask, and it will be given to you; seek, and you will find; knock, and it will be opened to you.*
> – Luke 11:9

REFLECTION

Faith keeps asking, seeking, and knocking, even when answers are delayed. God's will is always perfect, even when it is unclear. He opens and closes doors with purpose and timing that surpass understanding. Trusting His goodness steadies us as we lean on His promises. Seeking His will above our own aligns us with His best.

APPLICATION

† Keep asking in faith for God's will
† Seek Him continually through prayer
† Trust His perfect response and timing

CONNECTION

Thank You, Lord, for hearing every prayer. Help me rest in Your perfect will and timing. Strengthen my faith to keep seeking until You open the right door. In Jesus' name, Amen.

HIGHLIGHT QUOTE

God's will is always perfect, even when it is unclear.

JOURNAL PROMPT

What area of your life do you need to keep asking, seeking, and knocking in faith?

DAY 154
Rooted and Built Up in Christ

> *As you therefore have received Christ Jesus the Lord, so walk in Him, rooted and built up in Him and established in the faith, as you have been taught, abounding in it with thanksgiving.*
> – Colossians 2:6–7

REFLECTION

Faith in Christ is not merely intellectual; we live it out daily. Being rooted in Him gives stability in trials, while being built up produces growth in grace. As we walk with Him, His truth shapes our character and strengthens our faith. Gratitude overflows as we recognize His work within us.

APPLICATION

† Spend intentional time in prayer and Scripture today
† Let His presence anchor and strengthen your faith
† Express gratitude for His ongoing work in your life

CONNECTION

Thank You, Lord, for rooting and building me up in Christ. Strengthen my walk and let my life overflow with thanksgiving. In Jesus' name, Amen.

HIGHLIGHT QUOTE

To be rooted in Christ is to grow in grace and to overflow with gratitude.

JOURNAL PROMPT

How can you stay rooted in Christ today and let gratitude overflow from your heart?

DAY 155
Do We Need Wisdom?

> *If any of you lacks wisdom, let him ask of God, who gives to all liberally and without reproach.*
> *– James 1:5*

REFLECTION

God delights in giving wisdom when we ask. Knowing what to do and how to do it represents our heart's desire. We hesitate to ask because we question our hearing. Our faith needs to be more in His speaking than in our hearing. As we walk closely with Him, His voice becomes clearer and His guidance becomes sure.

APPLICATION

† Ask boldly for wisdom
† Release past failures into His grace
† Tune your heart daily to the Spirit's voice

CONNECTION

Thank You, Lord, for generously giving wisdom. Help me trust that You will speak to me clearly and lovingly guide each step. In Jesus' name, Amen.

HIGHLIGHT QUOTE

God delights in giving wisdom when we ask in faith.

JOURNAL PROMPT

What decision do you need to bring before God and ask boldly for wisdom?

DAY 156
Free from Guilt and Shame

> *In You, O LORD, I put my trust; Let me never be put to shame.*
> *– Psalm 71:1*

REFLECTION

Shame whispers, "You are your past," but Jesus declares, "You are new." Guilt reminds us of what we've done; grace reminds us of what He's done. Shame relates to who we are; guilt to what we do. Jesus Christ nailed both guilt and shame to the cross. We now walk in freedom as beloved children of God, fully accepted and restored.

APPLICATION

† Reject lies of shame and guilt

† Embrace your identity as a new creation

† Walk boldly in forgiveness and grace

CONNECTION

Thank You, Lord, for removing guilt and shame through Your cross. Help me live in the truth of who I am in You—free, loved, and restored. In Jesus' name, Amen.

HIGHLIGHT QUOTE

Jesus Christ nailed both guilt and shame to the cross, and grace declares us free.

JOURNAL PROMPT

What lies of shame do you need to replace today with God's truth about your new identity?

DAY 157
The Spirit of Truth

> When He, the Spirit of truth, has come, He will guide you into all truth.
> – John 16:13

REFLECTION

The Holy Spirit reveals truth beyond human understanding. He exposes deception, clarifies confusion, and reminds us of what Jesus said. When we seek His guidance, He leads us safely through uncertainty. The Spirit of Truth is not distant; He dwells within, gently leading us into wisdom and freedom.

APPLICATION

- † Ask the Holy Spirit for discernment before reacting or deciding
- † Study Scripture, trusting the Spirit to reveal deeper meaning
- † Walk daily in the confidence that truth will always set you free

CONNECTION

Thank You, Holy Spirit, for leading me into truth. Silence every false voice, and help me follow Your peace and clarity in all things. In Jesus' name, Amen.

HIGHLIGHT QUOTE

The Spirit of Truth brings clarity where confusion once ruled.

JOURNAL PROMPT

Where do you need the Spirit's truth to bring clarity in your life today?

DAY 158
One Spirit-Led Moment

Trust in Him at all times, you people; Pour out your heart before Him; God is a refuge for us.
— Psalm 62:8

REFLECTION

One Spirit-led moment can shift the entire course of a day. Pausing to acknowledge God realigns our hearts and multiplies grace. Yielding to His presence opens the way for His wisdom and peace to flow. The enemy opposes our taking time to commune with the Holy Spirit because of the breakthroughs that come from these moments.

APPLICATION

† Pause before decisions and acknowledge God
† Invite His wisdom into your daily steps
† Trust His presence to multiply your efforts

CONNECTION

Thank You, Lord, for meeting me in each moment. Help me pause and yield to You throughout my day. In Jesus' name, Amen.

HIGHLIGHT QUOTE

One Spirit-led moment can shift the course of a day and open the way for a breakthrough.

JOURNAL PROMPT

Where can you pause today to invite God's presence?

DAY 159
It Changes Everything

> *My Presence will go with you, and I will give you rest.*
> – Exodus 33:14

REFLECTION

The presence of God brings peace where there is pressure and rest where there is striving. Moses refused to move without God's presence, knowing that success without Him is empty. The same presence that filled the tabernacle now dwells in us. When we recognize Him, everything shifts from burden to blessing.

APPLICATION

- † Invite God's presence into every part of your day
- † Rest in His companionship rather than rushing ahead
- † Acknowledge His nearness through prayer and gratitude

CONNECTION

Thank You, Lord, for Your presence that brings peace and rest. Let me never move without You. Keep me aware of Your Spirit guiding and strengthening me each day. In Jesus' name, Amen.

HIGHLIGHT QUOTE

God's presence turns striving into stillness and burden into blessing.

JOURNAL PROMPT

Where can you pause today to rest in God's presence instead of rushing ahead?

DAY 160
Blessed Peacemakers

Blessed are the peacemakers, For they shall be called sons of God.
– Matthew 5:9

REFLECTION

Peace doesn't always mean agreement; it means choosing God's presence over strife. Peacemakers carry calm into conflict, responding with wisdom instead of emotion. They prioritize love and unity over being right. Choosing peace invites God's blessing and reflects His nature in our relationships.

APPLICATION

- † Pause and pray before responding in conflict
- † Choose words that build bridges, not walls
- † Let God's peace rule your reactions and decisions

CONNECTION

Thank You, Lord, for calling me to be a peacemaker. Help me respond in love and carry Your peace into every situation. In Jesus' name, Amen.

HIGHLIGHT QUOTE

Choosing peace reflects the heart of the Prince of Peace.

JOURNAL PROMPT

Where do you need to bring peace instead of reacting in frustration?

DAY 161
Enduring Faith

But he who endures to the end shall be saved.
– Matthew 24:13

REFLECTION

Endurance is faith stretched over time. It's the quiet determination to keep going when we do not see the answers and our strength feels gone. God sustains those who refuse to give up, empowering them with His grace. Endurance is not about perfection; it's about persistence in trust. Only by yielding to the Holy Spirit can we stand strong in His grace.

APPLICATION

- † Ask God to strengthen your perseverance today
- † Remind yourself of His past faithfulness
- † Keep pressing forward, even when progress seems slow

CONNECTION

Thank You, Lord, for renewing my strength. Help me endure in faith and run my race with steadfast hope. In Jesus' name, Amen.

HIGHLIGHT QUOTE

Endurance is not about perfection; it's about persistence in trust.

JOURNAL PROMPT

Where do you need to keep enduring in faith, trusting God's perfect timing?

DAY 162
A Heart After God

> *The LORD has sought for Himself a man after His own heart.*
> – 1 Samuel 13:14

A 365-Day Journey Walking with the Word & the Spirit

REFLECTION

David's heart wasn't perfect, but it was pursuing. God looks for hearts that long to please Him, not ones that perform perfectly. A heart after God is humble, teachable, and willing to repent quickly. When we align our desires with His, we find strength, joy, and renewed intimacy with Him.

APPLICATION

- † Ask God to shape your heart to reflect His
- † Repent quickly when you sense distance or pride
- † Worship freely, knowing God delights in your pursuit

CONNECTION

Thank You, Lord, for loving hearts that chase after You. Create in me a clean heart and renew a steadfast spirit within me. In Jesus' name, Amen.

HIGHLIGHT QUOTE

God doesn't seek perfection; He seeks pursuit.

JOURNAL PROMPT

What area of your heart needs to return to God's pursuit today?

DAY 163
The Joy of Obedience

> *If you love Me, keep My commandments.*
> – John 14:15

REFLECTION

Obedience flows from love, not obligation. When we understand God's heart, His commands no longer feel restrictive; they feel protective. Each step of obedience draws us closer to His will and fills us with peace and joy that disobedience can never provide. Our desire to obey Him empowers us to do it, surrendered to His leading.

APPLICATION

- † Reflect on God's goodness behind His commands
- † Obey quickly, trusting His wisdom over your understanding
- † Rejoice in the peace that follows surrender

CONNECTION

Thank You, Lord, for the joy that comes through obedience. Help me trust Your commands as love in action. Teach me to walk in cheerful surrender. In Jesus' name, Amen.

HIGHLIGHT QUOTE

Obedience rooted in love produces joy and peace.

JOURNAL PROMPT

What area of obedience is God inviting you to walk in today?

DAY 164
Stir Up the Gift

> *Therefore I remind you to stir up the gift of God which is in you.*
> – 2 Timothy 1:6

REFLECTION

The gifts and callings of God are precious flames that we must tend to. Life's distractions can dim the fire, but intentional devotion fans it bright again. The more we step out by faith, trusting the gift, the more opposition may arise. Through prayer, the Word, and fellowship, we stir the embers and guard what God has placed within.

APPLICATION

- † Spend time in God's presence to rekindle your spiritual fire
- † Protect your heart from distraction or discouragement
- † Use your gifts with boldness and gratitude

CONNECTION

Thank You, Lord, for the gifts You've entrusted to me. Help me guard them well and keep the fire of Your Spirit burning brightly. In Jesus' name, Amen.

HIGHLIGHT QUOTE

God's gifts remain alive as we tend the flames through devotion.

JOURNAL PROMPT

What spiritual gift or calling do you need to stir up again?

DAY 165
Heed to Yourselves

> *Therefore take careful heed to yourselves, that you love the LORD your God.*
> – Joshua 23:11

REFLECTION

God's love is the soil where our faith grows deep. When we are rooted in His love, storms cannot uproot us. His love grounds us in peace and gives us stability when life feels uncertain. As we dwell in Christ, we comprehend the vastness of His love; a love that sustains, strengthens, and secures us.

APPLICATION

† Meditate on God's love for you
† Let His love be your foundation, not your feelings
† Share His love with others through grace and kindness

CONNECTION

Thank You, Lord, for rooting me in Your love. Strengthen my faith through Your presence and help me walk daily in Your peace. In Jesus' name, Amen.

HIGHLIGHT QUOTE

When we are rooted in His love, storms cannot uproot us.

JOURNAL PROMPT

How can you let God's love be your anchor in uncertain times?

DAY 166
Breaking Chains

> *But at midnight Paul and Silas were praying and singing hymns to God, and the prisoners were listening to them.*
> – Acts 16:25

REFLECTION

Some chains break not by force but through faith expressed in praise. Paul and Silas sang before freedom came, and their worship shook the foundations of their prison. Praise doesn't ignore pain; it magnifies the God who breaks every bondage. When we praise amid struggle, we shift the focus from what binds us to the One who frees us. Our praise can open doors no key ever could.

APPLICATION

- † Praise God before a breakthrough arrives
- † Declare His power greater than your struggle
- † Let worship become your weapon of victory

CONNECTION

Thank You, Lord, that my praise invites Your power. Break every chain that holds me and fill my heart with faith to sing in hard places. I trust You to bring freedom and peace. In Jesus' name, Amen.

HIGHLIGHT QUOTE

Our praise can open doors no key ever could.

JOURNAL PROMPT

Where in your life do you need to sing before you see the breakthrough?

DAY 167
New Every Morning

> Through the Lord's mercies we are not consumed, Because His compassions fail not. They are new every morning; Great is Your faithfulness.
> – Lamentations 3:22–23

REFLECTION

Each new morning is a fresh page in God's story of mercy. Yesterday's failures do not define today's grace. His faithfulness meets us at dawn, reminding us that renewal is always possible. Even when we stumble, His compassion rewrites our narrative with hope. Looking back fuels gratitude; looking ahead builds confidence. In every sunrise, His mercy says, "Begin again."

APPLICATION

† Thank God for the new mercies of this day
† Release what no longer belongs to your present season
† Step forward, trusting His faithfulness for what's ahead

CONNECTION

Thank You, Lord, for Your mercy that never ends. Wipe away the weight of yesterday and renew my spirit with Your grace today. May my life echo the faithfulness of Your love. In Jesus' name, Amen.

HIGHLIGHT QUOTE

Every sunrise whispers that God's mercy begins again.

JOURNAL PROMPT

What new mercy is God offering you this morning?

DAY 168
A Teachable Spirit

Show me Your ways, O LORD; Teach me Your paths.
– Psalm 25:4

REFLECTION

The Spirit teaches those willing to learn. A teachable heart recognizes that wisdom is a lifelong journey, not a single lesson. God delights in shaping pliable hearts that listen, adjust, and grow. We seek His ways to walk in His will. Every moment of humility before Him opens new understanding and deepens grace.

APPLICATION

† Approach each day with humility and curiosity before God
† Listen before speaking and seek understanding before judgment
† Thank God for every lesson—both easy and hard

CONNECTION

Thank You, Lord, for being my Teacher. Keep my heart soft, my mind open, and my spirit teachable. In Jesus' name, Amen.

HIGHLIGHT QUOTE

A teachable heart invites continual growth in God's wisdom.

JOURNAL PROMPT

What lesson is God trying to teach you right now through this season?

DAY 169
Witnesses to the World

Let your light so shine before men, that they may see your good works and glorify your Father in heaven.
– Matthew 5:16

REFLECTION

When we worship through trials, others see God's reality through our response. Paul and Silas praised in prison, and the other prisoners listened. Our worship testifies of God's goodness when words fall short. Praise becomes a light in dark places and hope to those who've lost theirs. Someone's faith may wait on our song.

APPLICATION

† Praise God publicly as well as privately
† Let your joy point others toward Jesus
† See your worship as a living testimony

CONNECTION

Thank You, Lord. Let my praise draw others to You. Use my worship as a light in dark places so others can see Your faithfulness and hope. Make my life a song that leads hearts home. In Jesus' name, Amen.

HIGHLIGHT QUOTE

Your praise preaches louder than words—it shows the world who God is.

JOURNAL PROMPT

Who around you might need to see your faith through praise this week?

A 365-Day Journey Walking with the Word & the Spirit

DAY 170
The Power of Prayer

The effective, fervent prayer of a righteous man avails much.
– James 5:16

REFLECTION

Prayer is not a last resort; it is our first response. It shifts the unseen and strengthens our hearts. When we pray fervently, spiritual opposition gives way and faith rises for the impossible. God hears every whisper and responds with wisdom and love. Persistent prayer doesn't change who God is; it changes who we become as we trust Him deeper.

APPLICATION

† Set aside intentional time each day for prayer
† Bring even minor concerns before God
† Persevere in faith, trusting His perfect response

CONNECTION

Thank You, Lord, for the power of prayer. Help me pray with persistence and faith, believing You are at work in every detail. In Jesus' name, Amen.

HIGHLIGHT QUOTE

Prayer doesn't change God; it changes us.

JOURNAL PROMPT

What prayer have you stopped praying that God may still work on?

DAY 171
A Vision of Hope

> For I know the thoughts that I think toward you, says the LORD, thoughts of peace and not of evil, to give you a future and a hope.
> – Jeremiah 29:11

REFLECTION

God calls us to see in three directions through His Spirit: backward to remember His faithfulness, inward to welcome His transforming presence, and forward to trust His promises. Instead of gazing down in despair, we lift our eyes in expectation of His glory. Hope is not wishful thinking; it is confident trust in His unfolding plan.

APPLICATION

† Reflect on God's faithful hand in your past
† Allow His Spirit to illuminate and heal your heart
† Anticipate His future works with joyful expectation

CONNECTION

Thank You, Lord, for directing my vision. Help me look back with gratitude, within with humility, and forward with trust. In Jesus' name, Amen.

HIGHLIGHT QUOTE

Hope looks back with gratitude, within with grace, and forward with faith.

JOURNAL PROMPT

Where is God asking you to lift your eyes and see with hope today?

DAY 172
Don't Hold On to It

> *Therefore humble yourselves under the mighty hand of God, that He may exalt you in due time, casting all your care upon Him, for He cares for you.*
> – 1 Peter 5:6–7

REFLECTION

God's mighty hand is both strong and tender. He invites us to release every burden, no matter how small or repetitive, into His care. A humble heart doesn't handle cares alone; it surrenders them to the Lord. We are not called to carry life's weight ourselves but with our Lord, who can handle above and beyond what we ask or think.

APPLICATION

† Release your worries daily into God's care
† Trust His love to carry what you cannot
† Humble yourself by leaning on His strength

CONNECTION

Thank You, Lord, for caring so deeply for me. Help me cast my cares on You again and again, trusting Your faithful love. In Jesus' name, Amen.

HIGHLIGHT QUOTE

A humble heart doesn't handle cares alone; it surrenders them to the Lord.

JOURNAL PROMPT

What worry do you need to cast on Him today?

DAY 173
God Holds Tomorrow

> *Therefore do not worry about tomorrow, for tomorrow will worry about its own things. Sufficient for the day is its own trouble.*
> – Matthew 6:34

REFLECTION

When tomorrow's fears crowd today's peace, we must guard our thoughts and stay grounded in the Word. God invites us to trust Him fully, letting go of anxious scenarios we cannot control. His promises are stronger than our what-ifs, and His grace is sufficient for this day. Instead of trying to predict the future, we can rest in the One who holds our tomorrow.

APPLICATION

† Meditate on Matthew 6:34 and repeat it when anxiety arises
† Trust God's timing and refuse to entertain fearful what-ifs
† Set goals prayerfully but surrender the outcomes fully

CONNECTION

Thank You, Lord, for knowing every detail of my tomorrow and calming my heart today. Help me rest in Your faithfulness and stay focused on what You have for me now. I choose to trust You and walk by faith, not by sight. In Jesus' name, Amen.

HIGHLIGHT QUOTE

God's promises are more powerful than our what-ifs.

JOURNAL PROMPT

What worries about tomorrow do you need to release to God today?

DAY 174
Give Thanks to the Lord

> *Oh, give thanks to the LORD! Call upon His name; Make known His deeds among the peoples!*
> – 1 Chronicles 16:8

REFLECTION

Gratitude shifts our focus from what's lacking to what's lasting. When we give thanks to the Lord in all circumstances, we align our hearts with Heaven's perspective. Thankfulness invites God's peace and transforms ordinary moments into worship. As we share our gratitude with others, our faith strengthens and we grow in the knowledge of God's goodness.

APPLICATION

- † Start your day by listing three things you're thankful for
- † Choose gratitude amid difficulty
- † Let thankfulness shape your prayers and outlook

CONNECTION

Thank You, Lord, for the power of gratitude. Help me cultivate a thankful heart in every circumstance and see Your goodness all around me. In Jesus' name, Amen.

HIGHLIGHT QUOTE

Gratitude shifts our focus from what's lacking to what's lasting.

JOURNAL PROMPT

What blessings can you thank God for right now, even in difficulty?

DAY 175
The Pure in Heart

> *Blessed are the pure in heart, For they shall see God.*
> – Matthew 5:8

REFLECTION

Purity of heart isn't about flawlessness; it's about focus. It flows from the new life we have in Christ through the Holy Spirit. When our hearts are undivided, we see God's hand more clearly in every situation. A pure heart trusts His intentions, loves without condition, and pursues His truth above all else.

APPLICATION

- † Examine your motives before acting or speaking
- † Invite the Holy Spirit to purify your thoughts and desires
- † Look for God's presence in the ordinary moments

CONNECTION

Thank You, Lord, for making my heart Your home. Cleanse me from divided motives and help me see You more clearly in all things. In Jesus' name, Amen.

HIGHLIGHT QUOTE

Purity of heart clears our vision to see God in everything.

JOURNAL PROMPT

What distractions or divided motives do you need to surrender to keep your heart pure?

DAY 176
Seeking Him Diligently

But without faith it is impossible to please Him, for he who comes to God must believe that He is, and that He is a rewarder of those who diligently seek Him. – Hebrews 11:6

REFLECTION

Faith pleases God not through performance, but through trust. We come, believing in the fullness of the Trinity—Father, Son, and Holy Spirit—and seeking all that He is rather than relying on who we are. His presence opens the door to joy and strength. God meets us with grace in our struggles, deepening our faith as we draw near and seek Him wholeheartedly.

APPLICATION

† Choose to focus on God's character, not your failures
† Seek deeper trust in His presence daily
† Ask Him to increase your faith where doubts linger

CONNECTION

Thank You, Lord, for receiving me with grace. Grow my faith and help me to please You by trusting fully in who You are. In Jesus' name, Amen.

HIGHLIGHT QUOTE

Faith pleases God not through performance, but through trust.

JOURNAL PROMPT

What doubt do you need to exchange for faith today?

DAY 177
Hallelujah

> *Praise the LORD! Praise God in His sanctuary; Praise Him in His mighty firmament!*
> *– Psalm 150:1*

REFLECTION

"Hallelujah" may sound familiar, but its meaning carries unmatched power. "Hallel" means to boast boldly, and "Yah" is the name of God. Together, they form a declaration of confident worship. When we say "Hallelujah," we proclaim God's greatness in every circumstance. Bold praise shifts atmospheres, strengthens faith, and declares that God reigns here and now.

APPLICATION

- † Speak "Hallelujah" with faith, not formality
- † Let bold praise silence fear and doubt
- † Declare God's goodness in every situation

CONNECTION

Thank You, Lord, for the power in my praise. Let every "Hallelujah" rise with a faith that honors You and stirs others to believe. Teach me to boast boldly in who You are. In Jesus' name, Amen.

HIGHLIGHT QUOTE

Every "Hallelujah" is a bold declaration that God reigns here and now.

JOURNAL PROMPT

What situation today needs the power of a bold "Hallelujah"?

DAY 178
Hard-Pressed on Every Side

> But we have this treasure in earthen vessels, that the excellence of the power may be of God and not of us. We are hard-pressed on every side, yet not crushed; we are perplexed, but not in despair.
> – 2 Corinthians 4:7–8

REFLECTION

Though pressures surround us, they cannot destroy us. Like olives pressed for oil, trials release the anointing of the Holy Spirit within us. Pressure becomes the pathway for God's power to flow through our lives. Christ in us overcomes anything that comes upon us. When the weight feels overwhelming, His Spirit strengthens and sustains us with a peace that nothing can crush.

APPLICATION

† Remember that you carry a treasure greater than pressure
† Let trials drive you to rest in Christ's strength
† Trust God to release His anointing through pressure

CONNECTION

Thank You, Lord, for sustaining me through life's pressures. Let Your Spirit flow through me, even in trials, and reveal Your strength in my weakness. In Jesus' name, Amen.

HIGHLIGHT QUOTE

Pressure releases the anointing of God within us.

JOURNAL PROMPT

What pressure might God be using to release His purpose in you?

DAY 179
Putting On Love

> But above all these things put on love, which is the bond of perfection.
> – Colossians 3:14

REFLECTION

Love is the defining garment of Christ's followers. Our words and actions can wound or heal, divide or build. Putting on love shapes whether we respond with kindness, gentleness, and grace that reflect Christ in a broken world. We clothe ourselves in love through faith, trusting the Holy Spirit to flow through us with a divine affection that never fails.

APPLICATION

- † Examine if your words build up or tear down
- † Ask the Spirit to shape your responses in love
- † Clothe yourself daily in kindness and grace

CONNECTION

Thank You, Lord, for clothing me with Your love. Help me put it on in every interaction and let it define all I do. In Jesus' name, Amen.

HIGHLIGHT QUOTE

Love is the garment that reflects Christ to the world.

JOURNAL PROMPT

Where do you need to put on love more intentionally today?

DAY 180
My Heart Is Overwhelmed

> *When my heart is overwhelmed; Lead me to the rock that is higher than I.*
> *– Psalm 61:2*

REFLECTION

When sorrow and fear weigh us down, Jesus lifts us higher. In grief or confusion, He draws us to Himself, our sure and steady Rock. He answers our cries, heals our perspectives, and fills our hearts with a peace beyond understanding. Even in darkness, He is near and faithful to carry us through.

APPLICATION

- † Press into Jesus when your heart is heavy
- † Cry out, even when words fail
- † Rest in His love and let Him lead you forward

CONNECTION

Thank You, Lord, for lifting me when my heart is overwhelmed. Lead me to the Rock that is higher than I. Surround me with Your presence and peace. In Jesus' name, Amen.

HIGHLIGHT QUOTE

When sorrow and fear weigh us down, Jesus lifts us higher.

JOURNAL PROMPT

Where do you feel overwhelmed today, and how can you let Jesus lift you higher?

DAY 181
Refined by Fire

> When you walk through the fire, you shall not be burned, Nor shall the flame scorch you.
> – Isaiah 43:2

REFLECTION

God does not waste a single trial. Fire refines, revealing the gold of His work within us. It burns away what hinders and strengthens what remains. When life's heat feels unbearable, we remember His promise: He is in the fire with us. The flames that test us will never destroy us; they purify our faith for greater glory.

APPLICATION

† Trust that God is refining you, not destroying you
† Let go of what the fire can remove
† Praise Him, knowing His purpose is good

CONNECTION

Thank You, Lord, for walking with me through every fire. Purify my heart and strengthen my faith to shine brighter for Your glory. In Jesus' name, Amen.

HIGHLIGHT QUOTE

The flames that test us are the same ones that refine us.

JOURNAL PROMPT

What "fire" in your life might God be using to refine and strengthen your faith?

DAY 182
He Will Deliver Us

> *Who delivered us from so great a death, and does deliver us; in whom we trust that He will still deliver us.*
> – 2 Corinthians 1:10

REFLECTION

God's deliverance has a rhythm: He has delivered, He is delivering, and He will deliver again. Remembering past faithfulness builds confidence for today and hope for tomorrow. Fear often clings to the unknown, but faith holds fast to His unchanging nature. Each remembrance of His goodness strengthens our trust that the same God who delivered before will do it again.

APPLICATION

- † Recall a past deliverance and thank God aloud
- † Rest in His present faithfulness
- † Trust confidently that He will deliver again

CONNECTION

Thank You, Lord, for past, present, and future deliverance. Strengthen my trust in Your unchanging love and help me rest in Your continual faithfulness. In Jesus' name, Amen.

HIGHLIGHT QUOTE

Remembering past faithfulness builds confidence for today and hope for tomorrow.

JOURNAL PROMPT

What past deliverance strengthens your faith today?

DAY 183
Grace Over Rejection

> *But He turned and rebuked them, and said, "You do not know what manner of spirit you are of ...*
> *– Luke 9:55*

REFLECTION

When rejection strikes, it can awaken emotion and cloud spiritual clarity. The disciples reacted in the flesh, seeking judgment instead of mercy, but Jesus corrected them with grace. He reminded them of His mission to save, not destroy, calling them to higher discernment. In Him, we find strength to respond in love rather than retaliation, reflecting His Spirit instead of our hurt.

APPLICATION

† Resist reacting in the flesh when hurt—pause and pray before responding
† Ask the Holy Spirit to lead your heart with love and discernment
† Follow Jesus' example and walk in purpose, undeterred by rejection

CONNECTION

Thank You, Lord, for loving me through every rejection and for helping me respond in the Spirit. Fill me with Your grace, compassion, and strength to stay focused on Your calling. May my heart reflect Yours, full of mercy and truth. In Jesus' name, Amen.

HIGHLIGHT QUOTE

Jesus calls us to respond with grace, not retaliation.

JOURNAL PROMPT

How can you respond with grace the next time you feel rejected?

DAY 184
The Truth Shall Make You Free

> *Then Jesus said to those Jews who believed Him, "If you abide in My word, you are My disciples indeed. And you shall know the truth, and the truth shall make you free."*
> *– John 8:31–32*

REFLECTION

We grow in freedom by continuing in the Word—not merely reading it, but abiding in it. His truth becomes alive in us as we receive it by faith and walk in its power. What begins as head knowledge becomes personal revelation through experience. The Holy Spirit reveals truth, silences lies, and leads us into the fullness of who we are in Christ.

APPLICATION

† Spend time daily in the Word, seeking revelation through prayer and worship

† Stand on God's truth in every circumstance, even when it's tested

† Declare the living Word over your life until it takes root and bears fruit

CONNECTION

Thank You, Lord, for Your Word that reveals truth and brings freedom. Help me to abide in You and receive Your promises by faith. Let Your truth become living and active in my heart, transforming me daily. In Jesus' name, Amen.

HIGHLIGHT QUOTE

Abiding in God's Word turns truth into freedom.

JOURNAL PROMPT

What truth from Scripture do you need to continue abiding in this week?

DAY 185
Power of Praise

Whenever I am afraid, I will trust in You.
— Psalm 56:3

REFLECTION

Fear and praise cannot dwell in the same heart. When we choose praise, fear loses its voice. Worship doesn't deny reality; it declares a higher one: that God is greater than what threatens us. Praise shifts our focus from the storm to the Savior, from worry to worship. Each time we lift our voices in trust, fear retreats and faith rises.

APPLICATION

† Speak praise instead of rehearsing fear
† Declare who God is, not what fear says
† Let worship become your first response

CONNECTION

Thank You, Lord, that fear must flee when I praise You. Fill my heart with songs that silence anxiety and strengthen trust. Let faith be louder than every whisper of fear. In Jesus' name, Amen.

HIGHLIGHT QUOTE

When we choose praise, fear loses its voice.

JOURNAL PROMPT

When fear rises, what truth about God can you praise Him for right now?

DAY 186
Embrace the Now

> *Now faith is the substance of things hoped for, the evidence of things not seen.*
> — Hebrews 11:1

REFLECTION

The enemy loves to trap us in the regrets of yesterday or the fears of tomorrow, stealing the joy of today. We often miss divine moments by not being fully present. God isn't just near; He is here. His grace is for this moment, right now. As we rest in His presence and gratitude, we discover peace and purpose in the present.

APPLICATION

- † Turn away from distractions and focus on what's before you
- † Treasure moments with loved ones and with God's presence
- † Trust that today holds a divine purpose

CONNECTION

Thank You, Lord, for being present with me right now. Help me live fully in this moment with gratitude and peace. Teach me to recognize and embrace Your presence in today. In Jesus' name, Amen.

HIGHLIGHT QUOTE

God's grace is not distant; it's present in the now.

JOURNAL PROMPT

How can you be more present and aware of God's grace in today's moments?

DAY 187
Recognizing the Battle

> *For we do not wrestle against flesh and blood, but against principalities, against powers, against the rulers of the darkness of this age.*
> – Ephesians 6:12

REFLECTION

Much of what we face daily isn't merely natural; it's spiritual. A battle rages beyond what our eyes can see, where darkness resists God's purpose in our lives. When we live unaware, we become vulnerable to unseen attacks. But when we recognize the battle, we stay alert in prayer, faith, and the Word. Awareness leads to readiness, and readiness leads to victory in Christ.

APPLICATION

- † Acknowledge the unseen spiritual battle around you
- † Stay prayerful and alert in every circumstance
- † Put on the armor of God before the day begins

CONNECTION

Thank You, Lord, for opening my eyes to the unseen battles around me. Help me stand strong in Your power and walk daily in spiritual awareness and faith. Keep me rooted in Your truth. In Jesus' name, Amen.

HIGHLIGHT QUOTE

Awareness of the unseen battle equips us to fight the war effectively.

JOURNAL PROMPT

What area of your life do you need to view with spiritual, not just natural, eyes?

DAY 188
The "Yet" Praise Life

> *Though the fig tree may not blossom ... Yet I will rejoice in the LORD, I will joy in the God of my salvation.*
> – Habakkuk 3:17–18

REFLECTION

"Yet" praise is the purest form of worship. It rises when nothing seems right, declaring that God is still good. It's faith that stands unshaken when answers delay and hope feels dim. This kind of praise is not about circumstances but confidence in His character. When we choose to say, "Yet I will praise You," Heaven hears unwavering trust.

APPLICATION

† Praise God, even when you don't see results
† Let gratitude rise above disappointment
† Declare His goodness in every season

CONNECTION

Thank You, Lord, for teaching me to praise even in the "yet." Strengthen my heart to trust when I cannot see and to rejoice when life feels uncertain, and to know that You are still worthy. In Jesus' name, Amen.

HIGHLIGHT QUOTE

"Yet" praise declares that God's goodness is greater than life's gaps.

JOURNAL PROMPT

Where do I need to say, "Yet I will praise You, Lord," today?

DAY 189
Free to Flee

> *Flee also youthful lusts; but pursue righteousness, faith, love, peace with those who call on the Lord out of a pure heart.*
> – 2 Timothy 2:22

REFLECTION

The Holy Spirit gives us discernment and courage to flee from anything that endangers our walk with God. Temptation rarely announces itself; it disguises itself as harmless or helpful. But when the Spirit prompts us, obedience becomes our protection. In Christ, fleeing is not weakness; it is Spirit-led strength that preserves our purity and peace.

APPLICATION

† Stay alert to temptation and obey quickly when the Spirit warns you
† Pursue righteousness and fellowship with those who strengthen your faith
† Run into God's presence and stay grounded in His Word

CONNECTION

Thank You, Lord, for giving me discernment and courage to flee what hinders me. Help me obey Your Spirit promptly and pursue Your righteousness with passion. In Jesus' name, Amen.

HIGHLIGHT QUOTE

Fleeing temptation is not weakness but Spirit-led strength.

JOURNAL PROMPT

What temptation is God prompting you to flee from immediately?

A 365-Day Journey Walking with the Word & the Spirit

DAY 190
Belonging to Our Redeemer

> *You were bought at a price; therefore glorify God in your body and in your spirit, which are God's.*
> — 1 Corinthians 6:20

REFLECTION

Redemption is deeply personal. God didn't just find us; He bought us back at the highest price imaginable. The blood of Jesus paid for every sin, securing our freedom forever. We are no longer bound to shame or striving; we belong to the King. Chosen and never forsaken, we live from a place of security, where identity shifts from insecurity to inheritance.

APPLICATION

† Remember that you are God's possession, not the enemy's
† Walk in freedom as one fully redeemed
† Live with gratitude for the price He paid

CONNECTION

Thank You, Lord, for buying me back with Your precious blood. Help me live from the truth of belonging, free from fear and striving. Let my life reflect the worth You placed on me. In Jesus' name, Amen.

HIGHLIGHT QUOTE

In Christ, identity shifts from insecurity to inheritance.

JOURNAL PROMPT

How does knowing you were bought at a price change how you see yourself today?

DAY 191
Joy and Peace in Believing

> Now may the God of hope fill you with all joy and peace in believing, that you may abound in hope by the power of the Holy Spirit.
> – Romans 15:13

REFLECTION

As the world grows darker, God fills us with supernatural joy and peace—not based on circumstances but rooted in faith. We revive hope when we believe what God says more than what we see. The Holy Spirit strengthens us to stand firm and overflow with a hope that encourages others to trust Him again.

APPLICATION

- † Anchor your hope in God, not in your circumstances
- † Speak words of faith and encouragement
- † Stay filled with the Spirit through prayer, worship, and the Word

CONNECTION

Thank You, Lord, for being the God of hope. Fill me with Your joy and peace as I trust You. Let my life overflow with hope by the power of the Holy Spirit. In Jesus' name, Amen.

HIGHLIGHT QUOTE

Hope comes alive when we believe God's Word more than what we see.

JOURNAL PROMPT

What promise can you cling to in faith so joy and peace overflow in you?

DAY 192
Speak Life

> *Death and life are in the power of the tongue, And those who love it will eat its fruit.*
> — Proverbs 18:21

REFLECTION

Our words shape atmospheres, relationships, and even our own hearts. God designed speech to build, bless, and bring forth life. When we speak words of faith and gratitude, we align with His purposes. The Holy Spirit teaches us to pause before we speak so that our mouths become instruments of peace, not pain.

APPLICATION

† Speak words that encourage and uplift others
† Replace negative talk with declarations of faith
† Ask the Holy Spirit to guide your words before you respond

CONNECTION

Thank You, Lord, for giving me the power to speak life. Help me use my words wisely to reflect Your truth and bring healing where hurt lives. In Jesus' name, Amen.

HIGHLIGHT QUOTE

Our words shape atmospheres, relationships, and even our own hearts.

JOURNAL PROMPT

How can you use your words to bring life to someone today?

DAY 193
Walking in Wisdom

> *But the wisdom that is from above is first pure, then peaceable, gentle, willing to yield, full of mercy and good fruits.*
> – James 3:17

REFLECTION

True wisdom reflects God's nature: pure, peaceful, gentle, and full of mercy. Earthly wisdom, rooted in pride, divides and destroys. As we invite the Holy Spirit to shape our thinking, we learn to discern what is true and pleasing to Him. When we abide in His Word, His Word renews our minds, and our lives reflect His character more each day.

APPLICATION

- † Evaluate motives rooted in peace or pride
- † Ask the Spirit to reveal truth and align your heart
- † Walk humbly in God's wisdom each day

CONNECTION

Thank You, Lord, for wisdom from above. Fill me with Your Spirit to walk in purity, peace, and mercy. Let my choices reflect Your heart. In Jesus' name, Amen.

HIGHLIGHT QUOTE

Earthly wisdom, rooted in pride, divides and destroys.

JOURNAL PROMPT

Where do you need to exchange self-centered reasoning for God-centered wisdom?

DAY 194
A Song in the Night

> But at midnight Paul and Silas were praying and singing hymns to God, and the prisoners were listening to them.
> – Acts 16:25

REFLECTION

Worship in dark moments silences despair. Paul and Silas sang while chained, proving that praise depends not on circumstances but on faith. The presence of the Lord breaks through barriers, lifting hearts above hardship. Our midnight songs invite Heaven's power and turn prisons into places of praise. Worship changes the atmosphere until miracles break forth.

APPLICATION

† Worship even when you don't feel like it
† Praise God for who He is, not just what He's done
† Let your song of faith inspire others

CONNECTION

Thank You, Lord, for giving me a song in every season. Help me praise You even in the dark, trusting that You are working all things for good. In Jesus' name, Amen.

HIGHLIGHT QUOTE

Worship turns midnight moments into miracles.

JOURNAL PROMPT

What can you praise God for right now, even while you are waiting?

DAY 195
Living Water

Whoever drinks of the water that I shall give him will never thirst.
– John 4:14

REFLECTION

Jesus offers a satisfaction the world cannot imitate. His living water fills our deepest thirst and revives weary hearts. Many seek fulfillment elsewhere, only to return empty, but His presence restores continually. When we draw near daily, His Spirit renews, refreshes, and fills us again with joy and strength to pour into others.

APPLICATION

- † Spend time in prayer and worship daily to stay spiritually filled
- † Recognize when worldly distractions leave you dry
- † Share the hope and refreshment of Jesus with others

CONNECTION

Thank You, Lord, for being my living water. Refresh me by Your Spirit and help me pour out Your love to others. In Jesus' name, Amen.

HIGHLIGHT QUOTE

Jesus quenches the thirst that the world cannot touch.

JOURNAL PROMPT

Where do you need to drink again from the living water of His presence?

DAY 196
Our Provider

> *And Abraham called the name of the place, The-LORD-Will-Provide.*
> *– Genesis 22:14*

REFLECTION

When Abraham faced the test of surrender, he discovered God's faithfulness. In every trial, the Lord reveals Himself as our Provider. His provision may not arrive early, but it never comes late. He works through unexpected means, reminding us that He alone is our source. As we trust and obey, He meets our needs and strengthens our faith in the waiting.

APPLICATION

- † Thank God for His past provisions as reminders for today
- † Surrender what you fear losing
- † Expect God's provision to meet your need in His perfect way

CONNECTION

Thank You, Lord, for being my Provider. Teach me to trust You when provision seems delayed and to rest in Your perfect timing. In Jesus' name, Amen.

HIGHLIGHT QUOTE

Provision may not come early, but it never comes late.

JOURNAL PROMPT

Where have you seen God provide in unexpected ways?

DAY 197
Looking Unto Jesus

Looking unto Jesus, the author and finisher of our faith.
– Hebrews 12:2

REFLECTION

Distractions draw us away from faith's focus. But when our eyes remain fixed on Jesus, storms lose their power to intimidate. He is both the beginning and completion of our faith journey, guiding us through every wave of doubt and difficulty. When we choose to look to Him, our perspective shifts from fear to faith, from chaos to calm, from striving to rest.

APPLICATION

† Refocus on Jesus when distractions arise
† Declare His promises instead of your fears
† Trust that He will finish what He started in you

CONNECTION

Thank You, Lord, for being the Author and Finisher of my faith. Keep my eyes on You and steady my heart in every storm. In Jesus' name, Amen.

HIGHLIGHT QUOTE

Faith grows stronger when our eyes stay fixed on Jesus.

JOURNAL PROMPT

What distractions do you need to release so you can focus fully on Jesus?

When you walk through the fire, you shall not be burned, Nor shall the flame scorch you.

– Isaiah 43:2

DAY 198
God of the Impossible

> For with God nothing will be impossible.
> – Luke 1:37

REFLECTION

What seems impossible to us is already complete in God's plan. Faith doesn't deny reality; it surrenders it to divine possibility. Our limitations are invitations to encounter His limitless power. When we place the impossible in His hands, He transforms impossibility into testimony. Trust in the God who specializes in what we cannot do and delights in revealing His glory.

APPLICATION

† Declare God's power over every impossible situation
† Choose faith over fear when facing uncertainty
† Thank Him in advance for what He will do

CONNECTION

Thank You, Lord, that nothing is impossible for You. Strengthen my faith to believe beyond what I see and to rest in Your power. In Jesus' name, Amen.

HIGHLIGHT QUOTE

Faith turns impossibility into opportunity for God's glory.

JOURNAL PROMPT

What "impossible" situation can you trust God to handle this week?

DAY 199
Knowing Your Weapons

> *For the weapons of our warfare are not carnal but mighty in God for pulling down strongholds.*
> – 2 Corinthians 10:4

REFLECTION

God has not left His children defenseless. Through the blood of Jesus, the Word of God, and the armor of God, the Holy Spirit equips us for victory in every battle. These weapons are not symbolic—they carry real spiritual power. When we pray, declare the Word, and live under the covering of the blood of Jesus, we stand fully armed and secure in His strength.

APPLICATION

- † Apply the blood of Jesus over your life daily
- † Speak God's Word with authority in every battle
- † Clothe yourself with His armor before each day begins

CONNECTION

Thank You, Lord, for giving me powerful weapons in Christ. Teach me to use them faithfully and walk confidently in Your victory. Let Your Word and Spirit guard my steps. In Jesus' name, Amen.

HIGHLIGHT QUOTE

Believers aware of their weapons become unstoppable in battle.

JOURNAL PROMPT

Which spiritual weapon do you need to use more intentionally this week?

DAY 200
Don't Give Up!

> *But you, be strong and do not let your hands be weak, for your work shall be rewarded!*
> – 2 Chronicles 15:7

REFLECTION

We all face moments of discouragement when the fruit of our labor seems delayed. When we feel tempted to give up, the Holy Spirit renews our strength and gives us courage to continue. He never gives up on us. The end of ourselves becomes the beginning of God's strength, and every act of obedience draws us closer to the reward He has prepared.

APPLICATION

- † Keep sowing good seeds, even when results are unseen
- † Lean on the Spirit when you grow weary or discouraged
- † Encourage yourself by remembering past victories

CONNECTION

Thank You, Lord, for renewing my strength when I grow weary. Help me persevere in doing good and hold fast to Your promise of reaping in due season. My eyes are on You, my Redeemer. In Jesus' name, Amen.

HIGHLIGHT QUOTE

When we feel tempted to give up, we rise, knowing God never gives up on us.

JOURNAL PROMPT

Where do you need to press on in faith, trusting that He will reward your work?

DAY 201
Rivers in the Desert

> Behold, I will do a new thing ... I will even make a road in the wilderness And rivers in the desert.
> – Isaiah 43:19

REFLECTION

We should never limit God by what looks barren or finished. When familiar paths close and hope feels faint, He begins something entirely new. His Spirit moves in hidden ways, turning dry ground into places of fruitfulness. The same God who makes rivers flow in deserts transforms endings into divine beginnings and impossibilities into testimonies of His faithfulness.

APPLICATION

† Look for signs of transformation, not just refreshment
† Thank God for working in unseen and unexpected ways
† Stay open to the new thing He is bringing forth

CONNECTION

Thank You, Lord, for Your power to transform barren places. Breathe new life into what has felt stuck and bring beauty out of what seemed broken. I trust You to make all things new. In Jesus' name, Amen.

HIGHLIGHT QUOTE

God's new thing doesn't just refresh; it transforms what seemed beyond repair.

JOURNAL PROMPT

What area of your life might God be transforming into something new?

DAY 202
The Power of Surrender

> *Come to Me, all you who labor and are heavy laden, and I will give you rest.*
> – Matthew 11:28

REFLECTION

Jesus calls us not only to rest, but also to release control. His invitation to peace begins where striving ends. When we surrender the weights we've tried to carry alone, His strength meets our weakness. In surrender, we find stability. The hands that hold the universe also hold us, teaching us that we find true power when we yield to His care.

APPLICATION

† Release what you've been trying to manage on your own
† Breathe deeply and remember that He carries what you cannot
† Rest in the assurance that surrender brings strength

CONNECTION

Thank You, Lord, for calling me to lay everything at Your feet. Help me rest in Your perfect care and find peace in surrender. Teach me that letting go is where rest truly begins. In Jesus' name, Amen.

HIGHLIGHT QUOTE

Rest begins where striving ends.

JOURNAL PROMPT

What area of your life is God inviting you to surrender so you can find rest?

DAY 203
But You, O Lord

> But You, O LORD, are a shield for me, My glory and the One who lifts up my head.
> – Psalm 3:3

REFLECTION

When life feels overwhelming and opposition surrounds us, faith gives us a new focus. David faced betrayal and fear, yet turned his gaze upward with four words: "But You, O Lord." That shift changes everything. Our situation may not instantly change, but our confidence does. God remains greater than every enemy, stronger than every storm, and faithful through it all.

APPLICATION

† Acknowledge your situation honestly before the Lord
† Declare His greatness above what opposes you
† Let "But You, O Lord" become your daily declaration

CONNECTION

Thank You, Lord, for reminding me that You are greater than what surrounds me. Lift my eyes above fear and fix my heart on Your strength. I choose to rest in Your faithfulness. In Jesus' name, Amen.

HIGHLIGHT QUOTE

Four words, "But You, O Lord," can shift fear into faith.

JOURNAL PROMPT

Where do you need to lift your eyes and declare, "But You, O Lord"?

DAY 204
Unconquered Light

> *And the light shines in the darkness, and the darkness did not comprehend it.*
> – John 1:5

REFLECTION

Darkness can resist, but it cannot overcome the light of God. His presence cuts through despair and confusion with unwavering power. Every shadow must yield where His truth shines. Even in the world's darkest hour, His light remains steady, victorious, and unstoppable. As we walk in that light, we become reflections of His hope to those still searching.

APPLICATION

† Stand firm in faith when circumstances feel dark
† Let kindness and truth be your light to others
† Thank God that His victory shines through you

CONNECTION

Thank You, Lord, for being the light that nothing can extinguish. Fill me with Your presence and make me a beacon of hope to those around me. Let Your truth triumph in every dark place. In Jesus' name, Amen.

HIGHLIGHT QUOTE

Darkness can resist, but it cannot overcome the light of God.

JOURNAL PROMPT

Where can you shine God's unconquered light in someone's darkness today?

DAY 205
Beholding His Work

> *But we all, with unveiled face, beholding as in a mirror the glory of the Lord, are being transformed into the same image from glory to glory, just as by the Spirit of the Lord.*
> *– 2 Corinthians 3:18*

REFLECTION

Beholding God's glory in others shifts our perspective from flaws to faith. When we focus on weaknesses, we discourage, but when we notice His transforming work, we build up. Each life reflects His grace in progress. Instead of comparing, we celebrate how the Spirit shapes each of us from glory to glory, trusting in His unfinished work.

APPLICATION

† Celebrate others' progress, not their flaws
† Trust God's ability to transform lives
† Pray with faith for His work in others

CONNECTION

Thank You, Lord, for Your transforming work in all of us. Help me celebrate others' progress and keep my eyes on Your glory. In Jesus' name, Amen.

HIGHLIGHT QUOTE

It takes a Spirit-led perspective to see God's hand in others.

JOURNAL PROMPT

How can you encourage someone today by recognizing God's work in their life?

DAY 206
Bound in the Spirit

> *And see, now I go bound in the spirit to Jerusalem, not knowing the things that will happen to me there.*
> – Acts 20:22

REFLECTION

Paul went to Jerusalem, bound by the Spirit, ready for anything. God frees us from control, intimidation, and unhealthy ties. Being bound to Christ secures us in His covenant and calling. The Holy Spirit empowers us to walk boldly, unhindered. He leads our steps, and our stops, from faith to faith.

APPLICATION

† Stand firm in your bond with Christ
† Reject fear and manipulation by trusting His Spirit
† Walk boldly in the freedom of His call

CONNECTION

Thank You, Lord, for Your powerful presence. I desire to be bound to You alone. Free me from every tie that hinders my walk. In Jesus' name, Amen.

HIGHLIGHT QUOTE

Being bound to the Spirit frees us from fear and empowers us to walk boldly.

JOURNAL PROMPT

What attachments or fears do you need to release to be fully bound to God's Spirit?

DAY 207
Building on Christ

> *For no other foundation can anyone lay than that which is laid, which is Jesus Christ.*
> – 1 Corinthians 3:11

REFLECTION

Jesus is the only foundation strong enough to sustain a lasting life. Yet what we build on that foundation also matters. Our words, actions, and priorities become the structure rising from His truth. What's built on Him endures; what's built apart from Him fades. When Christ is the cornerstone, even the storms prove His strength.

APPLICATION

† Examine what you're building; does it rest on Christ's truth?
† Let Scripture shape every plan and pursuit
† Build with faith, humility, and eternal purpose

CONNECTION

Thank You, Lord, for being my unshakable foundation. Teach me to build wisely in a way that honors You. May my life reflect Your strength and truth. In Jesus' name, Amen.

HIGHLIGHT QUOTE

What's built on Christ stands when all else falls.

JOURNAL PROMPT

What area of your life needs rebuilding with Christ as the cornerstone?

DAY 208
He Restores My Soul

He restores my soul; He leads me in the paths of righteousness For His name's sake.
– Psalm 23:3

REFLECTION

God not only saves us; He restores us. His Spirit refreshes weary hearts and renews broken dreams. Restoration isn't about returning to what was but about becoming new in His presence. As we follow His leading, He strengthens our souls with peace and purpose, teaching us to walk in who we are in Him, from glory to glory.

APPLICATION

† Spend quiet time with God to receive restoration
† Release weariness and allow His Spirit to renew you
† Walk forward in the strength He provides

CONNECTION

Thank You, Lord, for restoring my soul. Refresh my heart and lead me in paths of righteousness for Your glory. In Jesus' name, Amen.

HIGHLIGHT QUOTE

Restoration is not returning to what was; it's becoming new in Him.

JOURNAL PROMPT

What part of your soul needs God's restoration today?

DAY 209
Genuine Anointing

> *But my horn You have exalted like a wild ox; I have been anointed with fresh oil.*
> – Psalm 92:10

REFLECTION

The anointing isn't about titles or recognition; it's divine empowerment to obey God. True anointing flows from intimacy, not applause. It's His Spirit working through surrendered hearts to bring freedom where there's bondage and hope where there's despair. When we stay humble and yield, our lives become vessels of His power and love to a hurting world.

APPLICATION

- † Let God's anointing flow through you to help others
- † Stay humble; His power works through surrendered hearts
- † Seek to serve, not to be seen

CONNECTION

Thank You, Lord, for Your anointing that breaks yokes and brings healing. Use me as a vessel of freedom and love wherever You lead. Let Your Spirit flow through me in power and grace. In Jesus' name, Amen.

HIGHLIGHT QUOTE

True anointing is not for status; it's for service.

JOURNAL PROMPT

How can you let God's anointing flow through you to lift someone else today?

DAY 210
Free to Be

And you shall know the truth, and the truth shall make you free.
— John 8:32

REFLECTION

As we grow in Christ, His unconditional love frees us from the need to perform or pretend. We no longer strive to earn acceptance—His grace transforms us from the inside out. Masks fall, wounds heal, and confidence rises. Secure in His love, we live as God created us to be: whole, joyful, and free in His truth.

APPLICATION

- † Embrace your identity in Christ without comparison or self-doubt
- † Let go of people-pleasing and rest in God's acceptance
- † Walk in the Spirit, letting His love shape your confidence

CONNECTION

Thank You, Lord, for loving and accepting me just as I am and setting me free to be who You've called me to be. Transform me by Your Spirit and help me walk in boldness, joy, and authenticity. In Jesus' name, Amen.

HIGHLIGHT QUOTE

God's love frees us from pretending and striving; it makes us secure in Him.

JOURNAL PROMPT

Where do you still feel pressure to perform, and how can you rest in God's love?

DAY 211
Sleeping in the Storm

> *I lay down and slept; I awoke, for the LORD sustained me. I will not be afraid of ten thousands of people Who have set themselves against me all around.*
> – Psalm 3:5–6

REFLECTION

Peace in the middle of chaos is the fruit of trust. David slept while surrounded by enemies because he knew God was in control. We can acknowledge the storm without surrendering to it. Faith whispers that we are in God's loving hands. When we rest in that truth, fear loses its voice and His presence guards our hearts and minds through the night.

APPLICATION

† End each day by entrusting every concern to God
† Believe that He watches over you while you rest
† Let His peace silence the storm within your soul

CONNECTION

Thank You, Lord, for guarding me through every storm. Teach me to rest in Your presence and trust You with what I cannot control. I will sleep in peace, knowing You fight for me. In Jesus' name, Amen.

HIGHLIGHT QUOTE

Peace isn't the absence of storms; it's the rest in the Sustainer.

JOURNAL PROMPT

What worries do you need to release tonight so you can rest in God's peace?

DAY 212
Our Faithful God

> *Through the LORD's mercies we are not consumed, Because His compassions fail not. They are new every morning; Great is Your faithfulness.*
> — Lamentations 3:22–23

REFLECTION

God's faithfulness is the steady thread through every season of change. Circumstances shift and people come and go, but His mercy remains. Each sunrise is proof that His compassion endures. Looking back, we can trace His hand carrying us through every valley and victory. The same God who was faithful before will be faithful again. His love never fades.

APPLICATION

- † Begin each day thanking God for His unchanging love
- † Remember a season when His mercy sustained you
- † Encourage someone with the story of His steadfast care

CONNECTION

Thank You, Lord, for Your faithful love that never changes. Remind me daily of Your compassion and help me rest in Your constancy. Let my life reflect Your enduring grace. In Jesus' name, Amen.

HIGHLIGHT QUOTE

God's faithfulness doesn't waver with our seasons; it anchors them.

JOURNAL PROMPT

Where have you seen God's steady hand guiding you through change?

DAY 213
The Power of His Name

> *For "whoever calls on the name of the LORD shall be saved."*
> – Romans 10:13

REFLECTION

The name of Jesus carries unmatched power and authority because of who He is. In His name, chains break, hearts heal, and salvation comes. His name silences fear and speaks peace into chaos. Every time we call Him, Heaven responds. His name is our refuge, our victory, and our song.

APPLICATION

- † Speak the name of Jesus over every fear and situation
- † Thank Him for the authority you have in His name
- † Share with someone how His name has changed your life

CONNECTION

Thank You, Lord, for the power of Your name. I call upon You today for strength, peace, and victory. Let Your name be exalted in my life. In Jesus' name, Amen.

HIGHLIGHT QUOTE

When we call on the name of Jesus, Heaven moves on earth.

JOURNAL PROMPT

What area of your life needs the power of Jesus' name declared over it?

DAY 214
He Goes with You

> *Be strong and of good courage, do not fear nor be afraid of them; for the LORD your God, He is the One who goes with you. He will not leave you nor forsake you.*
> – Deuteronomy 31:6

REFLECTION

We do not prove our faith by how we begin but by how we endure when battles intensify. The enemy is relentless, yet God's Spirit enables us to persevere with a strength that isn't our own. Prayer, worship, and service keep us aligned with His purposes and help us remain steadfast when enthusiasm fades. Courage births persistence, helping us to continue moving forward because He walks with us always.

APPLICATION

† Reflect on one area where your zeal has dimmed, and surrender it to God
† Ask Him for renewed persistence in that area
† Take one intentional step to reignite devotion

CONNECTION

Thank You, Lord, for giving me fresh courage and persistence. Help me to press forward in faith, leaning on Your strength. Thank You for never leaving me. In Jesus' name, Amen.

HIGHLIGHT QUOTE

Courage births persistence, helping us to continue moving forward because He walks with us always.

JOURNAL PROMPT

Where is God asking you to press on with persistent courage instead of weariness?

DAY 215
Consider the Lilies

Consider the lilies of the field, how they grow.
– Matthew 6:28

REFLECTION

Just as God tends the lilies, He faithfully cares for every detail of our lives. Anxiety grows when we focus on what we can't control, but Jesus invites us to release fear and trust in His care. The lilies flourish without worry; so can we, resting in His promises. When we stop striving and start trusting, peace flows and faith grows.

APPLICATION

- † Name the worries you carry and release them to God
- † Remind yourself that He delights in providing for you
- † Use faith as a shield when anxiety creeps in

CONNECTION

Thank You, Lord, for providing for me in every season. I lay my worries before You and trust Your perfect care. Help me grow in peace and faith like the lilies. In Jesus' name, Amen.

HIGHLIGHT QUOTE

The lilies flourish without worry; so can we, resting in His promises.

JOURNAL PROMPT

What specific worry do you need to release today to trust God's faithful provision?

DAY 216
Come Boldly to the Throne

> *Let us therefore come boldly to the throne of grace, that we may obtain mercy and find grace to help in time of need.*
> – Hebrews 4:16

REFLECTION

When we fail, our instinct is to retreat from God, feeling unworthy of His presence. But Jesus, our compassionate High Priest, understands our struggles. He doesn't just sympathize; He strengthens. The enemy wants us trapped in defeat, but God calls us to approach Him with confidence, knowing mercy awaits.

APPLICATION

Come honestly before God and expect His grace

Write one burden you've carried alone and release it in prayer

Thank Him for mercy that meets you, even when you feel unworthy

CONNECTION

Thank You, Lord, for Your throne of grace where I find mercy and help. When I feel unworthy, remind me of Your unchanging love. I come boldly, trusting in Your sufficiency. In Jesus' name, Amen.

HIGHLIGHT QUOTE

God calls us to approach Him with confidence, knowing His mercy is waiting.

JOURNAL PROMPT

What burden do you need to surrender before God's throne today?

DAY 217
More than Enough

> *And my God shall supply all your need according to His riches in glory by Christ Jesus.*
> – Philippians 4:19

REFLECTION

There are moments when we feel depleted of strength, patience, or hope. God promises to supply every need according to His riches, not our resources. Where we fall short, His abundance overflows. In weakness, He gives power; in hunger, He multiplies provision. Trusting Him means shifting from scarcity to sufficiency, knowing He is always more than enough.

APPLICATION

† Bring one area of lack before God and ask for His provision
† Reflect on past times when He met your needs abundantly
† Choose gratitude today for His sufficiency in every season

CONNECTION

Thank You, Lord, for meeting my needs according to Your riches, not my limits. Help me trust Your provision in every area of lack and rest in Your abundance. In Jesus' name, Amen.

HIGHLIGHT QUOTE

In weakness, He gives power; in hunger, He multiplies provision.

JOURNAL PROMPT

Where do you feel a lack today, and how can you invite God's sufficiency into it?

DAY 218
Our New Identity

> *Therefore, if anyone is in Christ, he is a new creation; old things have passed away; behold, all things have become new.*
> – 2 Corinthians 5:17

REFLECTION

In Christ, we are not who we once were. He gave us a new identity: redeemed, empowered, and seated with Him in heavenly places. The same Spirit that raised Jesus from the dead lives within us. An unaware believer is unarmed. When we know who we are in Christ, fear loses its hold, and confidence in His authority takes its place.

APPLICATION

† Declare your identity as a child of God each day
† Refuse lies that say you are powerless or unworthy
† Walk in the authority Christ has already given you

CONNECTION

Thank You, Lord, for making me new in Christ. Help me walk boldly in my identity and live from the victory You've already secured. Let my confidence rest in who You are within me. In Jesus' name, Amen.

HIGHLIGHT QUOTE

Knowing who you are in Christ silences every lie of the enemy.

JOURNAL PROMPT

What truth about your identity in Christ do you need to walk in today?

DAY 219
Breaking Through the Cocoon

> *The one who breaks open will come up before them; They will break out, Pass through the gate, And go out by it; Their king will pass before them, With the Lord at their head.*
> — Micah 2:13

REFLECTION

Like a cocoon around a caterpillar, God's protective boundaries allow transformation to unfold without interference. In those hidden seasons, it may seem like nothing is happening, but He is refining us for the breakthrough ahead. We cannot rush the process. Breaking out too soon would hinder the growth. Trusting His work within keeps us still until it's time to rise renewed.

APPLICATION

† Identify areas where you feel "stuck" and ask God for His perspective
† Trust His process, knowing He protects, even when you don't understand
† Surrender your timeline to His perfect timing for breakthrough

CONNECTION

Thank You, Lord, for guarding me in seasons of preparation. Help me to trust Your timing and embrace the refining work You are doing. Lead me into Your breakthrough. In Jesus' name, Amen.

HIGHLIGHT QUOTE

God's protective boundaries allow transformation to unfold without interference.

JOURNAL PROMPT

What "cocoon season" are you in, and how is God preparing you for a breakthrough?

DAY 220
Walking the Bright Path

> *But the path of the just is like the shining sun, That shines ever brighter unto the perfect day.*
> *– Proverbs 4:18*

REFLECTION

The path of the righteous is one of a steady, growing light. God's guidance doesn't rush; it unfolds with grace and purpose. Each step of obedience brings greater clarity and confidence. When guilt or pride pulls us off course, His mercy restores our direction and renews our focus. Walking with Him means continual transformation, with His light leading us ever closer to the fullness of His will.

APPLICATION

- † Ask God to reveal any area where you've drifted from His path
- † Choose humility over pride, grace over guilt
- † Thank Him for guiding your steps toward increasing light

CONNECTION

Thank You, Lord, for lighting my path and keeping me close to You. Lead me in righteousness and help me walk faithfully toward Your perfect plan. May my life shine brighter each day in Your presence. In Jesus' name, Amen.

HIGHLIGHT QUOTE

Each step of obedience makes the path of faith shine brighter.

JOURNAL PROMPT

Where is God inviting you to walk in greater light and maturity?

DAY 221
The God of Peace

Now may the Lord of peace Himself give you peace always in every way.
– 2 Thessalonians 3:16

REFLECTION

We do not find peace in quiet moments or solved problems but in the presence of God Himself. He is the Lord of peace—constant, personal, and unchanging. His presence calms our fear and confusion. His peace doesn't visit occasionally; it abides continually, guarding both heart and mind. We don't chase peace; we draw near to the One who is peace.

APPLICATION

† Invite God's presence into every anxious thought
† Speak His peace over your surroundings through prayer
† Rest in knowing His peace remains, even when circumstances shift

CONNECTION

Thank You, Lord, for being my peace. Teach me to rest in Your presence instead of striving for control. Fill my heart with Your calm so I can carry Your peace wherever I go. In Jesus' name, Amen.

HIGHLIGHT QUOTE

We don't chase peace; we rest in the God who is peace.

JOURNAL PROMPT

Where in your life do you need to remember that God Himself is your peace?

DAY 222
When God Said "Wait"

> *Rest in the LORD, and wait patiently for Him.*
> *– Psalm 37:7*

REFLECTION

Waiting is not wasted when it's spent in faith. God often works behind the scenes, preparing what we cannot yet see. Patience in waiting grows trust, and trust matures into peace. The delay is not denial; it's divine timing aligning for our good. Our waiting is not for what we want but for Him—believing His plan exceeds our expectations.

APPLICATION

† Surrender your timeline to God's perfect plan
† Use waiting seasons to grow in worship and wisdom
† Remember past times when His timing proved best

CONNECTION

Thank You, Lord, for teaching me to rest while I wait. Strengthen my faith to trust Your timing and purpose in every season. In Jesus' name, Amen.

HIGHLIGHT QUOTE

Waiting with faith transforms delay into preparation.

JOURNAL PROMPT

What are you waiting for that you can surrender into God's perfect timing today?

DAY 223
Overflowing Grace

And God is able to make all grace abound toward you.
– 2 Corinthians 9:8

REFLECTION

Grace doesn't trickle; it abounds. God's generosity meets every need and then spills over into blessings for others. His grace equips us for good work, sustains us in weakness, and turns scarcity into sufficiency. When we live open-handed before Him, grace flows through us, not only filling but overflowing. We become channels of the same kindness that continually renews us.

APPLICATION

† Receive God's grace daily with gratitude
† Let His abundance shape how you give and serve
† Thank Him for being enough in every circumstance

CONNECTION

Thank You, Lord, for the grace that overflows. Fill me until Your kindness pours out of my life to refresh others. Help me live from Your sufficiency, not my own. In Jesus' name, Amen.

HIGHLIGHT QUOTE

Grace never runs dry; it runs through.

JOURNAL PROMPT

How can you allow God's overflowing grace to reach someone else this week?

DAY 224
The Gift of Peace

> *Peace I leave with you, My peace I give to you.*
> – John 14:27

REFLECTION

Jesus gives a peace the world can't reproduce. It's not dependent on quiet conditions but on His living presence within us. His peace settles where worry once lived, calming anxious hearts and restoring clarity. This peace is more than a feeling; it's His gift, His promise, and His power at work in us. The peace we carry reflects Him to others.

APPLICATION

- † Receive His peace intentionally each day through prayer
- † When anxiety stirs, pause and welcome His Spirit's calm
- † Share His peace through gentleness and grace with others

CONNECTION

Thank You, Lord Jesus, for the gift of Your peace. Fill me with Your calm and teach me to live from it daily. Let Your peace overflow through me to bring comfort wherever I go. In Jesus' name, Amen.

HIGHLIGHT QUOTE

Jesus doesn't give peace as the world does—He gives Himself.

JOURNAL PROMPT

How can you live today as a carrier of Christ's peace to others?

DAY 225
Seasons of Growth

To everything there is a season, A time for every purpose under heaven.
– Ecclesiastes 3:1

REFLECTION

Each season carries a purpose, even a quiet, hidden one. Growth often happens beneath the surface where no one sees. When we assume a season wasted, we doubt God's faithful workings. Every phase allows His plan to unfold perfectly. Even dry seasons prepare us to thirst for His living water. Waiting seasons shape us for harvest and strengthen our trust in His timing.

APPLICATION

† Embrace your current season with faith and patience
† Ask God what He's teaching you right now
† Celebrate small steps of growth

CONNECTION

Thank You, Lord, for the seasons You've appointed in my life. Help me to trust Your timing and purpose in every moment. In Jesus' name, Amen.

HIGHLIGHT QUOTE

Hidden seasons are where deep roots of faith grow.

JOURNAL PROMPT

What lesson is God teaching you in this current season?

DAY 226
Standing in Authority

> *Behold, I give you the authority to trample on serpents and scorpions, and over all the power of the enemy.*
> – Luke 10:19

REFLECTION

Authority only works when it's exercised. Jesus gave His followers authority over the enemy—not to boast, but to walk in confidence and peace. True authority is not loud or forceful; it flows from humble faith in who Christ is within us. When we stand in His truth, darkness loses its grip. Knowing our position in Him, we walk with quiet strength for His glory.

APPLICATION

† Speak God's Word with calm confidence
† Stand firm against anything that opposes His truth
† Walk daily in the authority of Jesus' name

CONNECTION

Thank You, Lord, for entrusting me with Your authority. Help me use it wisely and boldly to stand firm in truth. Let every word I speak align with Your power and peace. In Jesus' name, Amen.

HIGHLIGHT QUOTE

Spiritual authority is quiet strength rooted in who Christ is within us.

JOURNAL PROMPT

Where do you need to stand in Christ's authority instead of shrinking in fear?

DAY 227
Directed Into God's Love

> *Now may the Lord direct your hearts into the love of God and into the patience of Christ.*
> – 2 Thessalonians 3:5

REFLECTION

God Himself directs our hearts into His love and the patience of Christ. We don't walk in love and patience by effort alone; it is the work of the Holy Spirit within us. As He guides our hearts, we learn to love deeply and endure faithfully. His love steadies our emotions, and His patience strengthens our perseverance. By grace, we stand, and by His Spirit, we grow.

APPLICATION

† Pray for God to direct your heart into His love daily
† Ask Him to grow Christlike patience in you
† Look for opportunities to show His love in action

CONNECTION

Thank You, Lord, for guiding my heart into Your love and the patience of Christ. Help me show Your love in all my interactions and wait patiently for the manifestation of Your promises. In Jesus' name, Amen.

HIGHLIGHT QUOTE

God Himself directs our hearts into His love and patience.

JOURNAL PROMPT

How can you let God guide your heart more fully into His love this week?

DAY 228
Anchored in Hope

This hope we have as an anchor of the soul, both sure and steadfast.
– Hebrews 6:19

REFLECTION

Hope anchors us when storms rage. It steadies our hearts and keeps faith from drifting. God's promises are unshakable, holding firm when everything else feels uncertain. Even when waves rise high, His Word secures us beneath the surface. To have hope in Him is not simply wishful thoughts, but a confident expectation, based on His faithfulness. It doesn't deny the storm; it endures through it, trusting His ultimate word.

APPLICATION

† Declare God's promises over areas of uncertainty
† Refuse to let discouragement loosen your grip on hope
† Encourage someone else who feels adrift in doubt

CONNECTION

Thank You, Lord, for being my anchor in every storm. Keep me grounded in Your promises and confident in Your faithfulness. In Jesus' name, Amen.

HIGHLIGHT QUOTE

Hope doesn't deny the storm; it anchors us through it.

JOURNAL PROMPT

What promise of God anchors you when life feels uncertain?

DAY 229
The Lifter of Your Head

> But You, O LORD, are a shield for me, My glory and the One who lifts up my head.
> – Psalm 3:3

REFLECTION

Discouragement can make us hang our heads in defeat, but God is the lifter of our heads. When He lifts us, our perspective shifts; darkness gives way to light, fear to faith, and despair to hope. The Lord meets us where we are but never leaves us there. He reminds us that our story isn't over and that His strength is enough for every step ahead.

APPLICATION

† Look up in faith when discouragement weighs you down
† Let God's promises replace shame with confidence
† Choose gratitude as He lifts you from sorrow to hope

CONNECTION

Thank You, Lord, for lifting my head when life presses me low. Restore my confidence in Your promises and fill me with renewed strength and joy. I look to You, my lifter and my hope. In Jesus' name, Amen.

HIGHLIGHT QUOTE

When God lifts your head, despair gives way to hope.

JOURNAL PROMPT

Where do you need to let God lift your head and restore hope today?

DAY 230
Don't Quit Before the Harvest

> *And let us not grow weary while doing good, for in due season we shall reap if we do not lose heart.*
> *– Galatians 6:9*

REFLECTION

Waiting can feel endless, but God's timing is exact. Beneath the surface, He is cultivating provision and grace. Patience is not inactivity; it's trust in motion. Every moment of endurance shapes our character and prepares a blessing. When we feel tempted to stop, we remember that the soil of perseverance produces the sweetest fruit.

APPLICATION

† Praise God for His unseen work
† Recall past answers to fuel present patience
† Thank Him in advance for the harvest to come

CONNECTION

Thank You, Lord, for being faithful in my waiting seasons. Teach me to trust Your process and hold fast until the harvest appears. In Jesus' name, Amen.

HIGHLIGHT QUOTE

Patience is active trust, believing God is working beneath the surface.

JOURNAL PROMPT

Where are you tempted to give up, and how can you choose patience?

DAY 231
Strength for Today

> *As your days, so shall your strength be.*
> – Deuteronomy 33:25

REFLECTION

God provides the exact strength needed for each day. His mercies are available every morning, not saved for a later date. When we draw from His grace instead of our own effort, what once felt impossible becomes possible. His strength is steady, personal, and sufficient. We can face each day, confident that His supply never runs out.

APPLICATION

† Ask daily for God's strength instead of relying on your own
† Focus on today instead of worrying about tomorrow
† Rest in His continual provision of grace

CONNECTION

Thank You, Lord, for giving me strength for this day. Teach me to draw from Your grace moment by moment. I rest in Your sufficiency. In Jesus' name, Amen.

HIGHLIGHT QUOTE

God provides the exact strength needed for each day.

JOURNAL PROMPT

Where do you need to depend on God's strength instead of your own today?

DAY 232
Faith Beyond Familiarity

> "A prophet is not without honor except in his own country and in his own house." Now He did not do many mighty works there because of their unbelief.
> – Matthew 13:57–58

REFLECTION

Many in Jesus' hometown missed His miracles because unbelief hid behind familiarity. They thought they knew Him, yet overlooked who He truly was. We often do the same, limiting what God can do through those closest to us or even through ourselves. Faith looks beyond the familiar and expects God to move in unexpected ways, through unexpected people, at unexpected times.

APPLICATION

† Ask God to reveal areas where familiarity has dulled your faith
† Choose to see those around you as vessels God can use
† Pray with a fresh expectation of His mighty works in your life

CONNECTION

Thank You, Lord, for moving in ways I least expect. Remove every barrier of unbelief and help me honor how You work through others and through me. I trust You for mighty works ahead. In Jesus' name, Amen.

HIGHLIGHT QUOTE

Faith looks beyond the familiar and expects God to move in unexpected ways.

JOURNAL PROMPT

Where has familiarity dulled your faith, and how can you choose a fresh expectation today?

DAY 233
Greater than Our Heart

> *For if our heart condemns us, God is greater than our heart, and knows all things.*
> — 1 John 3:20

REFLECTION

Feelings of unworthiness can cloud our view of God's grace. When our hearts condemn us, He reminds us that His love and knowledge are greater than our failures. Our confidence rests not in what we've done but in what Christ has accomplished for us. As we surrender self-doubt, we find the freedom to walk boldly in His forgiveness and live fully in His promises.

APPLICATION

† Identify areas where self-condemnation has hindered your confidence in God

† Declare His grace over your heart and mind today

† Step boldly into His promises, trusting His love over your feelings

CONNECTION

Thank You, Lord, for being greater than my heart. Silence my doubts and help me live boldly in Your forgiveness and love. In Jesus' name, Amen.

HIGHLIGHT QUOTE

When our hearts condemn us, God's love and truth are greater.

JOURNAL PROMPT

Where do you need to let God's truth silence self-condemnation today?

DAY 234
Broken for Breakthrough

> *He took the seven loaves and gave thanks, broke them and gave them to His disciples to set before them.*
> – Mark 8:6

REFLECTION

We can't find breakthroughs in outward fixes, only in inward transformation. As we break bread to share it, God allows our broken places to become vessels of blessing. In surrender, we find freedom; in weakness, His power flows. What feels like falling apart is often the moment He prepares to lift us and use us for His glory.

APPLICATION

† Bring your brokenness to Jesus, and thank Him for His presence in it
† Ask Him to transform pain into purpose for His glory
† Look for opportunities to bless others through what He's restored in you

CONNECTION

Thank You, Lord, for using my brokenness for breakthrough. Transform my pain into purpose, and let Your grace flow through me to others. In Jesus' name, Amen.

HIGHLIGHT QUOTE

God allows our broken places to become vessels of blessing.

JOURNAL PROMPT

How can you invite God to turn your brokenness into breakthrough today?

DAY 235
Trust and Obey

If you are willing and obedient, You shall eat the good of the land.
– Isaiah 1:19

REFLECTION

Trust and obedience walk hand in hand. God blesses not only our belief in Him but our willingness to act on that belief. When we obey His Word, even when difficult, we step into abundance. The Holy Spirit empowers what we surrender, and obedience opens doors that fear keeps closed. His way always leads to life and blessing.

APPLICATION

† Obey God promptly, even when you don't understand
† Trust His instructions as expressions of His love
† Expect His goodness to follow obedience

CONNECTION

Thank You, Lord, for guiding me with wisdom. Help me to trust and obey Your Word wholeheartedly. I know Your way leads to life and blessing. In Jesus' name, Amen.

HIGHLIGHT QUOTE

Obedience opens doors that fear keeps closed.

JOURNAL PROMPT

What step of obedience is God asking you to take right now?

DAY 236
Always On Call

> *Preach the word! Be ready in season and out of season. Convince, rebuke, exhort, with all longsuffering and teaching.*
> – 2 Timothy 4:2

REFLECTION

We are always on call for the Lord's work—ready to serve wherever we are. Readiness means staying sensitive to His Spirit, willing to obey even when it's inconvenient. God equips us for every assignment He places before us, drawing from what He has already deposited within. When He calls, He also provides the grace and strength to respond faithfully.

APPLICATION

- † Ask God to make you sensitive to His promptings throughout the day
- † Prepare your heart daily so you're ready for unexpected opportunities
- † Step into His assignments with confidence in His provision and grace

CONNECTION

Thank You, Lord, for calling me to be ready in every season. Keep me sensitive to Your Spirit and bold to respond when You lead. In Jesus' name, Amen.

HIGHLIGHT QUOTE

When God calls, His grace equips the willing heart.

JOURNAL PROMPT

How can you prepare your heart today to be ready for God's call?

DAY 237
Fear Not, for I Am with You

> *Fear not, for I am with you; Be not dismayed, for I am your God. I will strengthen you, Yes, I will help you, I will uphold you with My righteous right hand.*
> — Isaiah 41:10

REFLECTION

Fear arises from what we see or imagine, but God's nearness brings peace. As we face internal and external fears, His promise stands: He strengthens, helps, and upholds us. Trusting His presence frees us from fear's grip and anchors us in faith. When His love surrounds us, fear loses its power and we walk forward in quiet confidence.

APPLICATION

† Identify the fears you need to surrender to God today
† Declare His promises over areas where fear has taken hold
† Rest in the assurance of His presence and help

CONNECTION

Thank You, Lord, for upholding me with Your righteous hand. Replace my fear with faith and remind me that You are always near. In Jesus' name, Amen.

HIGHLIGHT QUOTE

God's presence drives out fear and upholds us with His righteous hand.

JOURNAL PROMPT

What fear do you need to surrender so you can rest in God's presence?

DAY 238
Watch Out for the Traps

> *Woe to the world because of offenses! For offenses must come, but woe to that man by whom the offense comes!*
> – Matthew 18:7

REFLECTION

Offense acts like a snare, luring us into bitterness and division. The enemy sets traps to derail our peace and unity, but Christ calls us higher—to walk in love. Refusing offense doesn't mean ignoring wrongs; it means addressing them with grace and humility. When we forgive and seek understanding, we escape the trap and keep our hearts free before God.

APPLICATION

† Ask God to reveal any hidden offenses lingering in your heart
† Choose forgiveness over bitterness when offense arises
† Seek clarity and communicate with grace to resolve conflicts

CONNECTION

Thank You, Lord, for giving me the power to overcome offense. Guard my heart from bitterness and teach me to respond with love and grace. In Jesus' name, Amen.

HIGHLIGHT QUOTE

Through humility and forgiveness, we escape the trap of offense.

JOURNAL PROMPT

What offense do you need to release to God so you can walk in freedom?

DAY 239
God Gives the Increase

> *I planted, Apollos watered, but God gave the increase. So then neither he who plants is anything, nor he who waters, but God who gives the increase.*
> – 1 Corinthians 3:6–7

REFLECTION

We are vessels in God's work—planting seeds, watering faithfully—but only He produces growth. Pride tempts us to take credit, yet all fruit belongs to Him. When we release results into His hands, peace replaces striving. Our part is faithfulness; His part is increase. True success is not what we build but what He blesses through our obedience.

APPLICATION

† Reflect on areas where you need to release results to God
† Give Him glory for any fruit produced through your service
† Pray for humility to remain a vessel pointing to Him alone

CONNECTION

Thank You, Lord, for giving the increase in every seed planted. Keep me humble and faithful, always pointing glory back to You. In Jesus' name, Amen.

HIGHLIGHT QUOTE

Our part is faithfulness—God gives the increase.

JOURNAL PROMPT

What results do you need to release to God and trust Him for the increase?

DAY 240
Recognizing the Lies

Then the serpent said to the woman, "You will not surely die ...
– Genesis 3:4

REFLECTION

Satan's deception often comes through subtle distortions, tempting us to doubt God's Word. The wide path he offers appears attractive but leads to destruction. God's commands, though narrow, bring life and freedom. Immersing ourselves in Scripture strengthens discernment, helping us to recognize lies and walk securely in truth. His Word keeps our hearts anchored in grace and guarded from deception.

APPLICATION

† Commit to daily Scripture reading to strengthen discernment
† Pray for humility to resist prideful temptations
† Replace lies with God's truth whenever doubts arise

CONNECTION

Thank You, Lord, for the truth of Your Word. Protect me from deception and guide me in the narrow path that leads to life. In Jesus' name, Amen.

HIGHLIGHT QUOTE

Immersing ourselves in Scripture equips us to recognize lies and walk in truth.

JOURNAL PROMPT

What lies do you need to replace with God's truth today?

DAY 241
Guarding Your Ears

> My son, give attention to my words; Incline your ear to my sayings. Do not let them depart from your eyes; Keep them in the midst of your heart.
> – Proverbs 4:20–21

REFLECTION

In a world filled with noise, countless voices compete for our attention and allegiance. Some distract; others distort God's truth. Scripture urges us to incline our ears to His words, guarding our hearts from deception. By giving priority to His voice and tuning out harmful influences, we strengthen faith and sharpen discernment. What we hear shapes who we become.

APPLICATION

† Evaluate the voices influencing your heart and mind today

† Replace negative or false inputs with God's Word and promises

† Commit to daily moments of quiet to hear His voice clearly

CONNECTION

Thank You, Lord, for speaking truth in a noisy world. Help me guard my ears and keep Your Word close to my heart. Strengthen my discernment and deepen my faith. In Jesus' name, Amen.

HIGHLIGHT QUOTE

What we hear shapes who we become.

JOURNAL PROMPT

What voices do you need to quiet so you can hear God's truth more clearly?

DAY 242
Greater Is He in You

> *You are of God, little children, and have overcome them, because He who is in you is greater than he who is in the world.*
> – 1 John 4:4

REFLECTION

Christ within us is greater than every opposition. Fear builds walls that isolate, but faith tears them down and opens us to God's peace. When we are clothed in His armor, the Holy Spirit empowers us to stand victoriously. Knowing He dwells in us changes how we face challenges—with boldness, not fear—for the Overcomer lives in us.

APPLICATION

† Declare today that Christ in you is greater than any opposition
† Tear down walls of fear and replace them with faith in Him
† Clothe yourself daily with the armor of God and walk in victory

CONNECTION

Thank You, Lord, that You in me is greater than anything against me. Help me live boldly in Your victory and peace. In Jesus' name, Amen.

HIGHLIGHT QUOTE

When we are clothed in His armor, the Holy Spirit empowers us to stand victoriously.

JOURNAL PROMPT

Where do you need to live boldly, remembering Christ is greater?

DAY 243
God Will Make a Way

> *Thus says the LORD, who makes a way in the sea And a path through the mighty waters.*
> – Isaiah 43:16

REFLECTION

God's ways often unfold beyond what we can predict. When life feels uncertain or the road unclear, His wisdom lights the path ahead. He provides direction in confusion and strength in delay. What seems impassable becomes possible when we walk with Him. The God who parted the sea still makes a way where none exists—faithful, steady, and unfailing.

APPLICATION

† Expect God to guide your steps, even when the way seems hidden
† Choose faith over fear by trusting His direction
† Rest in His presence and provision as you follow His lead

CONNECTION

Thank You, Lord, for leading me through uncertain places. Help me follow Your direction with peace and confidence. Where I see no path, show me You have already made the way. In Jesus' name, Amen.

HIGHLIGHT QUOTE

Where we see no path, God quietly prepares the way.

JOURNAL PROMPT

Where is God leading you to trust His direction more than your understanding?

DAY 244
Great and Awesome

Do not be afraid of them. Remember the Lord, great and awesome.
– Nehemiah 4:14

REFLECTION

Discouragement can come at us from all sides. Just like Nehemiah, we find ourselves surrounded by "rubbish," troubles, distractions, and minor annoyances that stack up. In those moments, our breakthrough starts with shifting our focus from the problem to God's promises. Magnifying the Lord minimizes our burdens and strengthens us.

APPLICATION

- † Pause and focus on God's character
- † Speak out loud: "The Lord is great and awesome!"
- † Take negative thoughts captive by meditating on God's Word

CONNECTION

Thank You, Lord, for helping me look beyond my troubles and remember Your greatness. Fill me with courage as I remember how awesome and mighty You are over every situation I face today. In Jesus' name, Amen.

HIGHLIGHT QUOTE

Magnifying the Lord minimizes our burdens and strengthens us.

JOURNAL PROMPT

In what situation do you need to shift your focus from problems to God's greatness?

A 365-Day Journey Walking with the Word & the Spirit

DAY 245
Unlocking the Impossible

> *His mother said to the servants, "Whatever He says to you, do it."*
> – John 2:5

REFLECTION

God's instructions often seem impossible or unreasonable. Like the servants at Cana, our obedience activates His supernatural power. Feelings of inadequacy and fear battle our faith, but He strengthens us in our weakness. Each act of obedience transforms our character and glorifies His name.

APPLICATION

† Respond quickly to God's promptings, even when unclear
† Trust His power more than your own ability
† Yield to His will daily, strengthening your walk of faith

CONNECTION

Thank You, Lord, for leading my steps. Empower me to obey Your voice without hesitation. I trust You to do the impossible through my surrender. In Jesus' name, Amen.

HIGHLIGHT QUOTE

Our obedience activates God's supernatural power.

JOURNAL PROMPT

What step of obedience has God asked you to take that seems "impossible"?

DAY 246
The Door of Fellowship

> *Behold, I stand at the door and knock. If anyone hears My voice and opens the door, I will come in to him and dine with him, and he with Me.*
> – Revelation 3:20

REFLECTION

Though omnipresent, Jesus never forces His way in. He waits for us to open the doors of our hearts. Through His Word and Spirit, He calls us to a deeper communion with Him. Like any relationship, intimacy grows as we invite Him into all areas of life. Fellowship with Christ transforms us as He becomes Lord of all.

APPLICATION

- † Invite Jesus into every area of your life
- † Respond to His Word with a heart of surrender
- † Seek fellowship with Him in prayer and worship

CONNECTION

Thank You, Lord, for Your amazing, unconditional love. I open the door of my heart to You. Dwell with me and lead me into deeper fellowship. In Jesus' name, Amen.

HIGHLIGHT QUOTE

Fellowship with Christ transforms us as He becomes Lord of all.

JOURNAL PROMPT

How can you open the door wider to Jesus in your daily routine this week?

DAY 247
The Light of Life

> Then Jesus spoke to them again, saying, "I am the light of the world. He who follows Me shall not walk in darkness, but have the light of life."
> – John 8:12

REFLECTION

When we follow Christ, His Spirit illuminates our path with wisdom and grace. The Light of Life doesn't simply reveal where to go; it transforms how we walk. His presence brings calm assurance in confusion and gentle correction when we drift. The Holy Spirit's promptings, those quiet nudges to pray, call, or pause, guide and protect us daily.

APPLICATION

† Ask the Holy Spirit to reveal His direction in every decision
† Respond quickly to His gentle promptings
† Let God's Word be the lamp that steadies your path

CONNECTION

Thank You, Lord, for being the Light of Life. Open my heart to hear Your Spirit's whisper and follow Your lead. Fill me with peace as I walk in Your truth. In Jesus' name, Amen.

HIGHLIGHT QUOTE

The Light of Life doesn't simply reveal where to go; it transforms how we walk.

JOURNAL PROMPT

Where is the Holy Spirit inviting you to walk more attentively with His light today?

DAY 248
As We Go

And so it was that as they went, they were cleansed.
– Luke 17:14

REFLECTION

The lepers were healed as they went, not before. Our obedience cannot be conditional on immediate results. The Lord manifests His healing and transformation in different ways, unfolding as we walk by faith. Often only in hindsight do we see how much He has touched us, from glory to glory.

APPLICATION

† Obey God's Word, even before seeing results
† Trust His timing in your healing and transformation
† Walk by faith, not by sight, daily

CONNECTION

Thank You, Lord. You are my Healer and Helper—always. Help me obey, even when I don't see immediate changes. Thank You for transforming me as I walk with You. In Jesus' name, Amen.

HIGHLIGHT QUOTE

God's transforming power often unfolds "as we go," not before.

JOURNAL PROMPT

Where do you need to obey first and trust God to reveal the results later?

DAY 249
What Shall We Do?

> Then they said to Him, "What shall we do, that we may work the works of God?" Jesus answered and said to them, "This is the work of God, that you believe in Him whom He sent."
> – John 6:28–29

REFLECTION

Like the disciples, we wonder if what we do is enough. Jesus reminds us that faith, not performance, pleases God. Our role is to believe in Him, trusting He will lead us into His works. Every act of love and prayer done in His name has an impact. We should do everything through our faith in Him and for Him.

APPLICATION

† Choose faith over striving to earn God's approval
† Believe that nothing done in His name is too small
† Rest as His vessel, ready for His work through you

CONNECTION

Thank You, Lord, for increasing my faith. Help me believe and rest in You. Lead me to works that glorify You, not myself. In Jesus' name, Amen.

HIGHLIGHT QUOTE

We should do everything through our faith in Him and for Him.

JOURNAL PROMPT

Where have you been striving instead of simply believing?

A 365-Day Journey Walking with the Word & the Spirit

DAY 250
Turning Aside to See God

> *Then Moses said, "I will now turn aside and see this great sight, why the bush does not burn."*
> – Exodus 3:3

REFLECTION

Moses encountered God at the burning bush when he stopped to observe. Likewise, God invites us to turn aside from distractions and notice His presence in daily life. As we pause, He speaks more clearly, drawing us deeper into fellowship. Our intentional seeking opens the door to revelation and closeness with Him.

APPLICATION

† Make space today to pause and seek God's presence
† Acknowledge His hand in the surrounding details
† Listen for His voice in quiet moments of stillness

CONNECTION

Thank You, Lord, for meeting me when I turn aside to seek You. Draw me closer and help me notice Your presence in my daily life. In Jesus' name, Amen.

HIGHLIGHT QUOTE

Turning aside from distractions opens the door to God's revelation.

JOURNAL PROMPT

What distractions do you need to turn aside from and notice God today?

DAY 251
Steps Ordered by the Lord

> *The steps of a good man are ordered by the LORD, And He delights in his way.*
> – Psalm 37:23

REFLECTION

Life pressures and distractions often tempt us to compare or shift lanes. Yet God calls us to stay focused on the unique path He's prepared. By keeping our eyes on Him, we resist frustration and trust His timing. Our lane may look different, but it's divinely ordered, and He delights in every step we take in faith.

APPLICATION

† Ask God for focus to stay in the lane He's assigned to you
† Resist comparing your journey to someone else's path
† Praise Him for guiding your steps toward His perfect plan

CONNECTION

Thank You, Lord, for ordering my steps and delighting in my way. Help me to stay focused on You and not let comparison distract me. In Jesus' name, Amen.

HIGHLIGHT QUOTE

By keeping our eyes on Him, we resist frustration and trust His timing.

JOURNAL PROMPT

Where are you tempted to compare instead of trusting God's ordered steps?

DAY 252
Walking in Divine Favor

> *For you bless the righteous, O LORD; you cover him with favor as with a shield.*
> *– Psalm 5:12*

REFLECTION

Divine favor isn't the absence of hardship; it's God's presence in every season. His favor doesn't always prevent difficulty, but it ensures purpose in it. Even in waiting, betrayal, or injustice, His unseen hand is working all things together. We can face life's valleys with confidence, knowing His favor surrounds us and His purpose will prevail.

APPLICATION

† Look for God's favor, even in uncomfortable or hidden seasons
† Trust that every setback is positioning you for purpose
† Let gratitude replace complaint as you watch His plan unfold

CONNECTION

Thank You, Lord, for surrounding me with Your favor like a shield. Teach me to recognize Your hand in every season and trust that You are working all things for my good. In Jesus' name, Amen.

HIGHLIGHT QUOTE

God's favor may not remove the challenge, but it always ensures purpose in it.

JOURNAL PROMPT

Where have you seen God's favor at work, even in hard seasons?

DAY 253
Established by Grace

It is good that the heart be established by grace.
– Hebrews 13:9

REFLECTION

Grace steadies what effort cannot. It anchors our hearts in truth when emotions shift and circumstances change. When we build on grace instead of performance, guilt loses its voice, and striving surrenders to peace. God's grace is not fragile; it's foundational. To be established in it is to live securely in the favor Christ has already finished and freely gives.

APPLICATION

† Stop striving, and rest in God's finished work
† Let grace, not guilt, shape your thoughts and actions
† Extend the same grace you've received to others

CONNECTION

Thank You, Lord, for the grace that grounds me in Your love. Establish my heart in confidence, not condemnation. Teach me to live from the security of Your favor every day. In Jesus' name, Amen.

HIGHLIGHT QUOTE

Grace is the firm ground beneath a restless heart.

JOURNAL PROMPT

Where do you need to stop striving so you can stand secure in God's grace today?

DAY 254
Prepared for the Test

> Now it came to pass after these things that God tested Abraham, and said to him, "Abraham!" And he said, "Here I am." Then He said, "Take now your son ... and offer him there as a burnt offering ... – Genesis 22:1–2

REFLECTION

God prepared Abraham's faith through years of trials before the ultimate test with Isaac. God uses our experiences to equip us for obedience today. His tests are not to produce faith, but to reveal it. Our preparation is hidden in our transitions. Every directive comes with His ability and presence to carry it out.

APPLICATION

- † Remember how God has prepared you for today's challenges
- † Trust His presence and ability in every test
- † Focus on your relationship with Him above all else

CONNECTION

Thank You, Lord, for preparing me for every test. Help me to trust Your faithfulness and obey with confidence. In Jesus' name, Amen.

HIGHLIGHT QUOTE

God's tests don't create faith; they reveal it.

JOURNAL PROMPT

What test are you facing that's revealing the strength of your faith in God's promises?

DAY 255
Test the Spirits

> *Beloved, do not believe every spirit, but test the spirits, whether they are of God; because many false prophets have gone out into the world.*
> – 1 John 4:1

REFLECTION

Because the Holy Spirit dwells in us, He helps us test both outside voices and inner thoughts. We ask, "Is this from You, Lord?" and wait for His peace, wisdom, and joy to confirm. Some thoughts appear good but are not God's best, so discernment is vital. Daily submission to Him enables us to capture every thought and walk in truth.

APPLICATION

- † Pray for discernment to test every spirit you encounter
- † Take every thought captive and bring it under Christ's authority
- † Submit daily to the Spirit's leading for wisdom and clarity

CONNECTION

Thank You, Lord. Help me discern truth from deception. Guide me by Your Spirit and guard my heart and mind in Christ Jesus. In Jesus' name, Amen.

HIGHLIGHT QUOTE

Discernment grows as we daily submit our thoughts and choices to the Holy Spirit.

JOURNAL PROMPT

Where do you need to pause and test what you are hearing or thinking before acting?

DAY 256
Enter the Ark

> Then the LORD said to Noah, "Come into the ark, you and all your household, because I have seen that you are righteous before Me in this generation ..."
> – Genesis 7:1

REFLECTION

Like Noah, we are called to obey God, even when His instructions seem unusual. The ark is a picture of Jesus, our refuge and rest. In Him, we stand strong against the enemy's attacks and remain secure in His love. God calls us to invite others to this refuge, where we find salvation in Christ alone.

APPLICATION

- † Rest in Jesus as your ark of safety
- † Stand firm in His righteousness amid the world's darkness
- † Invite others to find refuge in Christ

CONNECTION

Thank You, Lord, for being my ark of rest and salvation. I release all fear into Your caring hands. Keep me strong in You and help me point others to Your refuge. In Jesus' name, Amen.

HIGHLIGHT QUOTE

Jesus is our ark of refuge and rest, securing us in His love through every storm.

JOURNAL PROMPT

How can you rest more fully in Christ's protection and invite others into His refuge?

DAY 257
Launch Into the Deep

> *When He had stopped speaking, He said to Simon, "Launch out into the deep and let down your nets for a catch."*
> – Luke 5:4

REFLECTION

After fruitless labor, Peter obeyed Jesus' word and witnessed abundance. Our defeats can turn into victories when we let Him direct our steps. Even when instructions seem illogical, His Word brings breakthroughs. God prepares us through setbacks for blessings beyond expectation.

APPLICATION

† Trust God's Word, even when circumstances seem hopeless
† Obey Him promptly, despite past disappointments
† Expect His provision after seasons of frustration

CONNECTION

Thank You, Lord, I will launch into the deep at Your Word. Turn my defeat into victory by Your power. Help me hear, trust, and obey You. In Jesus' name, Amen.

HIGHLIGHT QUOTE

When we obey God's Word, even in the deep, He turns defeat into abundance.

JOURNAL PROMPT

What area of your life is God calling you to launch deeper into faith?

DAY 258
Living from His Strength

> *Come to Me, all you who labor and are heavy laden, and I will give you rest.*
> – Matthew 11:28

REFLECTION

Jesus never intended for us to live weary or self-reliant. His rest is not an escape from life but the power to live it through Him. When we depend on His strength instead of our own, peace steadies our hearts, even in motion. What once felt heavy becomes light in His hands. His rest flows through trust, reminding us that His grace is always enough.

APPLICATION

† Begin and end your day by leaning on His strength, not your own

† Invite His peace into your work, relationships, and decisions

† Let His presence renew your energy and focus throughout the day

CONNECTION

Thank You, Lord, that I can live from Your strength and not my own. Fill me with Your peace and steady my heart with Your grace. Teach me to walk in Your rhythm of rest and renewal. In Jesus' name, Amen.

HIGHLIGHT QUOTE

True rest is living every moment through His strength.

JOURNAL PROMPT

Where in your daily life do you need to lean more on God's strength than your own?

DAY 259
What Are We Building?

> *For we are God's fellow workers; you are God's field, you are God's building.*
> — 1 Corinthians 3:9

REFLECTION

We belong to God—not only His fellow workers but His building and His field. Our priority is to build His house with Christ as the cornerstone. Rather than leaning on our own strength, we rely on His wisdom and provision. Consecrated to Him, we become His glorious sanctuary.

APPLICATION

- † Surrender your entire self to His purpose
- † Build daily on Christ, your sure foundation
- † Rely on His provision above your own means

CONNECTION

Thank You, Lord, for Your wisdom, strength, and provision. Help me live as Your fellow worker, part of Your building and field, for Your glory. In Jesus' name, Amen.

HIGHLIGHT QUOTE

Consecrated to Him, we become His glorious sanctuary.

JOURNAL PROMPT

How can you build your life more intentionally on Christ, your foundation?

DAY 260
God's Thoughts for You

> *For I know the thoughts that I think toward you, says the LORD, thoughts of peace and not of evil, to give you a future and a hope.*
> – Jeremiah 29:11

REFLECTION

God's thoughts toward us are always good, even when we don't understand His ways. Like a parent weaning a child from milk to solid food, He leads us into growth that we may not understand at first. He removes the familiar to prepare us for greater things. We trust His wisdom and step forward with hope, from glory to glory.

APPLICATION

† Trust God's plans, even when they are unclear
† Yield willingly to His direction
† Step into the future with faith and hope

CONNECTION

Thank You, Lord, for Your good thoughts toward me. Help me to trust Your will, wisdom, and ways. Empower me to remain steadfast in faith, love, and hope. In Jesus' name, Amen.

HIGHLIGHT QUOTE

When God removes the familiar, He's preparing us for something greater.

JOURNAL PROMPT

What area of your life requires you to trust God's unseen plan right now?

DAY 261
Do We Know He Hears Us?

> Now this is the confidence that we have in Him, that if we ask anything according to His will, He hears us.
> – 1 John 5:14

REFLECTION

Prayer is powerful because it rests on God's attentive ear and loving heart. He hears more than words; He discerns the cries of our spirit. Confidence grows when we pray according to His will, knowing His answer is already at work. Even when outcomes look different from what we expect, His response is always best.

APPLICATION

† Pray with confidence, knowing God hears every word
† Seek His will in prayer instead of leaning on your desires
† Rest in the assurance that He is already working on your behalf

CONNECTION

Thank You, Lord, for the privilege to come boldly to Your throne of grace. Help me pray according to Your will and stand by faith when the answer doesn't meet my expectations. Strengthen my confidence in Your promises. In Jesus' name, Amen.

HIGHLIGHT QUOTE

He hears more than words; He discerns the cries of our spirit.

JOURNAL PROMPT

How can you align your prayers more with God's will this week?

DAY 262
Do We Glorify Jesus?

> *I will praise You, O Lord my God, with all my heart, And I will glorify Your name forevermore.*
> – Psalm 86:12

REFLECTION

One way to discern truth is by asking, "Does this glorify Jesus?" Anything that lifts the flesh or ego is not of God. The Holy Spirit always points to Christ, leaving us encouraged and edified. His work deepens faith and strengthens love. Our focus remains on His greatness, not our own. We live to glorify Him alone.

APPLICATION

† Discern if your words and actions glorify Christ
† Reject anything that elevates self over Jesus
† Seek to magnify His name in every situation

CONNECTION

Thank You, Lord. Help me discern what glorifies You. May my life always point others to Christ, never to myself. Glory to Your holy name, always and forever. In Jesus' name, Amen.

HIGHLIGHT QUOTE

The Spirit's work always points us to Jesus, never to ourselves.

JOURNAL PROMPT

What attitude or action in your life needs to shift so you can glorify Jesus more fully?

DAY 263
From Glory to Glory

> But we all, with unveiled face, beholding as in a mirror the glory of the Lord, are being transformed ... from glory to glory.
> – 2 Corinthians 3:18

REFLECTION

Transformation is a process, not a moment. As we behold Jesus, the Holy Spirit transforms us into His image. We reflect His glory in increasing measure. Growth may be slow, but it's steady. We don't notice it much because our self-centeredness diminishes as our Christ-centeredness increases. We reflect the One we behold, from glory to glory.

APPLICATION

- † Be patient with your spiritual growth
- † Keep your focus on Jesus, not your flaws
- † Celebrate progress, no matter how small

CONNECTION

Thank You, Lord, for transforming me by Your Spirit. Help me to trust the process and rejoice in every step of progress. In Jesus' name, Amen.

HIGHLIGHT QUOTE

Transformation takes time, but every step shines brighter with His glory.

JOURNAL PROMPT

What area of your life is God transforming little by little right now?

DAY 264
God Will Provide

> *And my God shall supply all your need according to His riches in glory by Christ Jesus.*
> *– Philippians 4:19*

REFLECTION

God meets our needs according to His riches, not ours. Worry shifts our gaze from the Giver to the need. His ways are higher; His supply is endless. He multiplies and provides supernaturally. We rest in His loving care and trust His abundant provision with childlike faith.

APPLICATION

† Look to God as your source today
† Trade worry for praise and thanksgiving
† Trust His provision beyond your reasoning

CONNECTION

Thank You, Lord, for being my Provider. Quiet my anxious thoughts and help me rest in Your abundant care. In Jesus' name, Amen.

HIGHLIGHT QUOTE

God's supply flows from His riches, not our resources.

JOURNAL PROMPT

What worry do you need to trade for faith in God's provision?

DAY 265
Give Me This Mountain

> *Now therefore, give me this mountain of which the LORD spoke in that day ... It may be that the LORD will be with me, and I shall be able to drive them out as the Lord said.*
> – Joshua 14:12

REFLECTION

At eighty-five, Caleb wasn't looking for comfort—he was claiming the mountain God had promised him years before. God's keeping power makes us more than conquerors, no matter our age or opposition. The Lord doesn't allow the mountains in our lives to defeat us, but uses them to display His strength through us. Each mountain becomes a stage for His glory and a testimony that faith still conquers giants.

APPLICATION

- † Face your mountains with courage rooted in God's promises
- † View challenges as opportunities for His faithfulness to shine
- † Declare victory before you see it, trusting His strength within you

CONNECTION

Thank You, Lord. Give me faith like Caleb to see challenges as opportunities for Your power. Strengthen my heart to conquer what seems impossible and to trust You for every victory. In Jesus' name, Amen.

HIGHLIGHT QUOTE

Mountains become a stage for God's glory when we face them with faith.

JOURNAL PROMPT

What mountain is God calling you to face in faith today?

DAY 266
The Lord Is My Light

> *The LORD is my light and my salvation; Whom shall I fear?*
> *– Psalm 27:1*

REFLECTION

God's light dispels fear and exposes truth. His presence brings clarity where confusion once ruled. Darkness cannot stay where He shines. When we walk in His light, courage rises, peace settles, and joy returns. His light not only guides our paths but also transforms our hearts, revealing the beauty of trust and the strength of His salvation.

APPLICATION

- † Invite God's light to lead your steps today
- † Replace fear with faith through prayer and worship
- † Shine His love into someone else's darkness

CONNECTION

Thank You, Lord, for being my light and salvation. Chase away every shadow of fear and fill me with Your radiant peace. Help me walk boldly in Your truth. In Jesus' name, Amen.

HIGHLIGHT QUOTE

God's light not only guides us, but it also changes everything it touches.

JOURNAL PROMPT

Where do you need to let God's light bring you courage and clarity today?

DAY 267
The Seed and the Harvest

Now may He who supplies seed to the sower, and bread for food, supply and multiply the seed you have sown and increase the fruits of your righteousness.
– 2 Corinthians 9:10

REFLECTION

As we desire to sow, God provides seed for planting. We release it in faith, trusting Him to bring increase. Though the enemy resists, God's incorruptible Word bears fruit. He supplies and multiplies what we plant or water from our hearts, regardless of its size. We are both sowers and seeds, planted by Him to display His righteousness, nourished by faith.

APPLICATION

† Sow generously in faith, trusting God's provision
† See yourself as a seed planted for His purpose
† Expect His increase in every area of your life

CONNECTION

Thank You, Lord, for giving me seed to sow. Multiply it for Your glory and let my life bear fruit for You. In Jesus' name, Amen.

HIGHLIGHT QUOTE

God supplies and multiplies what we plant or water from our hearts, regardless of its size.

JOURNAL PROMPT

What seed of faith or obedience is God asking you to plant today?

DAY 268
The Constant in Our Lives

> *Jesus Christ is the same yesterday, today, and forever.*
> – Hebrews 13:8

REFLECTION

Life's changes and challenges often shake us, but Jesus remains unchanging. Consistency in Him gives us perseverance to keep moving forward. Even in failure, His hand sustains us. He is our constant source of grace, strength, and hope. In moments of despair, His unwavering presence reminds us of His love that transcends understanding.

APPLICATION

- † Anchor your faith in Christ's unchanging nature
- † Persevere in good works, despite resistance
- † Rely on His grace when you stumble

CONNECTION

Thank You, Lord, for being the constant in my life. You never change. Forgive my inconsistency. Anchor me in Your constancy and sustain me in every season. In Jesus' name, Amen.

HIGHLIGHT QUOTE

When everything changes, Jesus remains the same: our anchor through every season.

JOURNAL PROMPT

Where do you need to rely more deeply on Christ's unchanging nature right now?

DAY 269
Following God Fully

> But My servant Caleb, because he has a different spirit in him and has followed Me fully, I will bring into the land where he went, and his descendants shall inherit it.
> – Numbers 14:24

REFLECTION

To follow God fully, wholeheartedly, is to say "yes" before knowing where He'll lead. It's choosing obedience when it's inconvenient and trust when His timing feels slow. This devotion isn't about perfection; it's about direction. Wholehearted hearts are steadfast, even when others shrink back. Partial obedience hesitates, but surrendered faith steps forward.

APPLICATION

† Examine your heart for areas of partial obedience
† Commit to following God completely, not selectively
† Rely on His strength to do what His Word requires

CONNECTION

Thank You, Lord. I choose to follow You with my whole heart. Help me to trust Your ways when I don't understand and to obey You in every season. Empower me by Your Spirit to walk fully in Your will. In Jesus' name, Amen.

HIGHLIGHT QUOTE

Wholehearted obedience says yes to God before knowing how.

JOURNAL PROMPT

What area of your life needs a wholehearted "yes" to God today?

DAY 270
Strength to Keep Going

> *And the LORD, He is the One who goes before you. He will be with you, He will not leave you nor forsake you; do not fear nor be dismayed.*
> – Deuteronomy 31:8

REFLECTION

Obedience can feel heavy when progress is slow, but the Holy Spirit renews those who lean on Him. Weariness whispers "quit"; grace whispers "continue." Each prayer, word of kindness, and act of faith builds what we cannot yet see. God rewards our perseverance in obeying Him. God is growing something eternal, even when the field looks bare.

APPLICATION

† Recommit tired areas of your life to God
† Stand on His promises when motivation fades
† Ask the Spirit to breathe fresh strength into your obedience

CONNECTION

Thank You, Lord, for renewing my strength when I am weary. Fill me with Your joy to keep sowing faithfully and to trust You for the harvest You've prepared. In Jesus' name, Amen.

HIGHLIGHT QUOTE

Perseverance plants seeds that time cannot erase.

JOURNAL PROMPT

What area of your life needs fresh strength to continue doing good?

DAY 271
God's Open Doors

> *He who has the key of David, He who opens and no one shuts, and shuts and no one opens.*
> *– Revelation 3:7*

REFLECTION

God opens doors that no one can shut and closes doors that no one can open. We trust not in opportunities themselves but in the One who holds the keys. Pursuing His presence over success positions us for His best. Even when the way forward is unclear, His purpose is always good and His timing is always right.

APPLICATION

† Walk through open doors with peace and confidence
† Wait with faith when unexpected doors close
† Trust His timing when clarity seems delayed

CONNECTION

Thank You, Lord, for holding every key in Your hands. Teach me to recognize Your openings and release every closed door to You. In Jesus' name, Amen.

HIGHLIGHT QUOTE

Peace comes from trusting the God who holds every key, not the doors themselves.

JOURNAL PROMPT

What open door is God inviting you to walk through, or release, today?

ns walking with the Word & the Spirit

DAY 272
Faith in Transition

I will instruct you and teach you in the way you should go; I will guide you with My eye.
— Psalm 32:8

REFLECTION

Transitions stretch us as God prepares us for what lies ahead. He often reveals the lesson only after we have walked through it. Restlessness can be His invitation to move with Him. Faith anchors us to trust His timing and embrace the unfamiliar, knowing He leads us into promise. Transition is preparation for position.

APPLICATION

† Trust God's unseen plan during seasons of change
† Reflect on the lessons He reveals after each trial
† Embrace holy restlessness as His preparation for what's next

CONNECTION

Thank You, Lord, for using transitions to prepare my heart. Help me release what is in the past and receive what You are bringing next. In Jesus' name, Amen.

HIGHLIGHT QUOTE

Transitions are not endings; they are invitations to trust God's next step.

JOURNAL PROMPT

What change are you resisting that may actually be God preparing you for growth?

DAY 273
Living and Powerful

> *For the word of God is living and powerful, and sharper than any two-edged sword.*
> – Hebrews 4:12

REFLECTION

The Word of God is not static; it is living and powerful. Jesus Himself is the Word made flesh, the Creator, and Redeemer who knows the depths of our hearts. His Word discerns thoughts and intentions, cutting through what is false to reveal what is true. As we read, hear, and obey it, the living Word shapes us from within, producing lasting transformation.

APPLICATION

- † Spend time in Scripture today, asking God to speak to your heart
- † Identify one truth from His Word to apply immediately to your life
- † Thank Him for the power of His living Word at work within you

CONNECTION

Thank You, Lord, for Your living and powerful Word. Let it penetrate my heart, renew my mind, and transform my life. Teach me to hear and obey Your truth each day. In Jesus' name, Amen.

HIGHLIGHT QUOTE

The Word of God is living and powerful, shaping us from within.

JOURNAL PROMPT

What truth from God's Word can you apply immediately today?

DAY 274
Guided by His Light

I am the light of the world. He who follows Me shall not walk in darkness, but have the light of life.
– John 8:12

REFLECTION

Jesus, the light of the world, guides us one faithful step at a time. Like a lighthouse cutting through fog, His presence brings direction and calm when the way ahead feels uncertain. As we follow His truth, confusion yields to clarity and fear gives way to faith. His light never flickers; it keeps us safe, centered, and walking toward life.

APPLICATION

† Ask Jesus to illuminate every choice before you
† Trade confusion for confidence by following His Word
† Walk forward, knowing His presence is your sure direction

CONNECTION

Thank You, Lord, for being my guiding light. Lead me through unclear paths with peace and purpose. Teach me to follow Your voice above every other. In Jesus' name, Amen.

HIGHLIGHT QUOTE

His light doesn't just show the way; it becomes the way.

JOURNAL PROMPT

Where do you need Jesus to bring clarity and direction today?

DAY 275
Word of Our Testimony

And they overcame him by the blood of the Lamb and by the word of their testimony.
– Revelation 12:11

REFLECTION

Our testimonies make the gospel visible and release hope to weary hearts. We may lack eloquence, but we know what Jesus has done. Sharing His work shifts the focus from our weakness to His strength. Each testimony becomes a declaration of victory—look what the Lord has done!

APPLICATION

- † Write one recent thing God has done
- † Share your story with someone today
- † Give Jesus the glory for every victory

CONNECTION

Thank You, Lord, for victories great and small. Give me boldness to share what You've done so others may find hope in You. In Jesus' name, Amen.

HIGHLIGHT QUOTE

Our stories of God's faithfulness become evidence of His power.

JOURNAL PROMPT

What recent victory can you testify about to encourage someone else?

DAY 276
From Adam to God's Family

> Christ has redeemed us from the curse of the law, having become a curse for us (for it is written, "Cursed is everyone who hangs on a tree"), that the blessing of Abraham might come upon the Gentiles in Christ Jesus.
> – Galatians 3:13–14

REFLECTION

Every person begins life in Adam's family, born with the same fallen nature of rebellion and separation from God. But through Christ, God adopts us into His family. The moment we believe, our spiritual DNA changes. We move from guilt to grace, from curse to blessing, from death to life. In God's family, our identity is secure, and we are safe.

APPLICATION

† Rejoice in your position in Christ
† Release the shame of your earthly past and embrace your new identity
† Live daily from the confidence of your divine inheritance

CONNECTION

Thank You, Lord, for redeeming me from the curse and adopting me as Your child. Let my life reflect the blessing of belonging to You and the joy of my new identity in Christ. In Jesus' name, Amen.

HIGHLIGHT QUOTE

We move from guilt to grace, from curse to blessing, from death to life.

JOURNAL PROMPT

How can you live more fully from your new identity in God's family?

DAY 277
Daily Bread

Give us this day our daily bread.
– Matthew 6:11

REFLECTION

As food sustains the body, God's Word sustains the soul. We hunger for fresh manna daily, whether we realize it. Feeding on His Word strengthens us, renews us, and keeps us anchored. The more we taste His truth, the more our hearts crave His presence, from glory to glory.

APPLICATION

- † Seek Scripture as daily nourishment
- † Honor your body as His temple with wise habits
- † Ask for fresh bread from Heaven today

CONNECTION

Thank You, Lord, for Your Word that feeds my spirit. Forgive me for neglecting my spiritual nourishment. Deepen my hunger for You and make Your truth my daily bread. In Jesus' name, Amen.

HIGHLIGHT QUOTE

Our spirits need daily bread as surely as our bodies need food.

JOURNAL PROMPT

What helps you stay spiritually nourished day by day?

DAY 278
Treasure Hunt

> *But we have this treasure in earthen vessels, that the excellence of the power may be of God and not of us.*
> *– 2 Corinthians 4:7*

REFLECTION

Our natural frame may seem ordinary, yet God has placed treasure within. Life in Christ becomes a treasure hunt as He reveals the riches of His Spirit. We look beyond weakness to see His strength at work. Through His Word, we uncover treasures of truth. The excellence of His power shines through fragile vessels, from glory to glory.

APPLICATION

† See yourself as a vessel of God's treasure
† Dig deeper into Scripture for hidden wisdom
† Focus on Christ within, not limitations without

CONNECTION

Thank You, Lord, for placing Your treasure within me. Help me live from Your power rather than my own. Let Your light shine through my life. In Jesus' name, Amen.

HIGHLIGHT QUOTE

Fragile vessels reveal the brilliance of God's treasure within.

JOURNAL PROMPT

How can you let the treasure of Christ within shine more freely through you?

DAY 279
Lift Your Eyes

> *Lift your eyes now and look from the place where you are—northward, southward, eastward, and westward.*
> – Genesis 13:14

REFLECTION

It was only after Abraham separated from Lot that God revealed His promise. Likewise, a new vision often follows release. God calls us to let go of attachments, regrets, and what-ifs so He can show us greater things. When we lift our eyes from the past, we see His promises unfolding before us.

APPLICATION

† Release the "if onlys" that weigh you down
† Invite God to bring closure to past wounds
† Trust Him with separations you don't understand

CONNECTION

Thank You, Lord, for shining light on my path. Help me to let go of the past and embrace the new opportunities You have prepared. In Jesus' name, Amen.

HIGHLIGHT QUOTE

God reveals a new vision when we release what no longer belongs to our journey.

JOURNAL PROMPT

What past attachment might God be asking you to release so you can see His new promise?

DAY 280
Unstoppable Growth

> *But the more they afflicted them, the more they multiplied and grew.*
> – Exodus 1:12

REFLECTION

When Pharaoh afflicted Israel, the Israelites multiplied and grew. Likewise, trials cannot stop divine fruitfulness. Pressure refines faith and produces endurance. The enemy may try to weary us, but the Spirit renews our strength. Under pressure, we grow taller, are rooted deeper, and rise stronger.

APPLICATION

- † Recognize that affliction can fuel growth
- † Ask the Holy Spirit to restore your strength
- † Stand firm when warfare feels relentless

CONNECTION

Thank You, Lord, for turning afflictions into growth. Strengthen me to keep pressing forward and multiply despite opposition. In Jesus' name, Amen.

HIGHLIGHT QUOTE

The more we're pressed, the deeper our roots grow in God.

JOURNAL PROMPT

How has God used pressure in your life to strengthen your faith?

DAY 281
Divine Opportunities

> *Therefore, as we have opportunity, let us do good to all, especially to those who are of the household of faith.*
> – Galatians 6:10

REFLECTION

Opportunities often appear in ordinary moments—a call, a meeting, a request. When we respond in faith, God turns small moments into significant ones. His timing leaves no room for hesitation or fear. Every open door is a chance to step into His extraordinary plan.

APPLICATION

- † Look for God in ordinary moments
- † Respond in faith to unexpected opportunities
- † Reject fear when opportunities seem too big

CONNECTION

Thank You, Lord, for every divine opportunity. Help me recognize them and respond in faith to Your leading. Forgive me for the chances I've missed and open my eyes to new ones. In Jesus' name, Amen.

HIGHLIGHT QUOTE

Ordinary moments often hold extraordinary opportunities from God.

JOURNAL PROMPT

What simple opportunity today might God be inviting you to see as divine?

DAY 282
A Secured Path

You enlarged my path under me, So my feet did not slip.
– Psalm 18:36

REFLECTION

When life feels unstable, God enlarges our path and keeps us from falling. His grace sustains us when we almost slip, almost give up, or almost break down. Christ is our sure foundation, upholding us with His right hand. He delivers us from every affliction, securing us in His strength.

APPLICATION

† Pray for God to steady your steps today
† Remember the times He has kept you from falling
† Stand on Christ, your sure foundation

CONNECTION

Thank You, Lord, for being my foundation. Uphold me with Your hand and keep me secure when I feel unsteady. Help me to trust Your sustaining power. In Jesus' name, Amen.

HIGHLIGHT QUOTE

When life feels uncertain, Christ is the firm ground beneath our feet.

JOURNAL PROMPT

Where do you need to let God steady your steps and enlarge your path?

DAY 283
Draw Near to God

> *For the law made nothing perfect; on the other hand, there is the bringing in of a better hope, through which we draw near to God.*
> – Hebrews 7:19

REFLECTION

The enemy whispers that we don't need prayer, worship, or the Word—but those are the very things that keep us alive. In hardship, our greatest need is deeper communion with God. His presence fills us with peace, love, and hope, enabling us to resist temptation and stand firm. We draw near and find Him near.

APPLICATION

- † Reject the lie that you don't need God today
- † Spend intentional time in His presence
- † Replace emotional relief with spiritual renewal

CONNECTION

Thank You, Lord, for drawing me near. Increase my hunger for You, and deepen my intimacy in Your presence. In Jesus' name, Amen.

HIGHLIGHT QUOTE

The closer we draw to God, the stronger we become against life's pressures.

JOURNAL PROMPT

What habit or distraction keeps you from drawing near to God daily?

DAY 284
Powerful Restoration

So he cut off a stick, and threw it in there; and he made the iron float.
– 2 Kings 6:6

REFLECTION

When the iron axe head sank, God made it float again. In the same way, He restores our passion, fire, and purpose when they seem gone. Even when we cannot trace the cause of loss, the Holy Spirit works to bring renewal. He lifts what feels unreachable back to the surface by His power.

APPLICATION

† Ask God to reveal areas of lost passion
† Invite Him to rekindle your spiritual fire
† Trust Him to restore what feels unreachable

CONNECTION

Thank You, Lord, for restoring what I lost. Renew my strength and vision. Rekindle my fire and lift me to a greater place in You. In Jesus' name, Amen.

HIGHLIGHT QUOTE

What sinks beyond our reach, God's power can still raise.

JOURNAL PROMPT

What passion or purpose do you need God to restore in this season?

DAY 285
Above and Beyond

> *Now to Him who is able to do exceedingly abundantly above all that we ask or think.*
> – Ephesians 3:20

REFLECTION

God's ability far exceeds our imagination. When we face impossibilities, He sees opportunities. Faith invites us to believe beyond what we understand. His blessings exceed our expectations and fill us with awe. Our limitations don't limit Him. We trust His ability beyond our understanding, resting in the abundance of His love and grace.

APPLICATION

† Thank God for exceeding your expectations
† Trust His power when you feel at your limit
† Stand in awe of His abundant blessings

CONNECTION

Thank You, Lord, for working above and beyond in my life. Help me to trust You with my unknowns and live in Your care. I yield to Your love and strength. In Jesus' name, Amen.

HIGHLIGHT QUOTE

Our limits never limit the limitless God who works above and beyond.

JOURNAL PROMPT

Where has God recently done more than you could have asked for or imagined?

DAY 286
Love Poured Out

> *Now hope does not disappoint, because the love of God has been poured out in our hearts by the Holy Spirit who was given to us.*
> – Romans 5:5

REFLECTION

The Holy Spirit pours God's love into our hearts in an unending supply that never runs dry. His love empowers us to love, even when others do not return it. Divine love disarms rejection and turns despair into hope. Nothing can separate us from the love of God in Christ Jesus, who fills every empty place.

APPLICATION

† Pray for God's love to overflow today
† Bless someone who may not return kindness
† Refuse rejection—receive His acceptance

CONNECTION

Thank You, Lord, for pouring Your love into my heart. Remove what blocks its flow. Let Your love overflow through me and lift despair into hope. In Jesus' name, Amen.

HIGHLIGHT QUOTE

God's love, poured into us by His Spirit, never runs dry, even when others do.

JOURNAL PROMPT

Where do you need to receive God's love more deeply so you can pour it out to others?

DAY 287
God Heals the Brokenhearted

The Spirit of the LORD is upon Me ... He has sent Me to heal the brokenhearted.
– Luke 4:18

REFLECTION

A broken heart can fence off future love, but Christ heals what fear defends. His love disarms our walls and restores trust where pain once ruled. God invites honest surrender so His Spirit can reach the places we cannot. In His presence, He unlocks old chains and brings wholeness through His unfailing love.

APPLICATION

† Name where your heart still hurts
† Invite Jesus to heal what you can't reach
† Take small steps of trust with safe people

CONNECTION

Thank You, Lord, for healing my broken heart. Tear down my defenses and restore freedom by Your Spirit. I surrender all. In Jesus' name, Amen.

HIGHLIGHT QUOTE

Jesus heals what fear defends, and love restores what pain has broken.

JOURNAL PROMPT

Where do you sense God inviting you to trust Him with your healing?

DAY 288
Walls Come Down

Now Jericho was securely shut up because of the children of Israel; none went out, and none came in.
– Joshua 6:1

REFLECTION

The Lord uses unexpected moments to break down the walls we build for self-protection. In His presence, barriers crumble and freedom comes. Walls keep others out and keep us from reaching out, but His Spirit brings healing and connection. Where fear builds distance, love restores peace.

APPLICATION

† Invite the Holy Spirit to reveal hidden walls
† Surrender wounded places to God's healing
† Choose connection where fear builds distance

CONNECTION

Thank You, Lord, for breaking down every wall that hinders Your best. Restore my soul and make me whole by Your grace. In Jesus' name, Amen.

HIGHLIGHT QUOTE

God breaks down the walls we build so His love can reach both in and out.

JOURNAL PROMPT

What wall, fear, pride, or hurt do you need to let God bring down?

DAY 289
Confident in His Work

> *Being confident of this very thing, that He who has begun a good work in you will complete it until the day of Jesus Christ.*
> – Philippians 1:6

REFLECTION

Though His work is often unseen, God faithfully brings it to completion. Each believer is part of His greater design, carefully placed and connected. Our confidence rests in His faithfulness, not our performance. As we follow His leading and trust His timing, He perfects all that concerns us.

APPLICATION

- † Trust God to finish the work He began in you
- † See yourself as part of His greater design
- † Stay faithful in your place until He moves you forward

CONNECTION

Thank You, Lord, for all You are doing in and through me. Strengthen my faith to trust You to complete the good work You began in me. In Jesus' name, Amen.

HIGHLIGHT QUOTE

God finishes every work He begins; His faithfulness never fails.

JOURNAL PROMPT

Where have you seen God's hand steadily working, even when you couldn't see results?

DAY 290
Worship That Wars

Then she came and worshiped Him, saying, "Lord, help me!"
— Matthew 15:25

REFLECTION

When Heaven seems silent and others reject us, worship keeps faith alive. The Canaanite woman pressed past offense and cried, "Lord, help me!" Worship lifts heaviness and drives out fear. As we adore Christ amid resistance, His peace and power replace despair with victory.

APPLICATION

† Turn rejection into worship
† Cry out, "Lord, help me!" with faith
† Let praise replace anxious thoughts

CONNECTION

Thank You, Lord, for Your abiding presence. Teach me to press through silence and offense with worship. Let my praise push back darkness and open Heaven's door. In Jesus' name, Amen.

HIGHLIGHT QUOTE

Worship is warfare; praise breaks through where words cannot.

JOURNAL PROMPT

Where can you respond with worship instead of worry or complain today?

DAY 291
Light in the Dark

> *The LORD is my light and my salvation; Whom shall I fear? The LORD is the strength of my life; Of whom shall I be afraid?*
> – Psalm 27:1

REFLECTION

Dark tunnels cannot cancel God's presence—they reveal it. In the shadows, His light shines brighter, guiding each step in wisdom and peace. When we walk by faith, His presence becomes our strength and courage. Fear fades as His light leads us forward from glory to glory.

APPLICATION

- † Acknowledge the tunnel you're walking through
- † Ask God to sharpen your spiritual sight
- † Trust His light to lead you one step at a time

CONNECTION

Thank You, Lord, for being my light and salvation. Steady my steps and drive out fear with Your presence. Teach me to trust the light of Your Word more than what I see. In Jesus' name, Amen.

HIGHLIGHT QUOTE

Even in darkness, God's light still shines enough for the next step.

JOURNAL PROMPT

What dark or uncertain area do you need to let God's light lead you through?

DAY 292
Pressing Toward the Prize

> *I press toward the goal for the prize of the upward call of God in Christ Jesus.*
> – Philippians 3:14

REFLECTION

Faith doesn't stand still; it reaches forward. The call of God continually draws us higher, inviting surrender, growth, and perseverance. Obstacles don't signal defeat; they strengthen our resolve and refine our dependence on Him. Even when the path ahead is uncertain, His presence guarantees direction.

APPLICATION

- † Press on when obstacles arise, knowing He is with you
- † Fix your focus on the upward call, not on past setbacks
- † Step beyond comfort to follow His leading in faith

CONNECTION

Thank You, Lord, for calling me to press toward Your higher purpose. Strengthen my heart to keep running with endurance and faith in what lies ahead. In Jesus' name, Amen.

HIGHLIGHT QUOTE

Faith reaches forward because God's best is always ahead.

JOURNAL PROMPT

What step of faith is God calling you to take as you press toward His purpose?

DAY 293
Faithful in the Hidden Season

> *And let us not grow weary while doing good, for in due season we shall reap if we do not lose heart.*
> – Galatians 6:9

REFLECTION

Much of faithfulness happens unseen. In quiet obedience, God shapes character and prepares fruit long before it appears. The world values results, but Heaven celebrates endurance. When we stay connected to the vine, His life flows through every simple act of love. We keep sowing, doing it unto the Lord, and trusting that His timing is perfect.

APPLICATION

† Keep serving with love, even when no one notices
† Guard your heart from discouragement in the waiting seasons
† Trust that God sees and rewards hidden obedience

CONNECTION

Thank You, Lord, for seeing what others never do. Strengthen me to stay faithful in the hidden seasons and to trust You for the fruit that only You can bring. In Jesus' name, Amen.

HIGHLIGHT QUOTE

Faithfulness in secret places prepares visible harvests.

JOURNAL PROMPT

Where might God be calling you to stay steady, even when the results are unseen?

DAY 294
Becoming a Chain Breaker

Christ has redeemed us from the curse of the law ... that the blessing of Abraham might come upon the Gentiles in Christ Jesus.
– Galatians 3:13–14

REFLECTION

Each of us can shape the spiritual direction of our family line. The enemy uses familiar patterns to keep generations bound, but in Christ, we have the power to break them. Every Spirit-led choice creates a new inheritance of blessing. The moment one believer stands firm in faith, the cycle shifts—from curse to favor, from defeat to victory.

APPLICATION

† Identify and reject generational patterns that oppose God's truth
† Choose daily obedience that plants seeds of blessing for generations
† Declare that God redeemed your family line to be favored and free

CONNECTION

Thank You, Lord, for empowering me to be a chain breaker in my family. Use my life to establish a legacy of blessing and freedom that brings You glory for generations to come. In Jesus' name, Amen.

HIGHLIGHT QUOTE

One Spirit-led choice can break generations of bondage and begin a legacy of blessing.

JOURNAL PROMPT

What pattern or habit in your family line is God calling you to break through faith?

DAY 295
Deep Calls Unto Deep

Deep calls unto deep at the noise of Your waterfalls; All Your waves and billows have gone over me.
– Psalm 42:7

REFLECTION

The Lord uses hardship to call us deeper into His presence. While the enemy provokes complaint, God invites contentment. His waves wash away insecurity and insufficiency, revealing His strength in us. As we rest beneath His waterfalls of grace, we discover His greatness through our trials.

APPLICATION

† Trust God to reveal His greatness through hardship
† Choose gratitude over grumbling
† Seek His presence daily, thirsting for more of Him

CONNECTION

Thank You, Lord, for Your grace and mercy. Help me abide in You and remain content in Your presence. Draw me deeper as I thirst for more of You. In Jesus' name, Amen.

HIGHLIGHT QUOTE

Every wave of trial carries a deeper revelation of His grace.

JOURNAL PROMPT

What recent hardship is calling you to a deeper place in God?

I am the light of the world. He who follows Me shall not walk in darkness, but have the light of life.

– John 8:12

DAY 296
A Thankful Heart

> And one of them, when he saw that he was healed, returned, and with a loud voice glorified God, and fell down on his face at His feet, giving Him thanks. And he was a Samaritan.
> – Luke 17:15–16

REFLECTION

Gratitude distinguishes the healed from the whole. Ten lepers were cleansed, but only one returned to thank Jesus, and he received more. Thankfulness completes the work of grace, keeping our hearts humble and full. A thankful heart sees God's hand in every gift and glorifies Him continually.

APPLICATION

† Thank God for both answered and unanswered prayers
† Express gratitude to others who have blessed your life
† Turn every prayer into an opportunity for praise

CONNECTION

Thank You, Lord, for every good and perfect gift. Teach me to live with a thankful heart and to see blessings in all things. In Jesus' name, Amen.

HIGHLIGHT QUOTE

Gratitude doesn't just thank God for what He's done; it invites more of His presence.

JOURNAL PROMPT

Who or what in your life do you need to stop and thank God for today?

DAY 297
Watered and Refreshed

> *The generous soul will be made rich, And he who waters will also be watered himself.*
> *– Proverbs 11:25*

REFLECTION

God often calls us to encourage or pray for others, even when our own strength feels low. As we pour out, He quietly renews what we thought was empty. The harvest comes in time. The same Spirit who empowers us to love others also refreshes us in the process. In serving, we receive; in watering others, we find our own souls restored.

APPLICATION

† Pray for someone else's need today
† Encourage others, even when you feel weary
† Trust God for unseen fruit that follows your faithfulness

CONNECTION

Thank You, Lord, for renewing me as I pour into others. Strengthen my heart to serve with love and perseverance, trusting You to refresh me in return. In Jesus' name, Amen.

HIGHLIGHT QUOTE

When we pour out in love, God fills us again with His renewing grace.

JOURNAL PROMPT

Who can you encourage or pray for today, even when you feel weary yourself?

DAY 298
Overcome Evil with Good

> *Do not be overcome by evil, but overcome evil with good.*
> – Romans 12:21

REFLECTION

The enemy tries to consume our focus with evil, but God calls us to release His goodness. Just as light dispels darkness, His presence within us overcomes the evil around us. We shine brighter not by striving, but by living in His Spirit, responding with love and truth. In every challenge, our response in Christ pushes back the darkness and reveals His glory.

APPLICATION

- † Ask God to show you where you can release His goodness today
- † Choose to respond to evil with love, prayer, and truth
- † Let His light shine through you in words and actions

CONNECTION

Thank You, Lord, that Your light overcomes darkness. Help me overcome evil with good and let Your love shine through me. In Jesus' name, Amen.

HIGHLIGHT QUOTE

God's presence within us overcomes the evil around us.

JOURNAL PROMPT

Where can you respond to evil with God's goodness today?

DAY 299
People of God

> Who once were not a people but are now the people of God, who had not obtained mercy but now have obtained mercy.
> — 1 Peter 2:10

REFLECTION

Once distant, now drawn near—this is our new identity in Christ. Each day, transformation continues as we walk in His mercy and light. Rather than fixating on what is unfinished, we celebrate progress. We are no longer who we were, and His grace keeps carrying us forward.

APPLICATION

† Celebrate progress in your walk of faith
† Rest in His mercy and new identity
† Trust His promises, even in the "not yet"

CONNECTION

Thank You, Lord, for calling me into Your marvelous light. Help me celebrate progress, walk in mercy, and trust Your promises. In Jesus' name, Amen.

HIGHLIGHT QUOTE

God's mercy makes strangers into His people and wanderers into His beloved.

JOURNAL PROMPT

What evidence of transformation can you thank God for in your walk with Him today?

DAY 300
Grace to the Humble

God resists the proud, But gives grace to the humble.
– James 4:6

REFLECTION

Pride closes the door to grace; humility opens it wide. When we depend on God instead of self, He releases divine strength to accomplish what we cannot. Humility is not self-deprecation—it's God-dependence. It keeps our focus on who He is, not on who we are. As we choose humility, His presence fills the space that pride once occupied. In that surrendered place, grace flows freely, restoring peace, power, and fellowship with Him.

APPLICATION

- † Confess any prideful or self-reliant attitudes to God
- † Choose humility in words, attitudes, and daily interactions
- † Depend on His grace rather than your own ability

CONNECTION

Thank You, Lord, for the grace that meets me in humility. Forgive my prideful ways and teach me to depend fully on You. Let Your presence dwell richly in my surrendered heart. In Jesus' name, Amen.

HIGHLIGHT QUOTE

Pride resists grace; humility makes room for it to flow.

JOURNAL PROMPT

Where might you need to humble yourself so God's grace can flow freely?

DAY 301
Seeds of Thought

> *Whatever things are true, whatever things are noble, whatever things are just, whatever things are pure, whatever things are lovely, whatever things are of good report ... meditate on these things.*
> – Philippians 4:8

REFLECTION

Our hearts are gardens, and our thoughts are seeds. Seeds of faith and hope produce peace, while seeds of fear yield weeds of anxiety. Overthinking the wrong things chokes our joy, but meditating on the truth restores life. As we guard our thoughts, we cultivate a mind that flourishes in God's peace.

APPLICATION

- † Meditate on what is true and praiseworthy
- † Replace negative thoughts with God's promises
- † Sow seeds of faith, love, and hope each day

CONNECTION

Thank You, Lord, for helping me take every thought captive to Christ. Guard my mind and let my thoughts bear fruit for Your glory. In Jesus' name, Amen.

HIGHLIGHT QUOTE

What we meditate on today will bloom in our hearts tomorrow.

JOURNAL PROMPT

What "thought seeds" are you planting: faith-filled or fear-filled?

DAY 302
Torches in Clay Pots

> *Then the three companies blew the trumpets and broke the pitchers—they held the torches in their left hands and the trumpets in their right.*
> – Judges 7:20

REFLECTION

Gideon's men broke their clay pots, revealing the torches within—a picture of God's treasure in earthen vessels. As we humble ourselves, His glory shines through. Brokenness releases the light that nothing can hide. The Holy Spirit removes pride and self-reliance so the flame of Christ can shine brighter through surrendered hearts.

APPLICATION

† Acknowledge that your sufficiency comes from God alone
† Allow Him to break your pride and self-reliance
† Abide in Christ in surrender and humility

CONNECTION

Thank You, Lord, for being my sufficiency. Break my pride and self-dependence so Your glory can shine through me. Let my life be a vessel of Your light. In Jesus' name, Amen.

HIGHLIGHT QUOTE

The flame of Christ can shine brighter through surrendered hearts.

JOURNAL PROMPT

What part of your life needs surrender so God's light can shine more clearly through you?

DAY 303
Like the Bars of a Castle

> *A brother offended is harder to win than a strong city, And contentions are like the bars of a castle.*
> – Proverbs 18:19

REFLECTION

Offense builds invisible prisons around our hearts, locking us in bitterness and isolation. But God's grace gives the key to freedom—love and forgiveness. As we mature in Christ, we learn to release hurt quickly and guard against resentment. Reconciliation opens the gate to peace and restores our witness of grace.

APPLICATION

- † Pray for wisdom when dealing with offense or conflict
- † Choose to release hurt and walk in love
- † Trust God's timing to heal and restore relationships

CONNECTION

Thank You, Lord, for Your mercy and patience. Help me to let go of offenses quickly and extend grace to others as You extend it to me. Restore unity and peace in my relationships. In Jesus' name, Amen.

HIGHLIGHT QUOTE

Forgiveness unlocks the heart and tears down the walls that offense builds.

JOURNAL PROMPT

Whom do you need to forgive or release to walk in freedom today?

DAY 304
The Touch of Faith

> And Jesus said, "Who touched Me?" When all denied it, Peter and those with him said, "Master, the multitudes throng and press You, and You say, "Who touched Me?" But Jesus said, "Somebody touched Me, for I perceived power going out from Me." – Luke 8:45–46

REFLECTION

Many pressed around Jesus, but only one reached out in faith. Her desperate touch overcame obstacles, fear, and doubt. In the same way, when we press through our fears and reach for Him with believing hearts, His power meets us in our need. Every prayer, every tear, and every act of faith becomes a touch that moves His heart and releases His power. His healing touch still awaits ours.

APPLICATION

- † Seek Jesus with perseverance and faith
- † Press through obstacles that hinder your reach
- † Trust His touch to bring healing and transformation

CONNECTION

Thank You, Lord, for Your loving and restoring touch. Help me persevere in faith, pressing through every obstacle to reach for You. In Jesus' name, Amen.

HIGHLIGHT QUOTE

People of faith don't just brush against Jesus; they reach until He touches them.

JOURNAL PROMPT

What area of your life needs a fresh, faith-filled touch from Jesus?

DAY 305
Abide in the Vine

I am the vine, you are the branches. He who abides in Me, and I in him, bears much fruit; for without Me you can do nothing.
– John 15:5

REFLECTION

Our position in Christ is one of trust, safety, and peace. Abiding in the vine means living in continual communion with Jesus, our life source. As branches, we cannot create fruit—we simply bear it as we remain in Him. When we strive apart from Him, unrest comes; when we abide, fruit flows.

APPLICATION

† Remain connected to Christ through prayer and worship
† Rely on His life as your constant source of strength and peace
† Rest in His presence and allow His Spirit to bear fruit through you

CONNECTION

Thank You, Lord, for being the vine and giving me life as Your branch. Help me to remain steadfast in every season. May my life bear much fruit that glorifies Your name. In Jesus' name, Amen.

HIGHLIGHT QUOTE

We don't produce fruit by striving but by abiding in the life of the vine.

JOURNAL PROMPT

Where are you striving instead of resting in your connection to Christ?

DAY 306
Faith, Hope, and Love

> We give thanks to God always for you all, making mention of you in our prayers, remembering without ceasing your work of faith, labor of love, and patience of hope in our Lord Jesus Christ in the sight of our God and Father. – 1 Thessalonians 1:2–3

REFLECTION

Faith works, love labors, and hope endures. Each reveals Christ's character through us. Love fuels our service, faith strengthens our walk, and hope anchors us in waiting seasons. Under pressure, these three remain, shining as evidence of the Holy Spirit's transforming power.

APPLICATION

† Live out your faith with works that glorify the Lord
† Labor in love, serving others sincerely
† Look to the future with unwavering hope

CONNECTION

Thank You, Lord, for the faith, hope, and love poured into my heart by Your Spirit. Help me live in their power every day. In Jesus' name, Amen.

HIGHLIGHT QUOTE

Faith acts, love serves, and hope holds fast when everything else shakes.

JOURNAL PROMPT

Which of the three: faith, hope, or love, needs strengthening in your life right now?

DAY 307
The Ministry of Reconciliation

> Now all things are of God, who has reconciled us to Himself through Jesus Christ, and has given us the ministry of reconciliation.
> – 2 Corinthians 5:18

REFLECTION

Reconciliation lies at the heart of the Gospel. In conflict, it's easy to take sides or defend pride, but Christ calls us to His side—peace. Reconciliation means valuing the person above the problem, keeping unity above opinion. Love doesn't erase differences; it invites grace to bridge them. Wherever division tries to dwell, His peace has the power to heal and restore.

APPLICATION

† Pray before speaking about any disagreement or dispute
† Choose peace over proving your point
† Value people above opinions, trusting the Spirit to bring truth and clarity

CONNECTION

Thank You, Lord, for reconciling me to Yourself through Jesus Christ. Help me reflect Your heart of peace in every conversation. Let Your grace guide my words and actions so I may be an instrument of unity and healing. In Jesus' name, Amen.

HIGHLIGHT QUOTE

Reconciliation values people above opinions and lets grace bridge the divide.

JOURNAL PROMPT

Where is God calling you to be an instrument of peace rather than a defender of your position?

DAY 308
Quench All the Fiery Darts

> *Above all, taking the shield of faith with which you will be able to quench all the fiery darts of the wicked one.*
> – Ephesians 6:16

REFLECTION

The enemy's darts—doubt, fear, accusation—fly without warning. Yet faith extinguishes every one. When we stand together in prayer and unity, our shields link to form an unbreakable defense. The battle is fierce, but Christ has already won the victory. Faith keeps us steady under His covering.

APPLICATION

- † Lift your shield of faith daily through prayer and declaration
- † Stand united with others for strength in battle
- † Trust that Christ's victory already secures your own

CONNECTION

Thank You, Lord, for shielding me with faith. Strengthen me to stand firm and confident in Your victory. Unite me with others to walk in faith and power. In Jesus' name, Amen.

HIGHLIGHT QUOTE

The battle is fierce, but Christ has already won the victory.

JOURNAL PROMPT

What fiery dart has tried to pierce your peace, and how can you lift your shield of faith against it?

DAY 309
Haste Makes Waste

> *Behold, I lay in Zion a stone for a foundation ... Whoever believes will not act hastily.*
> – Isaiah 28:16

REFLECTION

Impatience leads to error, but faith waits on God's timing. When we move under pressure, we risk stepping outside His will. Trusting in Christ, the sure foundation, steadies our hearts. Believing means pausing until His peace gives permission to move. Haste fades; His timing stands firm.

APPLICATION

† Pause and seek God before acting under pressure
† Pray for His wisdom in every decision
† Wait for His peace as your green light to move

CONNECTION

Thank You, Lord, for being my sure foundation. Teach me to trust Your timing and resist haste. Lead me by Your peace and patience. In Jesus' name, Amen.

HIGHLIGHT QUOTE

Faith walks slowly enough to hear God's heartbeat.

JOURNAL PROMPT

Where are you tempted to rush ahead instead of waiting on God's timing?

DAY 310
Do You Not Know?

> *Or do you not know that your body is the temple of the Holy Spirit who is in you ... and you are not your own?*
> – 1 Corinthians 6:19

REFLECTION

Our bodies are not our own—they are sacred temples of the Holy Spirit. This awareness transforms how we live, rest, and care for ourselves. Every decision becomes an act of worship when we treat our bodies as vessels for His glory. Honor invites His presence; surrender makes us radiant.

APPLICATION

- † Honor God by treating your body with care and respect
- † Dedicate your choices to glorify Him daily
- † Rely on His grace to strengthen healthy habits

CONNECTION

Thank You, Lord, for making my body Your temple. Help me glorify You in body and spirit through all I do. Strengthen me to walk in holiness and gratitude. In Jesus' name, Amen.

HIGHLIGHT QUOTE

When we treat our bodies as His temple, our lives become acts of worship.

JOURNAL PROMPT

How can you honor God more intentionally with your body and choices?

DAY 311
Receiving Faith Over Fear

For God has not given us a spirit of fear, but of power and of love and of a sound mind.
– 2 Timothy 1:7

REFLECTION

Fear silences boldness and stirs anxiety, but it is not from God. His Spirit fills us with courage, love, and stability. When fear speaks loudly, faith must speak louder still. Our fears reach toward the future, but faith abides in the present. We move forward, not because we feel fearless, but because the Holy Spirit within us is greater than our fear.

APPLICATION

† Recognize moments of intimidation and resist them
† Focus on faith in God, not the fear of circumstances
† Move forward through the Spirit's power

CONNECTION

Thank You, Lord, for Your Spirit of power, love, and a sound mind. Replace fear with faith and strengthen me to walk boldly in Your truth. In Jesus' name, Amen.

HIGHLIGHT QUOTE

Fear flees when faith finds its voice.

JOURNAL PROMPT

Where is fear trying to silence you, and how can you respond in faith instead?

DAY 312
Strength in Submission

But He gives more grace. Therefore He says: "God resists the proud, But gives grace to the humble." Therefore submit to God. Resist the devil and he will flee from you.
— James 4:6–7

REFLECTION

Greater grace flows through greater surrender. We cannot humble ourselves in our own strength—it comes through submitting to God's will. In that surrender, He empowers us to stand firm against the enemy. Pride gives the adversary access; humility removes his footing. When our hearts bow to God, His strength rises within us.

APPLICATION

† Begin each day by surrendering your will to God
† Repent quickly when pride or self-reliance appears
† Stand firm in grace when facing temptation or opposition

CONNECTION

Thank You, Lord, for the strength that comes through submission. Teach me to humble myself before You daily and to resist the enemy by Your power and grace. In Jesus' name, Amen.

HIGHLIGHT QUOTE

Surrender disarms the enemy and releases the power of grace.

JOURNAL PROMPT

What area of your life needs greater humility and surrender to God's will?

DAY 313
The Power of Redemption

> Bless the LORD, O my soul,
> And forget not all His benefits:
> Who forgives all your iniquities,
> Who heals all your diseases,
> Who redeems your life from destruction, Who crowns you with lovingkindness and tender mercies.
> – Psalm 103:2–4

REFLECTION

When Jesus redeemed us, He bore every curse, every failure, and every generational stronghold so we could live free. He carried our pain, broke the power of the past, and exchanged our bondage for blessing. We are no longer victims but victors who establish new legacies of grace. Redemption rewrites the story of our lives in the ink of mercy.

APPLICATION

† Worship with gratitude for the complete redemption Christ secured
† Declare freedom from every generational pattern of defeat
† Walk in the blessings and authority of your redeemed identity

CONNECTION

Thank You, Lord, for redeeming my life and breaking every chain of the past. Help me live in the fullness of Your blessing and reflect Your freedom to generations after me. In Jesus' name, Amen.

HIGHLIGHT QUOTE

Redemption rewrites your story, turning every curse into a channel of blessing.

JOURNAL PROMPT

What area of your life needs to be rewritten by the power of redemption?

DAY 314
Seeking the Holy Spirit

If you then, being evil, know how to give good gifts to your children, how much more will your heavenly Father give the Holy Spirit to those who ask Him!
– Luke 11:13

REFLECTION

In the rush of life, we often seek worldly solutions before seeking the Holy Spirit. True power flows only from His presence. He strengthens, guides, and fills us with wisdom beyond our own. Our strength without His weakens us and keeps us bound. When we invite Him in, our efforts become grace-filled and our lives bear lasting fruit.

APPLICATION

† Ask daily for the Holy Spirit's guidance and power
† Pause before decisions to listen for His direction
† Welcome His presence into every part of your life

CONNECTION

Thank You, Lord, for the gift of Your Holy Spirit. I long for His presence and power. Lead me in wisdom, fill me with grace, and manifest Your glory through me. In Jesus' name, Amen.

HIGHLIGHT QUOTE

Power without the Spirit fades, but power from the Spirit bears eternal fruit.

JOURNAL PROMPT

What area of your life most needs the Holy Spirit's guidance today?

DAY 315
What Do You See?

> *There we saw the giants ... and we were like grasshoppers in our own sight.*
> – Numbers 13:33

REFLECTION

Fear distorts our vision, shrinking God and magnifying obstacles. The Israelites saw giants instead of grace and retreated in defeat. When we view ourselves through insecurity, we empower our challenges instead of our God. Through faith, we see differently—giants become grasshoppers in His presence.

APPLICATION

- † Reject fearful thoughts that diminish your worth
- † See yourself through the eyes of Christ
- † Trust Him to conquer every giant in your path

CONNECTION

Thank You, Lord, for making me strong in You. Open my eyes to see through faith, not fear. Let Your power silence every giant that intimidates me. In Jesus' name, Amen.

HIGHLIGHT QUOTE

Faith changes how we see; giants shrink when God stands tall.

JOURNAL PROMPT

What "giant" in your life do you need to see through the eyes of faith?

DAY 316
Our Dot-to-Dot Journey

And we know that all things work together for good to those who love God, to those who are the called according to His purpose.
– Romans 8:28

REFLECTION

God is always connecting the dots, even when we can't see the picture forming. Each joyful or painful season links to another, revealing His purpose in time. Faith walks one step at a time, trusting His design before it's visible. What we assume are ends become steppingstones in His glorious plan. Every dot is a preparation for the next work of grace.

APPLICATION

† Trust God's bigger picture, even when it's unclear
† Rest in His care through each new season
† Believe He's working all things together for good

CONNECTION

Thank You, Lord, for working all things together for my good. Strengthen my trust when the picture is incomplete. Help me see each step as part of Your purpose. In Jesus' name, Amen.

HIGHLIGHT QUOTE

When we can't see the full picture, faith holds the pen while God connects the dots.

JOURNAL PROMPT

What season in your life might be one of God's "dots in progress"?

DAY 317
Reach for His Saving Hand

> But when he saw that the wind was boisterous, he was afraid; and beginning to sink he cried out, saying, "Lord, save me!" And immediately Jesus stretched out His hand and caught him, and said to him, "O you of little faith, why did you doubt?" – Matthew 14:30–31

REFLECTION

Peter walked on water until he focused on the storm. Likewise, when fear captures our focus, faith sinks. Jesus doesn't scold; He saves. The moment we cry, "Lord, save me," His hand reaches out in grace. Each rescue deepens our trust and reminds us of His greatness. His powerful presence never leaves us helpless.

APPLICATION

- † Refocus on Jesus when distraction causes doubt
- † Call on Him immediately when faith falters
- † Rest in His rescue and timing

CONNECTION

Thank You, Lord, for stretching out Your hand when I start to sink. Anchor my faith and steady my steps upon Your Word. In Jesus' name, Amen.

HIGHLIGHT QUOTE

Even when our faith falters, His hand never fails.

JOURNAL PROMPT

Where is Jesus asking you to take His hand and trust Him again?

DAY 318
Set Apart from the Start

> *But when it pleased God, who separated me from my mother's womb and called me through His grace.*
> – Galatians 1:15

REFLECTION

God's call began long before we recognized it. His grace marked us from the womb, guiding us through every detour and delay. Every member of the body of Christ is unique and valuable to the whole. Looking back reveals His hand at work in all things. When we yield to His leading, purpose unfolds and grace abounds.

APPLICATION

† Reflect on the times God protected you before salvation
† Pray for clarity of His purpose today
† Trust His grace for your future path

CONNECTION

Thank You, Lord, for calling me and setting me apart by Your grace. Help me walk in confidence and faith in Your plan. In Jesus' name, Amen.

HIGHLIGHT QUOTE

Our calling is older than our awareness; it began in God's heart.

JOURNAL PROMPT

Where can you see evidence of God's hand guiding you long before you knew Him?

DAY 319
When the Night Shines

> *Indeed, the darkness shall not hide from You, But the night shines as the day; The darkness and the light are both alike to You.*
> – Psalm 139:12

REFLECTION

What feels hidden to us is still visible to God. Darkness may surround us, but it cannot surround Him. His light sees through confusion, grief, and fear, revealing direction and purpose we can't yet see. When we cannot find our way, His eyes never lose sight of us. The same God who created the night watches over us within it, turning our deepest uncertainty into a shout of praise.

APPLICATION

† Rest in the truth that God sees clearly, even when you cannot
† Invite His presence into the areas that feel hidden or uncertain
† Let His light turn fear into quiet trust

CONNECTION

Thank You, Lord, for being the light, even in my darkest moments. When I cannot see the way forward, help me rest in the truth that You can. Let Your presence turn my night into peace. In Jesus' name, Amen.

HIGHLIGHT QUOTE

God's light doesn't just remove the night; it transforms it.

JOURNAL PROMPT

Where have you mistaken darkness for God's absence when He was working unseen?

DAY 320
Another Touch

> *Then He put His hands on his eyes again and made him look up. And he was restored and saw everyone clearly.*
> – Mark 8:25

REFLECTION

One touch of salvation changed us forever, but continual touches keep transforming us. The Lord meets us in ordinary moments, renewing vision and reviving faith. His touch heals the pain of wrong experiences and reshapes our desires to align with His. Again and again, He restores us by His power, leading us from glory to glory until we see clearly through His eyes.

APPLICATION

† Notice His presence in life's ordinary moments
† Seek His renewing touch daily in prayer
† Trust Him to heal and restore you

CONNECTION

Thank You, Lord, for touching my life again and again. Restore my sight where it has dimmed, heal my wounds, and shape me into Your likeness. In Jesus' name, Amen.

HIGHLIGHT QUOTE

God's touch not only saves; it continually restores and renews us by grace.

JOURNAL PROMPT

What area of your life needs "another touch" from the Lord today?

DAY 321
Hidden in His Quiver

> *And He has made My mouth like a sharp sword; In the shadow of His hand He has hidden Me, And made Me a polished shaft; In His quiver He has hidden Me.*
> – Isaiah 49:2

REFLECTION

Like polished arrows, God shapes us in hidden seasons. He straightens, smooths, and anoints us so we will hit the mark. Waiting in His quiver builds patience and trust. When His timing comes, He launches us with precision into destiny. His preparation is always active, working toward His best for us.

APPLICATION

- † Trust God's shaping in hidden seasons
- † Embrace patience while waiting in His quiver
- † Be ready for His timing to launch you forward

CONNECTION

Thank You, Lord, for shaping me for Your purposes. I yield to Your preparation, even when I don't see it. Release me into Your perfect will in Your perfect timing. In Jesus' name, Amen.

HIGHLIGHT QUOTE

Hidden seasons are not wasted; they are God's workshop for destiny.

JOURNAL PROMPT

How is God shaping or preparing you during your current "hidden" season?

DAY 322
Be Anxious for Nothing

> *Be anxious for nothing, but in everything by prayer and supplication, with thanksgiving, let your requests be made known to God.*
> – Philippians 4:6

REFLECTION

Anxiety fades when we continually release our cares to God. Worry tries to reclaim what faith has surrendered, but peace guards what we give to Him. Prayer and thanksgiving turn fear into trust and invite His calm to rule our minds. The peace of God surpasses understanding and sustains us daily.

APPLICATION

† Release every worry to God in prayer
† Thank Him continually for His care and provision
† Trust His peace to guard your heart and mind

CONNECTION

Thank You, Lord, for Your peace that surpasses understanding. Teach me to release every anxiety and rest in Your love. Guard my heart and mind in Christ Jesus. In Jesus' name, Amen.

HIGHLIGHT QUOTE

Peace remains where thanksgiving replaces worry.

JOURNAL PROMPT

What specific worry do you need to release to God right now?

DAY 323
What Do You Remember?

> *Some trust in chariots, and some in horses; But we will remember the name of the LORD our God.*
> – Psalm 20:7

REFLECTION

It's easy to forget God's past faithfulness when faced with new challenges. Yet remembrance fuels faith. We don't rely on human strength or recognition but on the steadfast name of the Lord. Remembering His goodness transforms discouragement into confidence and keeps our hearts steadfast in gratitude.

APPLICATION

† Forgive when others forget your efforts or kindness
† Remember God's faithfulness in your past
† Praise Him for His goodness in every season

CONNECTION

Thank You, Lord, for Your constant faithfulness. Help me never forget Your goodness or depend on anything above You. I will remember Your name and trust in You always. In Jesus' name, Amen.

HIGHLIGHT QUOTE

Remembering what God has done strengthens faith for what He will do next.

JOURNAL PROMPT

What past act of God's faithfulness do you need to remember and thank Him for today?

DAY 324
Shake Off the Enemy's Attacks

> *But he shook off the creature into the fire and suffered no harm.*
> – Acts 28:5

REFLECTION

Paul shook off the viper that had latched onto him, and no harm came. Likewise, we can shake off attacks of fear, accusation, or discouragement through faith. God's fire purifies and protects, consuming every scheme meant for harm. The power of the Holy Spirit enables us to rise unharmed and keep walking in victory.

APPLICATION

† Refuse fear or accusation when the enemy strikes
† Stand firm in your authority in Christ
† Shake off every attack through prayer and praise

CONNECTION

Thank You, Lord, for the power of Your Spirit. Help me shake off every attack and walk boldly in Your victory. Let Your fire consume all that is not of You. In Jesus' name, Amen.

HIGHLIGHT QUOTE

Faith doesn't ignore the bite; it shakes it off into the fire of God's power.

JOURNAL PROMPT

What attack or discouragement do you need to "shake off" by faith today?

DAY 325
Waves of Glory

> *Then they cry out to the LORD in their trouble, And He brings them out of their distresses. He calms the storm, So that its waves are still.*
> *– Psalm 107:28–29*

REFLECTION

God treasures every tear we've shed and every storm we've endured. Even when His presence feels different from yesterday, He is still near, ready to calm the chaos within and around us. The storms that once threatened to sink us become the very waves that carry us into deeper intimacy with Him. These waves wash away the residue of trials and make room for more of His glory.

APPLICATION

† Remember a storm God has calmed in your past, and thank Him for it
† Invite His presence into the areas of turbulence in your life today
† Ask Him to use your testimony to bring peace to others facing storms

CONNECTION

Thank You, Lord, for calming every storm and bringing me into deeper places with You. Help me to welcome Your waves of glory and trust Your peace in every situation. In Jesus' name, Amen.

HIGHLIGHT QUOTE

The storms that once threatened to sink us become the very waves that carry us into deeper intimacy with Him.

JOURNAL PROMPT

How has God used past storms to draw you closer to Him?

DAY 326
Strengthened in the Inner Man

> *That He would grant you, according to the riches of His glory, to be strengthened with might through His Spirit in the inner man.*
> – Ephesians 3:16

REFLECTION

Human strength runs out quickly, but the Holy Spirit strengthens us from within. His power fortifies us far beyond our natural ability, equipping us to fulfill God's purpose with grace and endurance. When we feel weak, His might rises in us. Spiritual strength flows from His glory and never runs dry.

APPLICATION

- † Pray daily for strength from the Holy Spirit
- † Depend on His power, not your own effort
- † Expect His abundance beyond what you can ask or think

CONNECTION

Thank You, Lord, for strengthening me with might in my inner being. Remind me that Your Spirit never fails and that Your power sustains me in every trial. In Jesus' name, Amen.

HIGHLIGHT QUOTE

When our strength ends, His begins and never runs out.

JOURNAL PROMPT

What area of your life needs inner strength from the Holy Spirit today?

DAY 327
The Power of Gratitude

In everything give thanks; for this is the will of God in Christ Jesus for you.
— 1 Thessalonians 5:18

REFLECTION

Gratitude shifts our focus from what's wrong to Who is right—God. Complaining clouds the heart, but thanksgiving clears it. When we choose gratitude, joy replaces heaviness, and peace flows freely. Gratitude doesn't change every circumstance, but it changes the way we walk through it, aware of grace, steady in faith, and full of hope.

APPLICATION

† Replace complaints with words of gratitude
† Encourage others to notice God's goodness
† Give thanks, even in waiting or hardship

CONNECTION

Thank You, Lord, for the transforming power of gratitude. Guard my heart from negativity and help me stay mindful of Your faithfulness in every season. In Jesus' name, Amen.

HIGHLIGHT QUOTE

Gratitude doesn't change our circumstances; it changes us.

JOURNAL PROMPT

What blessing can you thank God for that you often overlook?

DAY 328
Rejoice, Pray, and Give Thanks

> *Rejoice always, pray without ceasing, in everything give thanks; for this is the will of God in Christ Jesus for you.*
> – 1 Thessalonians 5:16–18

REFLECTION

Joy, prayer, and gratitude are sacred companions that sustain the believer's heart. Rejoicing lifts our eyes from the storm to the Savior. Prayer aligns our will with His. Thanksgiving anchors our faith in His goodness. When these rhythms shape our days, ordinary moments become worship. As we rejoice, pray, and give thanks continually, peace becomes our posture and joy our song.

APPLICATION

† Rejoice in the Lord, even when life feels uncertain
† Pray continually, staying aware of His presence
† Give thanks daily for His steadfast love and care

CONNECTION

Thank You, Lord, for the joy of Your presence and the peace that comes through prayer and gratitude. Let my life reflect continual praise in every season. In Jesus' name, Amen.

HIGHLIGHT QUOTE

When we rejoice, pray, and give thanks, every season becomes sacred.

JOURNAL PROMPT

Which of these—rejoicing, praying, or giving thanks—do you need to practice more intentionally?

DAY 329
Reflecting Christ's Love

> *We love Him because He first loved us.*
> — 1 John 4:19

REFLECTION

Our love for God is always a response to His love for us, never a way to earn it. Out of this love, we extend grace and compassion to others, even when they are not returned. Love becomes a reflection of Christ shining through us. In action, it testifies to His presence and power in our lives. We cannot produce it; it flows from Him.

APPLICATION

† Look for opportunities to show love in action today
† Choose patience and kindness when it is difficult
† Reflect God's love in both small and significant ways

CONNECTION

Thank You, Lord, for loving me first. Teach me to love others as You have loved me. Help me embrace Your love and share it in my actions. Let each act of love reveal the truth of Your perfect love for me. In Jesus' name, Amen.

HIGHLIGHT QUOTE

Love in action is the visible evidence of Christ within us.

JOURNAL PROMPT

Who can you intentionally show Christ's love to today?

DAY 330
Lift Your Eyes

> *Lift your eyes now and look ... for all the land which you see I give to you and your descendants forever.*
> – Genesis 13:14–15

REFLECTION

Separation often precedes blessings. As God led Abram to lift his eyes after parting ways with Lot, He invites us to release what hinders us and to trust His greater plan. Letting go is rarely easy, but it positions us to receive what's next. When we surrender distractions or relationships that no longer align with His will, He lifts our vision to see His promises anew.

APPLICATION

- † Identify something God may be asking you to release in this season
- † Pray for courage to trust His greater purpose in letting go
- † Thank Him for the new vision He is bringing into focus

CONNECTION

Thank You, Lord, for calling me to lift my eyes beyond what I've left behind. Help me to trust Your plan and see the promises You've prepared for me. In Jesus' name, Amen.

HIGHLIGHT QUOTE

Letting go positions us to lift our eyes and see God's promises anew.

JOURNAL PROMPT

What is God asking you to release so He can lift your eyes to His promises?

DAY 331
Held by His Hand

> Nevertheless I am continually with You; You hold me by my right hand. You will guide me with Your counsel, And afterward receive me to glory.
> – Psalm 73:23–24

REFLECTION

Before we knew Christ, we leaned on our own strength. Now we learn dependence, trusting His hand to guide us day by day. The more we rely on Him, the more we discover His presence is constant and His counsel unfailing. Often, He solves problems before we even notice them. He holds us securely and leads us faithfully to glory.

APPLICATION

† Surrender an area where you've been trying to stay in control
† Declare your trust in God's faithful hand through prayer
† Look back at His past guidance and thank Him for it today

CONNECTION

Thank You, Lord, for holding me by Your right hand and guiding me with Your counsel. Help me depend on You in every unknown and trust that You are always near. In Jesus' name, Amen.

HIGHLIGHT QUOTE

God's hand holds us securely and guides us faithfully to glory.

JOURNAL PROMPT

Where are you trying to stay in control instead of relying on God's hand?

DAY 332
Standing Out in Faith

> *God has chosen the foolish things of the world to put to shame the wise.*
> – 1 Corinthians 1:27

REFLECTION

Faith sets us apart in a world chasing applause and approval. Standing out for God means resisting pressure to conform and holding firm to His truth. Like a lighthouse in the dark, our lives can guide others to Christ. The power isn't in us but in His Spirit working through us, shining brightly so others can see His transforming grace at work.

APPLICATION

- † Examine areas where you feel pressured to blend in with the crowd
- † Ask God for boldness to stand for Him, even when it's unpopular
- † Seek to reflect Christ's light rather than seek human approval

CONNECTION

Thank You, Lord, for calling me to stand out in faith. Give me the courage to shine for You and guide others to Your truth. Let my life reflect Your transforming grace. In Jesus' name, Amen.

HIGHLIGHT QUOTE

Faith stands out by reflecting Christ's light, not seeking human approval.

JOURNAL PROMPT

Where is God asking you to stand out in faith instead of blending in?

DAY 333
Called Into Fellowship

> *God is faithful, by whom you were called into the fellowship of His Son, Jesus Christ our Lord.*
> *– 1 Corinthians 1:9*

REFLECTION

When God calls us, He calls us not only out of darkness but also into His marvelous light. Every calling removes something that hinders us and replaces it with something better. We are called out of despair into hope, out of rejection into belonging. His call is constant and faithful, drawing us closer to Christ and deeper into His purposes each day.

APPLICATION

- † Reflect on what God has called you out of and what He's called you into
- † Thank Him for the fellowship you have with Christ today
- † Ask for a deeper revelation of His calling on your life

CONNECTION

Thank You, Lord, for calling me into fellowship with You. Draw me closer each day and deepen my understanding of Your call. Help me to walk worthy of it with gratitude and faith. In Jesus' name, Amen.

HIGHLIGHT QUOTE

God's call always moves us from darkness to light, from isolation to intimacy with Christ.

JOURNAL PROMPT

What has God called you out of, and what is He calling you into now?

DAY 334
Strength in Stillness

> *In returning and rest you shall be saved; In quietness and confidence shall be your strength.*
> – Isaiah 30:15

REFLECTION

Stillness before God does more than quiet the soul; it strengthens it. When we return to Him in rest, we find salvation from fear and weariness. Quietness is not withdrawal but confidence in His working while we wait. As we release control, His strength fills the space our striving once occupied. Trust becomes the anchor that steadies every storm.

APPLICATION

- † Set aside quiet time with God each day
- † Choose rest over restless striving when anxiety rises
- † Let confidence in His sovereignty replace fear of the unknown

CONNECTION

Thank You, Lord, for meeting me in the quiet and restoring my strength. Teach me to rest in Your presence and trust Your perfect timing. Let my confidence stand in You alone. In Jesus' name, Amen.

HIGHLIGHT QUOTE

Stillness is not weakness; it's strength found in quiet confidence before God.

JOURNAL PROMPT

Where is God calling you to pause, return, and draw strength from resting in Him?

DAY 335
The Sound of Abundance

> *Then Elijah said to Ahab, "Go up, eat and drink; for there is the sound of abundance of rain."*
> — 1 Kings 18:41

REFLECTION

Faith hears what sight cannot. Elijah heard the sound of abundance long before rain appeared. God calls us to listen beyond the silence of delay. When expectation replaces discouragement, we hear Heaven's promise before it manifests on earth. His abundance is not distant; it's already on its way.

APPLICATION

† Believe God's promises, even in the waiting
† Guard your heart against doubt and weariness
† Expect more than enough from your faithful God

CONNECTION

Thank You, Lord, for the sound of abundance. Strengthen my faith to keep believing for more than I can see. Teach me to expect the overflow of Your goodness. In Jesus' name, Amen.

HIGHLIGHT QUOTE

Faith hears the rain before a single drop falls.

JOURNAL PROMPT

Where do you need to expect God's "sound of abundance" again?

DAY 336
Using Our God-Given Gifts

Having then gifts differing according to the grace that is given to us, let us use them."
– Romans 12:6

REFLECTION

God places unique gifts in each of us to serve His purpose and bless others. Some are visible, others are hidden, but all are valuable. When we steward them faithfully, His grace multiplies. Comparison steals joy, but gratitude refines purpose. As we use what He's given, our lives become instruments of His glory.

APPLICATION

- † Identify and nurture the gifts God has placed within you
- † Use your gifts to serve others and glorify Him
- † Celebrate the grace in your life without comparison

CONNECTION

Thank You, Lord, for the gifts You've given me. Teach me to use them wisely and joyfully. Let my talents reflect Your love and serve Your Kingdom. In Jesus' name, Amen.

HIGHLIGHT QUOTE

Every gift, large or small, becomes powerful when placed in God's hands.

JOURNAL PROMPT

What gift or passion has God placed in you that you can use more intentionally?

DAY 337
Your Glory Revealed

> *But You, O LORD, are a shield for me, My glory and the One who lifts up my head.*
> *– Psalm 3:3*

REFLECTION

In a world that measures worth by appearance and approval, God reminds us that He Himself is our glory. Success or failure does not define our identity; His presence within us does. When we live aware of His glory, insecurity fades and confidence grows. Criticism loses its sting because of our value in Him. We no longer strive to prove; we simply rest in Him.

APPLICATION

† Affirm your worth as one who carries God's glory
† Reject comparison and rest in His acceptance
† Reflect His light through humility and gratitude

CONNECTION

Thank You, Lord. You are my glory and the source of my worth. Let Your light shine through me so others can see Your goodness. Keep my heart humble, secure, and full of praise. In Jesus' name, Amen.

HIGHLIGHT QUOTE

When we rest in God's glory, we stop striving for the world's approval.

JOURNAL PROMPT

Where have you been seeking validation that only God can give?

DAY 338
Led by the Spirit

> *So he answered and said to me: "This is the word of the LORD to Zerubbabel: 'Not by might nor by power, but by My Spirit,' says the LORD of hosts ...*
> *– Zechariah 4:6*

REFLECTION

The Holy Spirit leads us through peace, conviction, and truth. His direction may come softly, but His guidance is sure. When peace disappears, it's an invitation to pause and pray. True maturity is not independence but dependence on His leading. Being Spirit-led keeps us walking in alignment with the Father's will.

APPLICATION

- † Pause when peace is missing, and seek God's direction
- † Surrender your will to His at every decision point
- † Listen for His leading through Scripture and prayer

CONNECTION

Thank You, Lord, for leading me by Your Spirit. Teach me to listen, trust, and follow with a yielded heart. Let Your peace guide every choice I make. In Jesus' name, Amen.

HIGHLIGHT QUOTE

Spiritual maturity isn't about control; it's about surrender.

JOURNAL PROMPT

Where do you need to slow down and invite the Holy Spirit's guidance today?

DAY 339
Filled to the Brim

> Jesus said to them, "Fill the waterpots with water." And they filled them up to the brim.
> – John 2:7

REFLECTION

The servants filled the jars completely, and Jesus transformed the water into wine. Partial obedience limits miracles, but wholehearted obedience invites transformation. When we fill our lives with the Word and Spirit, God fills every space with His presence until our lives overflow with His goodness.

APPLICATION

- † Fill your heart daily with God's Word and Spirit
- † Obey His voice completely, not halfway
- † Overflow into others with encouragement and love

CONNECTION

Thank You, Lord, for filling me to the brim with Your presence. Let my obedience invite Your transformation and overflow into others. In Jesus' name, Amen.

HIGHLIGHT QUOTE

Full surrender fills the jars; Jesus turns the water into wine.

JOURNAL PROMPT

Where is God calling you to obey fully so He can fill you completely?

DAY 340
The Breaker Goes Before You

I will go before you And make the crooked places straight; I will break in pieces the gates of bronze And cut the bars of iron.
– Isaiah 45:2

REFLECTION

God, our Breaker, goes ahead of us, clears the path, and prepares the way. He has already conquered what feels impossible to us. Every obstacle becomes an opportunity for His glory to shine. We walk forward with confidence, knowing the Breaker moves before us and secures our victory.

APPLICATION

- † Trust God to remove obstacles in His timing
- † Declare His promises over difficult situations
- † Walk forward in faith, confident in His power

CONNECTION

Thank You, Lord, for going before me and breaking through barriers I cannot see. Straighten my path and reveal Your glory through my life. In Jesus' name, Amen.

HIGHLIGHT QUOTE

When God goes before us, nothing can stand against us.

JOURNAL PROMPT

What obstacle do you need to trust the Breaker to go before you and remove?

DAY 341
United as One Body

> *From whom the whole body, joined and knit together by what every joint supplies ... causes growth of the body for the edifying of itself in love.*
> – Ephesians 4:16

REFLECTION

We are one body in Christ, connected through His Spirit. Every believer has a purpose and a part to play. Unity doesn't erase diversity; it celebrates it. When we encourage, uplift, and honor one another, the whole body grows stronger. Love is the bond that keeps us knit together in grace.

APPLICATION

† Encourage others rather than comparing yourself
† Value every member of Christ's body
† Stay connected to God and His people in love

CONNECTION

Thank You, Lord, for placing me in Your body with purpose. Help me strengthen others and walk in unity. Teach me to serve in love and humility. In Jesus' name, Amen.

HIGHLIGHT QUOTE

Unity doesn't mean sameness; it means togetherness in purpose and love.

JOURNAL PROMPT

How can you build unity and strengthen others in the body of Christ today?

DAY 342
Called by His Word

> God, who gives life to the dead and calls those things which do not exist as though they did.
> – Romans 4:17

REFLECTION

God spoke Abraham's identity before the promise came to pass. In the same way, He calls us chosen, beloved, and victorious—even when circumstances suggest otherwise. Our role is to align our words and faith with His, declaring His promises until they manifest. We walk not by what we see, but by what He has spoken over us.

APPLICATION

- † Speak God's truth over your life, even when it's hard to see
- † Reject false labels and embrace the identity He declares over you
- † Thank Him for promises in progress, trusting that He will fulfill them

CONNECTION

Thank You, Lord, for calling me by name and declaring truth over my life. Help me align my words and faith with Yours. In Jesus' name, Amen.

HIGHLIGHT QUOTE

God calls us chosen, beloved, and victorious long before we see it.

JOURNAL PROMPT

What promise has God spoken over you that you need to declare today?

DAY 343
Sowing in Tears

*Those who sow in tears
Shall reap in joy.*
– Psalm 126:5

REFLECTION

In God's economy, our tears are valuable. Every prayer sown in sorrow prepares a harvest of joy. In dry seasons, He is still near, watering our faith and nurturing unseen growth. When joy seems delayed, remember that He is working beneath the surface, and your tears are watering tomorrow's breakthrough.

APPLICATION

† Trust that God's presence remains, even when you can't feel it
† Pray and persevere through dry seasons
† Expect joy to rise where tears once fell

CONNECTION

Thank You, Lord, for turning my tears into seeds of joy. Help me to trust Your timing and press forward in faith. In Jesus' name, Amen.

HIGHLIGHT QUOTE

Every tear sown in faith becomes a seed for future joy.

JOURNAL PROMPT

What situation do you need to trust will one day yield joy from your tears?

DAY 344
Mindful of the Things of God

> *You are not mindful of the things of God, but the things of men.*
> *– Matthew 16:23*

REFLECTION

Like Peter, we can easily view life through human reasoning instead of a divine perspective. The mind of Christ focuses on eternity, not temporary gain. When we renew our thoughts with Scripture, our focus shifts from fear to faith, from obstacles to opportunity. Godly mindfulness anchors peace during chaos.

APPLICATION

- † Replace anxious thoughts with God's truth
- † Ask the Holy Spirit to renew your perspective
- † Keep your focus on eternal things, not the temporary

CONNECTION

Thank You, Lord, for giving me the mind of Christ. Renew my thoughts to align with Your will and keep me mindful of eternal truth. In Jesus' name, Amen.

HIGHLIGHT QUOTE

When our minds align with God's truth, peace becomes our natural state.

JOURNAL PROMPT

What thought or worry do you need to surrender to God's perspective today?

> We love Him because He first loved us.
> – 1 John 4:19

DAY 345
Cheerful Giving

> *So let each one give as he purposes in his heart, not grudgingly or of necessity; for God loves a cheerful giver.*
> – 2 Corinthians 9:7

REFLECTION

True generosity flows from love, not obligation. When we give cheerfully, our hearts mirror God's own nature. Giving is never about the amount but about the attitude. A joyful giver turns resources into worship and seeds into harvest. The value of a gift is the love behind it. In giving freely, we reflect the grace that was first given to us.

APPLICATION

† Give with joy and purpose, not pressure
† Look for opportunities to bless others generously
† Remember that giving is an act of worship

CONNECTION

Thank You, Lord, for being the ultimate Giver. Teach me to give from a cheerful heart and reflect Your generosity in all I do. In Jesus' name, Amen.

HIGHLIGHT QUOTE

Generosity transforms giving from obligation to worship.

JOURNAL PROMPT

How can you give with more joy and gratitude in this season?

DAY 346
Beholding His Glory

> *But we all, with unveiled face, beholding as in a mirror the glory of the Lord, are being transformed ... from glory to glory.*
> – 2 Corinthians 3:18

REFLECTION

We become what we behold. As we fix our gaze on Christ, His glory reshapes our hearts. Rushing through life blinds us to His beauty, but beholding Him restores focus and joy. The more we look to Him, the more His Spirit transforms us, reflecting His image in our thoughts, words, and ways.

APPLICATION

- † Pause daily to behold the Lord through prayer and Scripture
- † Notice divine moments hidden in ordinary life
- † Reflect His glory by being present with others

CONNECTION

Thank You, Lord, for helping me behold Your glory. Open my eyes to see You in every moment. Transform me as I fix my gaze on You. In Jesus' name, Amen.

HIGHLIGHT QUOTE

We reflect the glory we behold, so let our eyes stay on Jesus.

JOURNAL PROMPT

What can you do today to slow down and behold God?

DAY 347
Arrows of Victory

> Then he said, "Take the arrows" ... "Strike the ground"; so he struck three times, and stopped.
> – 2 Kings 13:18

REFLECTION

Joash stopped too soon, forfeiting full victory. Likewise, we sometimes pray or believe halfway. God calls us to keep striking until He tells us to stop. Persistence in faith brings breakthroughs. Every act of obedience is an arrow of victory—when we persevere, we overcome.

APPLICATION

- † Keep striking in prayer until God brings the victory
- † Silence discouragement and press forward in faith
- † Obey fully and consistently, even when progress seems slow

CONNECTION

Thank You, Lord, for calling me to persevere in faith. Strengthen me to keep striking and never give up until You manifest Your promise. In Jesus' name, Amen.

HIGHLIGHT QUOTE

Persistence turns arrows of faith into arrows of victory.

JOURNAL PROMPT

Where do you need to "strike the ground" again in prayer or perseverance?

A 365-Day Journey Walking with the Word & the Spirit

DAY 348

Seeking the Lord

> *Sow for yourselves righteousness; Reap in mercy; Break up your fallow ground, For it is time to seek the LORD.*
> – Hosea 10:12

REFLECTION

Life's distractions can cloud our spiritual sight, but we are called to seek the Lord with fervor. Just as we search urgently when we lose something valuable, so we should pursue His presence with our whole hearts. Seeking Him above all brings clarity, peace, and renewed confidence in His promises.

APPLICATION

- † Seek the Giver more than the gifts
- † Sharpen your focus on His presence daily
- † Trust His promises with renewed vision

CONNECTION

Thank You, Lord, for calling me to seek You above all else. Sharpen my vision, clear distractions, and keep me aligned with Your presence. In Jesus' name, Amen.

HIGHLIGHT QUOTE

Those who seek the Lord with all their hearts find clarity, peace, and purpose.

JOURNAL PROMPT

What distractions do you need to clear to seek God more intentionally?

DAY 349
The Light of the World

> Then Jesus spoke to them again, saying, "I am the light of the world. He who follows Me shall not walk in darkness, but have the light of life."
> – John 8:12

REFLECTION

Jesus' light exposes deception and reveals what is true. In a world clouded by confusion, His Word brings clarity and courage to stand firm. The closer we walk with Him, the brighter truth shines and the faster fear fades. Darkness loses its hold where His presence reigns. In Him, we find victorious life: radiant, pure, and unshakable.

APPLICATION

- † Let Scripture shape your thoughts and decisions
- † Reject every lie that hides in the shadows
- † Reflect His truth through compassion and integrity

CONNECTION

Thank You, Lord, for being the light that conquers darkness. Shine through me so Your truth is seen in my words and actions. Keep me rooted in Your victorious light. In Jesus' name, Amen.

HIGHLIGHT QUOTE

Where Christ shines, darkness has no power to remain.

JOURNAL PROMPT

What area of your life needs the clarity of Christ's light today?

DAY 350
God's Plan in Disruptions

So it was, that while they were there, the days were completed for her to be delivered.
– Luke 2:6

REFLECTION

Mary and Joseph's disrupted plans led them to Bethlehem, exactly where God would fulfill prophecy. God's purpose often unfolds through detours. What feels like delay or disappointment may be divine direction. His sovereignty turns interruptions into intersections with destiny.

APPLICATION

† Trust God's plan when the enemy disrupts yours
† Rest in His timing, even when it feels delayed
† Look for His purpose in unexpected changes

CONNECTION

Thank You, Lord, for turning every disruption into divine direction. Help me rest in Your timing and trust Your plan when life feels uncertain. In Jesus' name, Amen.

HIGHLIGHT QUOTE

What feels like a detour to us is often a direct route in God's plan.

JOURNAL PROMPT

What recent "disruption" might God be using to position you for purpose?

DAY 351
The Power of Perfect Love

> *There is no fear in love; but perfect love casts out fear, because fear involves torment. But he who fears has not been made perfect in love.*
> – 1 John 4:18

REFLECTION

Fear loses its grip when God's perfect love takes hold of our hearts. His love reassures us of His presence and replaces anxiety with peace. As we fix our eyes on His unchanging love, we cast out fear. Living in this freedom, we walk confidently, knowing His love never fails. It remains constant amid all uncertainties.

APPLICATION

- † Read and meditate on Scriptures about God's love
- † Reject fear by affirming His promises aloud
- † Invite His love to bring peace into anxious moments

CONNECTION

Thank You, Lord, for showering me with love and dispelling fear from my soul. I embrace Your peace and strength. Help me be quick to reject fear and receive Your love instead. In Jesus' name, Amen.

HIGHLIGHT QUOTE

As we fix our eyes on His unchanging love, we cast out fear.

JOURNAL PROMPT

What fear do you need to surrender to God's love today?

DAY 352
Glorious Lights

For it is the God who commanded light to shine out of darkness, who has shone in our hearts.
— 2 Corinthians 4:6

REFLECTION

The light of Christ shines through us, even when we feel dim. The Holy Spirit within us radiates hope and grace to a dark world. We may not see how far our light reaches, but others do. Together as His body, our lights merge into a brilliance that drives out darkness and magnifies His glory.

APPLICATION

† Let His light shine through words and deeds
† Encourage others who feel dim or weary
† Join other believers to shine brighter together

CONNECTION

Thank You, Lord, for shining Your light in my heart. Let me reflect Your love and truth wherever I go, and unite me with others to brighten the world for Your glory. In Jesus' name, Amen.

HIGHLIGHT QUOTE

The Holy Spirit within us radiates hope and grace to a dark world.

JOURNAL PROMPT

Where can you shine the light of Christ in someone's life this week?

DAY 353
The Living Word

For the word of God is living and powerful, and sharper than any two-edged sword.
– Hebrews 4:12

REFLECTION

God's Word is alive—it cuts through confusion, heals hidden pain, and builds faith. Like a surgeon's scalpel, it divides soul from spirit, exposing truth with precision. His Word never returns void; it equips, restores, and sustains us. When we wield it in faith, darkness flees and victory comes.

APPLICATION

† Feed daily on the living Word of God
† Trust its power to heal and renew your heart
† Use Scripture as your weapon in every battle

CONNECTION

Thank You, Lord, for Your living Word. Let it renew my mind, strengthen my spirit, and guide my steps. Teach me to wield it with bold faith. In Jesus' name, Amen.

HIGHLIGHT QUOTE

The Word of God doesn't just speak; it transforms.

JOURNAL PROMPT

What Scripture is God highlighting for you to live by today?

DAY 354
God Knows Our Frame

> *For He knows our frame; He remembers that we are dust.*
> — Psalm 103:14

REFLECTION

God understands our weaknesses and limitations, yet loves us without measure. He knows every wound, every fear, and every need. Where others may misjudge, He sees the truth of our hearts. Our weakness doesn't stop his compassion; it makes it bigger. We rest in His love and trust His patient, transforming work.

APPLICATION

† Rest in God's unconditional love and understanding
† Surrender your weaknesses for His transforming strength
† Rejoice that He cares for every detail of your life

CONNECTION

Thank You, Lord, for knowing me fully and loving me completely. Help me rest in Your care and trust Your patient hand at work within me. In Jesus' name, Amen.

HIGHLIGHT QUOTE

Our weakness doesn't stop his compassion; it makes it bigger.

JOURNAL PROMPT

Where do you need to let God's understanding replace your self-criticism?

DAY 355
Making Room for Jesus

> *And she brought forth her firstborn Son ... and laid Him in a manger, because there was no room for them in the inn.*
> *– Luke 2:7*

REFLECTION

Jesus entered the world in simplicity, welcomed in a humble manger because there was no room elsewhere. Even now, He seeks hearts willing to make space for His presence. We easily fill our lives with noise, plans, and distractions that crowd Him out, yet He longs not for a moment's attention but a permanent dwelling.

APPLICATION

- † Set apart quiet moments each day for Jesus
- † Surrender what distracts you from His presence
- † Welcome Him as Lord over every part of your life

CONNECTION

Thank You, Lord, for desiring to dwell with me. Clear the clutter of my heart and fill it with Your peace and presence. Let my life be a place where You are always welcome. In Jesus' name, Amen.

HIGHLIGHT QUOTE

Jesus doesn't seek a place to visit; He seeks a heart to call home.

JOURNAL PROMPT

What part of your life needs to make more room for Jesus today?

DAY 356
Loving One Another

> *Beloved, if God so loved us, we also ought to love one another.*
> *– 1 John 4:11*

REFLECTION

Love is the genuine evidence of God at work in us. It's expressed through kindness, forgiveness, and patience. Genuine love sees the best, believes the best, and endures the worst. When we love one another, God's presence becomes visible to the world—His love perfected in us.

APPLICATION

† Express love in practical, simple ways
† Forgive freely and extend grace
† Reflect God's love through your actions daily

CONNECTION

Thank You, Lord, for filling my heart with Your love. Teach me to love others unconditionally and show Your presence through every word and deed. In Jesus' name, Amen.

HIGHLIGHT QUOTE

Love is the genuine evidence of God at work in us.

JOURNAL PROMPT

Who can you show God's love to in a tangible way today?

DAY 357
God's Good Gifts

How much more will your Father who is in heaven give good things to those who ask Him!
— Matthew 7:11

REFLECTION

Our heavenly Father delights in blessing His children. His gifts are perfect and purposeful, meeting needs we didn't know we had. Every good thing flows from His heart of love. As we dwell in His presence, He fills us with peace, equips us for purpose, and calls us to share His goodness with others.

APPLICATION

† Ask boldly for the good things He desires to give
† Receive every gift with gratitude and humility
† Become a vessel of blessing to others

CONNECTION

Thank You, Lord, for every good and perfect gift. Help me live with open hands—ready to receive and eager to give. In Jesus' name, Amen.

HIGHLIGHT QUOTE

Every good gift reminds us of the Giver's perfect heart.

JOURNAL PROMPT

What good gift from God are you thankful for today?

DAY 358
Worship in Spirit and Truth

The true worshipers will worship the Father in spirit and truth; for the Father is seeking such to worship Him.
– John 4:23

REFLECTION

True worship isn't about music or moments; it's about heart posture. In worship, our focus shifts from problems to God's presence. Whether in joy or sorrow, worship awakens faith and draws Heaven near. As we exalt Him in spirit and truth, His glory fills the atmosphere, and peace replaces fear.

APPLICATION

† Magnify the Lord, not your circumstances
† Engage in both private and corporate worship
† Expect His presence to transform your heart and surroundings

CONNECTION

Thank You, Lord, for calling me into true worship. Teach me to lift Your name above everything else and encounter You in spirit and truth. In Jesus' name, Amen.

HIGHLIGHT QUOTE

Worship shifts the focus from what's wrong around us to Who is right within us.

JOURNAL PROMPT

How can you make worship a daily lifestyle, not just an event?

A 365-Day Journey Walking with the Word & the Spirit

DAY 359
The Greatest Gift

For there is born to you this day in the city of David a Savior, who is Christ the Lord.
– Luke 2:11

REFLECTION

The birth of Jesus is the greatest gift ever given—the gift of salvation, love, and eternal life. His coming changed history and still changes every heart that welcomes Him. The manger reminds us that glory often enters through humility and that we find true joy in His presence. The love of Christ is not seasonal; it's steadfast, offered daily to all who will receive it.

APPLICATION

† Thank God for the gift of salvation through Christ
† Share His love and kindness with someone today
† Celebrate His presence as your greatest treasure

CONNECTION

Thank You, Lord, for being the greatest gift of all. Fill my heart with Your love and joy. Help me share Your hope and peace wherever I go. In Jesus' name, Amen.

HIGHLIGHT QUOTE

The greatest gift we can ever receive, or share, is Jesus Himself.

JOURNAL PROMPT

How can you reflect the joy and love of Jesus in practical ways today?

DAY 360
God With Us

> *They shall call His name Immanuel, which is translated, "God with us."*
> – Matthew 1:23

REFLECTION

Immanuel, God with us, is the miracle that changes everything. His presence turns fear into peace and loneliness into joy. We are never beyond His reach, never outside His care. Whether in triumph or trial, His nearness is our greatest assurance. He walks beside us in every step, filling ordinary days with extraordinary grace.

APPLICATION

- † Seek His presence more than His provision
- † Recognize His nearness in your daily moments
- † Let His peace steady your heart in uncertainty

CONNECTION

Thank You, Lord, for being Immanuel—ever near, ever faithful. Help me live aware of Your presence in every circumstance. Let Your peace rule my heart and Your joy fill my days. In Jesus' name, Amen.

HIGHLIGHT QUOTE

His presence turns fear into peace and loneliness into joy.

JOURNAL PROMPT

Where have you recently seen evidence of God's presence with you?

DAY 361
Inseparable Love

> For I am persuaded that neither death nor life, nor angels nor principalities nor powers, nor things present nor things to come, nor height nor depth, nor any other created thing, shall be able to separate us from the love of God which is in Christ Jesus our Lord.
> – Romans 8:38–39

REFLECTION

God's love is unbreakable. No trial, tribulation, or force in Heaven or on earth can separate us from His love, not even death. Even when we stumble or feel distant, His love remains unchanged. This assurance strengthens our faith and deepens our trust in Him. Nothing can sever the bond of His love that holds us secure in Christ.

APPLICATION

† Declare daily that nothing can separate you from His love
† Reject the lie that hardship means God has abandoned you
† Rest in His unshakable presence, no matter your circumstance

CONNECTION

Thank You, Lord, for Your unbreakable love. When I feel distant, remind me You are always with me. Strengthen my heart in the assurance that nothing can separate me from You. In Jesus' name, Amen.

HIGHLIGHT QUOTE

No power in Heaven or on earth can separate us from God's love in Christ Jesus.

JOURNAL PROMPT

How does knowing His love is unbreakable change the way you face trials?

DAY 362
Wonderfully Made

I will praise You, for I am fearfully and wonderfully made.
– Psalm 139:14

REFLECTION

Our focus shapes our perspective. When we fixate on flaws, they grow in our eyes, but God calls us to see His marvelous workmanship in us. We are fearfully and wonderfully made, crafted with intention and beauty. As we dwell on His truth, we silence the enemy's lies and embrace the identity He gives us, living with gratitude and confidence in His design.

APPLICATION

- † Replace self-criticism with gratitude for how God created you
- † Declare His truth over your identity throughout the day
- † Praise Him for His marvelous workmanship in you

CONNECTION

Thank You, Lord, for making me fearfully and wonderfully. Help me see myself through Your eyes and silence every lie of the enemy. In Jesus' name, Amen.

HIGHLIGHT QUOTE

We are fearfully and wonderfully made, crafted with God's intention and beauty.

JOURNAL PROMPT

What truth from Psalm 139:14 can you declare over yourself today?

DAY 363
Praise at All Times

I will bless the LORD at all times; His praise shall continually be in my mouth.
– Psalm 34:1

REFLECTION

Life brings both joy and sorrow, but praise steadies the heart in every season. Our cries of despair transform into declarations of faith as we choose to bless the Lord. When we dwell on the works of our adversary, we praise him where none is due. Praise shifts our focus from what is wrong to Who is right—our faithful God who never changes.

APPLICATION

- † Choose to praise God aloud, even in difficulty
- † Replace fearful thoughts with words of worship
- † Write reasons you can bless the Lord today

CONNECTION

Thank You, Lord, for filling my heart with praise. Help me lift Your name high in every season of life. You are always worthy. In Jesus' name, Amen.

HIGHLIGHT QUOTE

Praise transforms despair into faith and fear into peace.

JOURNAL PROMPT

What situation today can you turn into an act of praise?

DAY 364
Amen to His Promises

For all the promises of God in Him are Yes, and in Him Amen, to the glory of God through us.
– 2 Corinthians 1:20

REFLECTION

God fulfilled His promises through Jesus, not through pending future acts. At the cross, He secured salvation, redemption, and victory. We respond in faith, saying amen to His yes in Christ. Daily, we believe, receive, and live from His finished work. In Him, it is not if and then, but yes and amen.

APPLICATION

† Lay hold of His promises by faith
† Agree with God—say amen to His yes
† Rest in Christ's finished work today

CONNECTION

Thank You, Lord, that every promise finds its yes in Christ. Align my heart to believe and my life to agree with Your Word. In Jesus' name, Amen.

HIGHLIGHT QUOTE

In Christ, God's promises are not if and then but yes and amen.

JOURNAL PROMPT

Which of God's promises do you need to say "amen" to and believe anew today?

DAY 365
Jesus Upholds All Things

Who being the brightness of His glory and the express image of His person, and upholding all things by the word of His power.
— Hebrews 1:3

REFLECTION

When we struggle to hold things together, we can rest in knowing that Jesus is holding us together. He upholds all creation by His powerful Word, sustaining life and peace. When our strength fails, His never does. Nothing falls apart beyond His reach. What He holds, He restores, and what He restores, He secures forever.

APPLICATION

- † Trust Jesus to uphold you when life feels heavy
- † Receive His peace when your mind feels overwhelmed
- † Rest in His hands, knowing nothing can snatch you away

CONNECTION

Thank You, Lord, for upholding me by the word of Your power. When I am weak, You remain strong. Help me rest in Your steady hands and reflect Your peace in all I do. In Jesus' name, Amen.

HIGHLIGHT QUOTE

When everything feels unstable, remember that Jesus never lets go.

JOURNAL PROMPT

What part of your life do you need to trust Jesus to hold together today?

A Blessing at the Journey's End

As this journey draws to a close, may your heart rest in the faithfulness of God, who has carried you every step of the way.

Each page you've walked through is a testimony that His promises stand and His presence sustains.

Let every victory stir your gratitude, every challenge reveal His grace, and every day ahead unfold with renewed hope.

You have seen His goodness behind you, His mercy beside you, and His purpose before you. Step into the new season with confidence, walking with the Word and the Spirit, from glory to glory!

With love and blessings,

Dr. Joelle Suel

About the Author

Dr. Joelle Suel is a Spirit-filled minister, speaker, and author with a passion to ignite revival and empower believers to walk in the Spirit, from glory to glory. Known for her prophetic insight and passion to stir faith and fire, she carries a deep hunger to see lives transformed by the presence and power of God.

Through Glory to Glory Ministries, she teaches, equips, and encourages believers through devotionals, books, courses, her podcast, and Glory Splash Gatherings.

Her anointed messages help believers grow spiritually, overcome battles, and discover their divine purpose.

Originally from France and now a proud American citizen, Dr. Joelle holds a Doctor of Ministry degree and brings decades of leadership and ministry experience.

She ministers globally through online platforms, livestreams, and Spirit-led resources published through her imprint, Word Feed Press.

When she is not writing or teaching, Dr. Joelle enjoys time with her daughters, grandchildren, and great-grandchildren—and walking with the Lord from glory to glory.

Connect at drjoelle.org

Let's Stay Connected

Thank you for allowing me to walk with you on this 365-day journey.

My heart is to encourage and equip believers to walk in the Spirit, grow in the Word, and live from glory to glory.

If you would like to receive:
- † daily devotional encouragement
- † prophetic insights
- † teaching moments
- † ministry updates
- † new resources & invitations

You're warmly invited to connect with me online:
- † drjoelle.org
- † Find me on YouTube, podcast platforms, and social media

I'd be honored to continue walking with you as we grow in Him, day by day, from glory to glory.

FREE BONUS
for Readers

I created a special prayer resource to strengthen and encourage your daily walk with the Lord.

It's my gift to bless your journey as you read this devotional.

- † 10 Prayers for Walking in the Word & the Spirit
- † A beautifully designed printable with ten Spirit-led prayers to help you:
- † Walk in daily alignment with the Holy Spirit
- † Renew your mind with the Word
- † Receive fresh strength
- † Experience breakthrough
- † Grow from glory to glory

May these prayers refresh your spirit and draw you deeper into His presence.

Dr. Joelle

Scan the QR Code or visit:
subscribepage.io/tenprayers

Scripture Index

OLD TESTAMENT

Genesis 3:4 – Day 240
Genesis 7:1 – Day 256
Genesis 13:14 – Day 279
Genesis 13:14–15 – Day 330
Genesis 13:17 – Day 83
Genesis 16:13 – Day 29
Genesis 22:1–2 – Day 254
Genesis 22:14 – Day 43, Day 196
Genesis 26:15 – Day 70
Genesis 26:22 – Day 71
Exodus 1:12 – Day 280
Exodus 3:3 – Day 250
Exodus 14:30 – Day 87
Exodus 33:14 – Day 159
Exodus 33:15 – Day 138
Numbers 13:33 – Day 315
Numbers 14:24 – Day 269
Deuteronomy 31:6 – Day 214
Deuteronomy 31:8 – Day 270
Deuteronomy 32:11–12 – Day 122
Deuteronomy 33:25 – Day 231
Joshua 1:9 – Day 119
Joshua 6:1 – Day 288
Joshua 14:12 – Day 265
Joshua 23:11 – Day 165
Judges 7:20 – Day 302
1 Samuel 13:14 – Day 162
1 Samuel 16:7 – Day 104
1 Kings 18:41 – Day 335
1 Kings 19:12 – Day 143
2 Kings 3:15 – Day 126
2 Kings 6:6 – Day 284
2 Kings 13:18 – Day 347
1 Chronicles 16:8 – Day 174
2 Chronicles 15:7 – Day 200
Nehemiah 4:14 – Day 244
Nehemiah 8:10 – Day 15
Psalm 3:3 – Day 23, Day 203, Day 229, Day 337
Psalm 3:5–6 – Day 211
Psalm 5:3 – Day 2
Psalm 5:12 – Day 252
Psalm 18:6 – Day 149
Psalm 18:36 – Day 282
Psalm 20:7 – Day 323
Psalm 23:1 – Day 22
Psalm 23:3 – Day 208
Psalm 25:4 – Day 168
Psalm 27:1 – Day 266, Day 291
Psalm 27:14 – Day 39
Psalm 29:2 – Day 8
Psalm 32:7 – Day 145
Psalm 32:8 – Day 272
Psalm 34:1 – Day 363
Psalm 37:1–2 – Day 59
Psalm 37:4 – Day 140
Psalm 37:5 – Day 111
Psalm 37:7 – Day 222
Psalm 37:23 – Day 9, Day 251
Psalm 42:7 – Day 295
Psalm 46:1 – Day 53
Psalm 46:10 – Day 65
Psalm 56:3 – Day 185
Psalm 61:2 – Day 180
Psalm 62:8 – Day 158
Psalm 71:1 – Day 156
Psalm 73:23–24 – Day 331
Psalm 73:26 – Day 90
Psalm 84:5–7 – Day 132
Psalm 86:12 – Day 262
Psalm 92:10 – Day 209

Psalm 100:3 – Day 80

Psalm 103:2–4 – Day 313

Psalm 103:14 – Day 354

Psalm 107:2 – Day 109

Psalm 107:13 – Day 91

Psalm 107:20 – Day 105

Psalm 107:28 – Day 113

Psalm 107:28–29 – Day 325

Psalm 112:4 – Day 58

Psalm 119:105 – How to Use This Devotional, Day 16

Psalm 126:5 – Day 343

Psalm 138:8 – Day 152

Psalm 139:12 – Day 319

Psalm 139:14 – Day 362

Psalm 139:23 – Day 63

Psalm 143:8 – Day 32

Psalm 145:8 – Day 41

Psalm 147:3 – Day 128

Psalm 150:1 – Day 177

Proverbs 3:5–6 – Day 33

Proverbs 4:18 – Day 88, Day 220

Proverbs 4:20–21 – Day 241

Proverbs 4:23 – Day 20, Day 66

Proverbs 11:25 – Day 297

Proverbs 18:14 – Day 12

Proverbs 18:19 – Day 303

Proverbs 18:21 – Day 192

Proverbs 21:23 – Day 25

Proverbs 24:16 – Day 116

Ecclesiastes 3:1 – Day 30, Day 225

Song of Solomon 2:15 – Day 19

Isaiah 1:19 – Day 235

Isaiah 10:27 – Day 124

Isaiah 12:4 – Day 74

Isaiah 28:16 – Day 309

Isaiah 30:15 – Day 334

Isaiah 40:8 – Day 47

Isaiah 40:31 – Day 4

Isaiah 41:10 – Day 237

Isaiah 43:2 – Day 181

Isaiah 43:16 – Day 243

Isaiah 43:18 – Day 5

Isaiah 43:19 – Day 10, Day 201

Isaiah 45:2 – Day 340

Isaiah 49:2 – Day 321

Isaiah 54:17 – Day 133

Isaiah 61:3 – Day 97

Isaiah 64:8 – Day 3

Jeremiah 2:13 – Day 48

Jeremiah 29:11 – Day 99, Day 171, Day 260

Lamentations 3:22–23 – Day 6, Day 167, Day 212

Daniel 3:17 – Day 21

Daniel 3:17–18 – Day 60

Hosea 10:12 – Day 348

Micah 2:13 – Day 219

Habakkuk 2:3 – Day 49

Habakkuk 3:17–18 – Day 188

Haggai 1:5 – Day 40

Zechariah 4:6 - Day 338

NEW TESTAMENT

Matthew 1:23 – Day 360

Matthew 5:8 – Day 175

Matthew 5:9 – Day 160

Matthew 5:16 – Day 169

Matthew 5:37 – Day 64

Matthew 6:6 – Day 135

Matthew 6:11 – Day 277

Matthew 6:28 – Day 215

Matthew 6:33 – Day 1

Matthew 6:34 – Day 173

Matthew 7:11 – Day 357

Matthew 8:8 – Day 123

Matthew 11:28 – Day 52, Day 202, Day 258

Matthew 13:57–58 – Day 232

Matthew 13:58 – Day 141
Matthew 14:30–31 – Day 317
Matthew 15:25 – Day 290
Matthew 16:16–17 – Day 45
Matthew 16:23 – Day 344
Matthew 17:20 – Day 11
Matthew 18:7 – Day 238
Matthew 18:18 – Day 67
Matthew 21:9 – Day 103
Matthew 22:37 – Day 131
Matthew 24:13 – Day 161
Matthew 26:39 – Day 107
Matthew 26:42 – Day 98
Mark 1:35 – Day 108
Mark 4:39 – Day 102
Mark 8:6 – Day 234
Mark 8:25 – Day 320
Mark 14:36 – Day 44
Luke 1:36–37 – Day 142
Luke 1:37 – Day 198
Luke 2:6 – Day 350
Luke 2:7 – Day 355
Luke 2:11 – Day 359
Luke 4:18 – Day 287
Luke 5:4 – Day 257
Luke 6:48 – Day 146
Luke 7:46–47 Day 134
Luke 8:45–46 Day 304
Luke 9:55 – Day 148, Day 183
Luke 10:19 – Day 226
Luke 11:9 – Day 153
Luke 11:13 – Day 314
Luke 16:10 – Day 26
Luke 17:5 – Day 27
Luke 17:14 – Day 248
Luke 17:15–16 – Day 296
Luke 19:5–6 – Day 78
Luke 24:32 – Day 42

John 1:5 – Day 204
John 2:5 – Day 245
John 2:7 – Day 339
John 4:14 – Day 195
John 4:23 – Day 358
John 4:23–24 – Day 17
John 6:28–29 – Day 249
John 6:35 – Day 51
John 8:12 – Day 247, Day 274, Day 349
John 8:31–32 – Day 184
John 8:32 – Day 210
John 10:14 – Day 36
John 11:25–26 Day 95
John 11:43–44 Day 114
John 14:15 – Day 163
John 14:27 – Day 224
John 15:1 – Day 62
John 15:5 – Day 305
John 16:13 – Day 157
John 16:33 – Day 125
John 21:7 – Day 112
Acts 4:29–30 – Day 115
Acts 4:31 – Day 50
Acts 16:25 – Day 166, Day 194
Acts 20:22 – Day 206
Acts 20:24 – Day 101
Acts 28:5 – Day 324
Romans 1:16 – Day 76
Romans 4:17 – Day 342
Romans 5:5 – Day 286
Romans 8:1 – Day 84
Romans 8:9 – Day 24
Romans 8:14 – Day 68
Romans 8:28 – Day 316
Romans 8:37 – Day 81
Romans 8:38–39 – Day 361
Romans 10:13 – Day 213
Romans 10:17 – Day 73

Romans 12:6 – Day 336	2 Corinthians 12:9 – Day 110
Romans 12:21 – Day 298	2 Corinthians 13:14 – Day 137
Romans 15:4 – Day 129	Galatians 1:15 – Day 318
Romans 15:13 – Day 191	Galatians 2:20 – Day 75
1 Corinthians 1:9 – Day 333	Galatians 3:3 – Day 77
1 Corinthians 1:18 – Day 92	Galatians 3:13–14 – Day 276, Day 294
1 Corinthians 1:27 – Day 332	Galatians 5:16 – Day 31
1 Corinthians 2:9 – Day 147	Galatians 6:9 – Day 230, Day 293
1 Corinthians 2:10 – Day 150	Galatians 6:10 – Day 69, Day 281
1 Corinthians 3:6–7 – Day 239	Ephesians 1:5 – Day 72
1 Corinthians 3:9 – Day 259	Ephesians 1:6 – Day 118
1 Corinthians 3:11 – Day 207	Ephesians 2:10 – Day 121
1 Corinthians 4:20 – Day 127	Ephesians 3:16 – Day 326
1 Corinthians 6:19 – Day 310	Ephesians 3:17 – Day 55
1 Corinthians 6:20 – Day 190	Ephesians 3:19 – Day 46
1 Corinthians 9:24 – Day 82	Ephesians 3:20 – Day 285
1 Corinthians 13:4, 8 – Day 130	Ephesians 4:16 – Day 341
1 Corinthians 15:57 – Day 94	Ephesians 4:22–24 – Day 7
1 Corinthians 16:9 – Day 35	Ephesians 4:26 – Day 37
1 Corinthians 16:13 – Day 56	Ephesians 6:12 – Day 187
2 Corinthians 1:10 – Day 182	Ephesians 6:16 – Day 308
2 Corinthians 1:20 – Day 364	Ephesians 6:17 – Day 89
2 Corinthians 2:10 – Day 38	Philippians 1:6 – Day 289
2 Corinthians 3:16 – Day 93	Philippians 1:12 – Day 136
2 Corinthians 3:18 – Day 205, Day 263, Day 346	Philippians 3:12 – Day 34
2 Corinthians 4:6 – Day 352	Philippians 3:14 – Day 292
2 Corinthians 4:7 – Day 120, Day 278	Philippians 4:6 – Day 322
2 Corinthians 4:7–8 – Day 178	Philippians 4:8 – Day 301
2 Corinthians 4:16 – Day 100	Philippians 4:19 – Day 217, Day 264
2 Corinthians 4:17–18 – Day 117	Colossians 1:13–14 – Day 96
2 Corinthians 5:17 – Day 218	Colossians 1:18 – Day 28
2 Corinthians 5:18 – Day 307	Colossians 2:6–7 – Day 154
2 Corinthians 9:7 – Day 345	Colossians 3:13–14 – Day 151
2 Corinthians 9:8 – Day 223	Colossians 3:14 – Day 179
2 Corinthians 9:10 – Day 267	1 Thessalonians 1:2–3 – Day 306
2 Corinthians 10:4 – Day 199	1 Thessalonians 5:16–18 – Day 328
2 Corinthians 10:5 – Day 139	1 Thessalonians 5:18 – Day 327
2 Corinthians 10:12 – Day 144	2 Thessalonians 3:1 – Day 61

2 Thessalonians 3:3 – Day 54
2 Thessalonians 3:5 – Day 227
2 Thessalonians 3:16 – Day 221
2 Timothy 1:6 – Day 164
2 Timothy 1:7 – Day 311
2 Timothy 2:22 – Day 189
2 Timothy 4:2 – Day 236
Hebrews 1:3 – Day 365
Hebrews 4:12 – Day 273, Day 353
Hebrews 4:16 – Day 216
Hebrews 6:19 – Day 228
Hebrews 7:19 – Day 283
Hebrews 11:1 – Day 186
Hebrews 11:6 – Day 176
Hebrews 11:11 – Day 14
Hebrews 12:2 – Day 197
Hebrews 13:8 – Day 268
Hebrews 13:9 – Day 253
Hebrews 13:15 – Day 85
James 1:5 – Day 155
James 3:17 – Day 193
James 4:6 – Day 300
James 4:6–7 – Day 312
James 5:16 – Day 170
1 Peter 1:23 – Day 86
1 Peter 2:10 – Day 299
1 Peter 5:6–7 – Day 172
1 Peter 5:8–9 – Day 79
1 John 2:27 – Day 106
1 John 3:20 – Day 233
1 John 4:1 – Day 255
1 John 4:4 – Day 242
1 John 4:6 – Day 57
1 John 4:11 – Day 18, Day 356
1 John 4:18 – Day 351
1 John 4:19 – Day 329
1 John 5:14 – Day 261
3 John 4 – Day 13
Revelation 3:7 – Day 271
Revelation 3:20 – Day 246
Revelation 12:11 – Day 275

Made in the USA
Coppell, TX
16 January 2026

68203216R00221